PUTTING IT ALL TOGETHER

Seven Patterns for Relating Science and the Christian Faith

RICHARD H. BUBE

Professor Emeritus of Materials Science
and Electrical Engineering
Stanford University - Stanford, California

UNIVERSITY
PRESS OF
AMERICA

Lanham • New York • London

Copyright © 1995 by
University Press of America,® Inc.
4720 Boston Way
Lanham, Maryland 20706

3 Henrietta Street
London WC2E 8LU England

Library of Congress Cataloging-in-Publication Data
Bube, Richard H.
Putting it all together : seven patterns for relating science and the
Christian faith / Richard H. Bube.
p.   cm.
Includes bibliographical references and index.
1. Religion and science.   I. Title.
BL240.2.B823   1995   261.5'5—dc20   94-24824 CIP

ISBN 0–8191–9755–6 (cloth : alk. paper)
ISBN 0–8191–9756–4 (pbk. : alk. paper)

"In the beginning was the Word, and the Word was with God, and the Word was God. He was in the beginning with God; all things were made through him, and without him was not anything made that was made. In him was life, and the life was the light of men." (John 1:1-4)

'For us there is one God, the Father, from whom are all things and for whom we exist, and one Lord, Jesus Christ, through whom are all things and through whom we exist." (I Corinthians 8:6)

".. because the creation itself will be set free from its bondage to decay and obtain the glorious liberty of the children of God. We know that the whole creation has been groaning in travail together until now; and not only the creation, but we ourselves, who have the first fruits of the Spirit, groan inwardly as we wait for adoption as sons, the redemption of our bodies. For in this hope we were saved." (Romans 8:21-24)

"but in your hearts reverence Christ as Lord. Always be prepared to make a defense to any one who calls you to account for the hope that is in you, yet do it with gentleness and reverence."
(I Peter 3:15)

Contents

Preface

A thinking person living in today's world can hardly avoid developing some kind of a pattern within which to express a personal reaction to both scientific and theological inputs. In many cases this pattern may be chosen without real awareness of the choice, which often results from a particular professional, cultural or ecclesiastical isolation. There are a number of such patterns - at least seven - each of which is held by an appreciable segment of the population, often with both Christians and non-Christians effectively advocating the same pattern.

It is the purpose of this book to attempt to clarify the identity of these possible patterns for relating science and the Christian faith, and to provide a balanced critique of each. Such an understanding of the issues involved is essential for an effective witness to Jesus Christ as Lord and Savior in a world dominated by the concepts and artifacts of science.

I would like to thank all of the people with whom I have interacted on these topics over the last forty or so years, especially those involved in the American Scientific Affiliation, its publications and its meetings. I would also like to thank the many students who participated in courses or seminars that I have led both at Stanford, in various churches, and on other college and university campuses. I am particularly indebted to my understanding and beloved wife Betty, who has provided me with unfailing support as well as the inputs of her perceptive and mature Christian insights throughout the writing of this book.

Stanford, California 1995   Richard H. Bube

Chapter 1

A Look at the Issues

The number of different ways that people have devised to relate science and the Christian faith is remarkable. Trying to reconcile the demands of our modern scientific world with the inputs of the Christian faith is often a formidable task. The more serious we are in trying to deal with issues confronting us in the world around us, the more difficult it is to decide how to deal with sometimes apparently contradictory inputs from science and from the Christian faith. So the problem is not only a theoretical one of concern to scholars, but an eminently practical one that concerns us all. A Bibliography for background reading is given in References 1 through 26, listed chronologically.

We have a love-hate relationship with science. On the one hand we complain about our loss of freedom to science-generated technology, the interference of science in human life, and problems of environmental pollution resulting from this technology; on the other we swallow the almost universal belief that science is the only reliable guide to truth. We have been permeated with the notion that what can be said scientifically is the only thing worth saying.

Purpose of this Book

Responses to many issues require a decision about the proper pattern for relating inputs from science and from Christian faith. Each way of resolving the tension between these two inputs has its origin in a

particular set of assumptions, and a particular orientation in the
scientific and theological worlds.

This book sets forth the main characteristics of seven principal
patterns for this interaction. Each of these patterns is adopted by a
sizable number of people living today, often with both Christians and
non-Christians choosing the same pattern. In each case the major
assumptions and conclusions of that particular pattern are indicated,
along with comments based on many years of being involved in the
dynamics of considering the interactions of science and the Christian
faith.

Why do we have such problems in trying to relate science and faith?
One of the main reasons is that there is a wide variety of opinions
about what these words "science" and "faith" really mean.   If we are
going to talk meaningfully about science and faith in this book, we
need to be clear at the beginning what we mean by these words.

Trying to state what something means requires the development of
some basic definitions.   Two people with different definitions may
well arrive at a different set of patterns and conclusions. As implied by
the Table of Contents, I would like to suggest that the meaningful
terms to define for our purposes in this book are primarily "science" and
"Christian theology."   We want to see how people who have made a
personal faith commitment to Jesus Christ as Lord and Savior can give
theological expression to that commitment in the midst of a
scientifically described world.

"Science" vs. "Faith"

To choose "science" and "faith" for our basic pair gets us into trouble
because these are not opposites of one another.   Faith - commitment
and action based on incomplete evidence (scientifically speaking) – is
present in all of the most significant activities of human life, in science
no less than in others.   Often "faith" and "reason" are contrasted as
essentially opposites, and in their extremes they may well be.   But in
the course of life we find that almost everything we encounter is made
up of some rational elements and some faith elements.

The dictionary definitions of these words might lead us to believe that
science is based on objective facts, whereas theology is based only on
personal feelings.   These distinctions are useful to point to some
differences between science and theology, but totally misleading if taken
to indicate some kind of exclusive disjunction between them.   Pure
objectivity in any human endeavor is a myth; no "fact" even in science
ever provides its own interpretation.   The entire scientific endeavor is

based ultimately upon a faith commitment: faith that the universe is intelligible to human beings and that the thoughts of our minds can be relevant to the structure of that universe. The analogous question to "Can you prove the existence of God?" is "Can you prove the validity of a scientific approach?" The answer to both questions is "No;" both must be chosen on faith before meaningful experience can follow.

If it is true that science is ultimately based on faith, it is no less true that theology involves a rational assessment of evidence. The Christian position is based on historical data that cannot be ignored in developing an authentic Christian theology. One of the reasons that the Christian faith receives so much opposition is that it is not totally relativistic and subjective. It does not allow an individual the freedom to construct whatever kind of religious system he subjectively chooses.

If the essential aspect of science is a rational approach to questions, it is no less true that major breakthroughs in science often occur as the result of guesses, intuition, flashes of insight, or instances of serendipity, rather than some kind of mechanical logical progression.

Christian faith on its side is a rational faith, a phrase that should not be regarded as an oxymoron. A rational faith is one in which the available evidence of every sort is assessed, whether from the biblical revelation, historical events, or community or personal experience, and then, guided partially by that assessment, humanly speaking, a personal choice is made and a faith commitment is formed.

To exhibit both faith and reason is an essential aspect of all human activities. We should not erect walls by appealing to false absolute dichotomies between faith and reason.

"Science" vs. "Bible"

Similarly to choose "science" and "the Bible" for our basic pair again gets us into trouble. Science is the result of interpretation of the world around us according to certain appropriate groundrules. "The Bible" itself is not the result of interpretation, but when the Bible is interpreted according to principles consistent with its nature, we have what we mean by "Christian theology." The equivalent concept to "the Bible" on the part of science would have to be "the universe." Science involves our interpretation of the universe; theology involves our interpretation of the Bible.

Pseudoscience and Pseudotheology

Sometimes people assign the name "science" when it is not appropriate, and similarly sometimes people assign the name "Christian theology" when it is not appropriate. Such inappropriate uses of the terms change "authentic science" into "pseudoscience," and "authentic theology" into "pseudotheology." What we mean by these terms will hopefully become clearer as we consider a variety of examples in this book.

Some Examples of Science-Theology Interactions

What is the significance of modern science for our theological understanding? This is the challenge that is being actively debated. The extremes of arguing that it has no significance, or that it totally invalidates all traditional Christian theology, are pitfalls to be avoided. But neither is the cause of Christ advanced when we speak nonsense about scientific topics or hold pseudoscientific positions that are clearly contradicted by authentic science.

Does science change our theology? It is commonly thought that modern science, by providing natural descriptions of events, is ruling out the necessity of God. In a universe in which we have come to understand the underlying physical mechanisms for so many processes, is there any room left for a God who interacts meaningfully with the world? We needed the concept of God to explain the unknown, it is argued, but now as we face a new century, science has shrunk the unknown to such an extent that the concept of God is thought by some to be no longer necessary.

It is extremely risky to tie a particular scientific model to the integrity of Christian theology. All too often a particular scientific model has fallen into disrepute and has carried contemporary regard for Christian theology with it. The often-repeated case of Galileo's interaction with the church of his day need not be belabored. But we should learn something from that historic catastrophe. What we should learn is not that there was in that case some kind of intrinsic conflict between science and Christianity, but rather that Christians of Galileo's day had become hopelessly bound by their identification of the inspired interpretation of the Bible with a Ptolemaic cosmology in which the earth was the unmoving center of the universe. Attempts to discredit the Ptolemaic scientific model were interpreted as attempts to discredit the validity of the biblical record. It was the assumed correlation between a particular biblical interpretation and Ptolemaic cosmology that was the real culprit.

Few other areas in modern science have received as much press as being significant for theology as has cosmology. Ever since the days of Copernicus and Galileo people have been having their ideas about God and the universe radically altered by our growing knowledge of cosmology. Those whose God was limited to some area on this earth, or who was only as high as the nearest mountain, have had to reckon with a God who is greater than the human mind can imagine. But those who have been willing to take a biblical view of our expanding knowledge of an expanding universe have always regarded God as the Creator of space-time, of the whole universe, of whatever size or character it may be found to be.

Nor does it follow that a God great enough to create all of the galaxies upon galaxies of the expanding universe cannot be a personal God who cares for human beings in a personal way. Our latest understanding of the origins of human life suggest strongly that the vast size of the universe is a necessary condition for the development of life on earth given the kind of universe that this is. Our appreciation of the great size of the universe, therefore, need not diminish our appreciation for the theological significance of the earth. If anything, its great size amplifies the importance of what has happened on earth. This world is so important to God that this incredibly large and powerful creation has been brought into being to make human life on earth possible. We need also to remember that no matter how large, energetic or powerful the stars are, not one of them can love like a human being can.

Because of the philosophical conclusions derived from the determinism of classical physics (not the classical scientific models themselves), people often thought in terms of a static, deterministic (totally predictable) universe. Concerned theologians sought to relate these perspectives to biblical teaching. Then modern science in the form of quantum mechanics emphasized an approach based on an intrinsic indeterminacy or unpredictability observable at the atomic level. Those seeking theological insight from scientific phenomena found great comfort in this change, for it offered them a scientific model for escape from determinism and the apparent possibility of speaking of "free will" and "responsible choice" with scientific approval. Is this interpretation a valid one and how far does it go?

Turning their backs on centuries of an uneasy alliance between science and the Judaeo-Christian tradition, today people who claim scientific credentials argue that recent findings in science show that Eastern religions are the answer to a science-religion integration. In the area of "mysticism for the millions," thousands flock to New Age meetings where they engage in channeling operations to receive wisdom from the dead, or gather together to experience moments of "harmonic convergence." Is this a valid synthesis of science and theology?

Faced with limited frontiers on earth, many are now openly urging massive colonization of space with the setting up of large space stations designed for human society. In the process it is hoped that we will finally be contacted with other intelligent life in the universe, which has solved our human problems and will lead us into a Utopian future.

Three Tricky Presuppositions

Often in discussions of the significance of modern science for Christian theology, three presuppositions creep in unnoticed. They are often treated as if they were scientific, but they are really philosophical choices.

The first presupposition is that the universe is by definition all that exists. If the universe is all that exists, then "God," if he exists, must be part of the universe. This approach leads to a "God" radically inferior to the God of the Bible. Such a "God" is not the Creator of space-time, but is part of space-time. He (or it) is not independent from the creation, but is to a considerable, if not total, extent identical with and perhaps even dependent on the creation.

There is absolutely no scientific imperative for this presupposition. It is a misguided philosophical extrapolation. Biblical theology should keep us aware of the fact that the universe is not all there is. Instead the universe, all space-time that exists, has been created by God who exists independently of the universe. One may choose not to accept this, but it is certainly the biblical position and there is no scientific necessity to abandon it. The universe is separate from God (His transcendence) but totally dependent on God (His immanence).

The second presupposition to watch out for is the claim that if something cannot be measured, it does not exist. Once again this presupposition is based totally on philosophical choice and not on scientific imperative. It removes from the category of "existence" most of the finest and most highly valued human qualities and experiences, not to mention, of course, God himself. There is only a part of reality that can be legitimately investigated by authentic science. To suppose that what science can investigate is the whole of reality is naive indeed.

The third presupposition that is extremely prevalent in all kinds of discussions relating science and theology is that something called "chance" rules out the reality and activity of God in the world. We develop the refutation of this presupposition at several places in the chapters ahead, but it is important to start at the very beginning by at least being forewarned about some common misunderstandings in this area. Worldviews, total frameworks of presuppositions from within which one views the world, are extremely important in dealing with the interaction between science and Christian faith. It is essential to distinguish between a particular type of scientific description (either deterministic or probabilistic, often called "chance") and the type of worldview within which one deals with the major issues of life. It is our contention throughout this book that a Christian worldview based upon the biblical revelation concerning God can correspond in our experience with either a deterministic or a chance scientific description. To speak of a scientific chance description is therefore *never* to imply that God is not acting, that God is not directing, or that God is not sustaining the very existence of the phenomenon being considered.

Cultural vs. Biblical Theology

Another challenge that we face is the difficult task of distinguishing between theology based on an authentic interpretation of the Bible and its application to our daily lives, and theology that is really a deeply-ingrained and hidden residue of our cultural background. All too often our theological views today are based, not on the intent of the biblical revelation itself, but on models derived from scientific views of past centuries, long since outdated in science, but perpetuated in Christian communities.

It is because our theological views are so often still reflections of past scientific perspectives that they appear so vulnerable to inputs from modern science. The example of the church's opposition to Galileo's geocentric model of the universe is one that we need to constantly learn from. The task of biblical interpretation is discerning between what we have always been told a certain passage means, and what the biblical writers intended to convey as God's revelation. This is not an easy or incidental task.

Scientific Description of a Human Being

Another challenge we face is integrating a scientific view of the human being as the consequence of physical-chemical reactions, with the theological view of the human being as a spiritual person made in the image of God. This integration is at the basis of a large number of critical ethical issues that challenge us in the future.

How do we relate such scientific terms as "gene," "malfunction," and "environmental effects," to such theological terms as "soul" and "spirit"? Are theological terms addressed to the whole person such as "sin", "grace," "justification," and "sanctification," as accurate descriptions of human reality as "chemical imbalance," "genetic defect," and "peer pressure"?

What are the causes of the drug culture that is expanding with explosive force at the present time, threatening to undermine the very structure of human society? Is this a problem to be dealt with by applied technology, or are their greater needs of human beings that can be met only through a renewed relationship with God?

New Abilities Developed by Science

Because of the advances of science, human beings can now do things that previously were beyond their ability. Are these abilities obligations for us to act on, dangers for us to shun, or possibilities for us to carefully evaluate?

In the past, many human problems were beyond the knowledge of contemporary medical professionals and as a result had to be "left in the hands of God." Now many of these problems can be solved through human effort. But the question is, "Should they?"

A woman applies to a sperm bank to find a blond, musically inclined father for her child to be conceived in vitro. A man and a woman contract with another woman to be the surrogate mother of their child. Now that scientific technique makes it possible, do people have a "right to have children" no matter what means are used? What are the theological inputs?

In former times disease took its course and the average life span was relatively short. Now through the use of modern technology individuals can be kept alive for a relatively long time. Is keeping a person alive the longest possible time the ultimate goal of medicine? Do people have the "right to die"? We've heard a lot of talk about the "right to life," but as science and technology progress, we are going to hear a lot more about the other end of human life. As the time approaches when it may be technically possible to prolong biological human life indefinitely - provided that someone is willing or can be forced to pay the cost - how will we deal with an individual's desire to leave this world and to be with God without great emotional and economic burdens to his or her family? How does our theology affect our use of science?

Because we can launch a manned space mission to Mars, should we? If we can control the ratio of male to female babies, should we? If we become able to make significant genetic changes in the human being, should we?

In all of these areas, we are dealing with new knowledge; each of the areas may need its own guidelines. As we try to arrive at these guidelines, what model of the human being do we use?

The Value of Human Life

What dimensions of human life give it value, and how much value does it give when preservation of one human life comes into conflict with the preservation of another human life? Is "life" itself sacred, or should we distinguish between different kinds of "life," such as "biological life" vs. "personal life"?

If we affirm the "sanctity of life" what does that really mean when we face difficult decisions about the beginning and ending of human life? Do we have a higher regard for the sanctity of life when we allow a severely deformed infant to die, or when we apply all of the technological resources available to prevent that death? Do we have more regard for the sanctity of life when we use machines, pumps and intravenous feeding to keep a terminally ill person alive, or when, with the person's consent, we pull the plug and let that person die?

All of these questions, already plaguing us with their difficulty, will become more difficult as our technical knowledge and abilities increase. To answer them we need to know how to relate science and theology. Is it proper to distinguish between procedures that should not be followed because they are intrinsically wrong, and others that should not be followed because of their overall social implications? Or, if an action can be shown not to be intrinsically wrong, is it always permissible?

Legal Responsibility

As we get a more accurate picture of what makes human beings act the way they do, we can easily be led to ascribe all of their actions to determinism by genes or by environment.   In view of this kind of social determinism, how do we maintain a proper perspective on social justice, penalties for crime, jail sentences, or capital punishment, all of which are based at least implicitly on the assumption that individuals can be held legally responsible for their actions?   How do we work out in a very practical way the dilemma between determinism and "responsible choice" with regard to those who break the law?

Ecological Responsibility

Every generation believes that the situations it faces are unique. Usually this belief tends to underrate the fact that problems tend to repeat themselves. But perhaps our present generation has more justification for holding such a belief than any generation in the past.

Never before have we faced so imminently the end of the availability of fossil fuels. Never before have we faced so imminently the end of the availability of many scarce natural resources. Never before have we so thoroughly polluted our air, water and lands in the effort to advance civilization. Never before have many new sources of non-renewable energy been so fraught with obvious danger. Never before has international competition reached such an intensity.

How do we responsibly act the role of "steward" or "caretaker" that is assigned to us by the Bible, with respect to technological use of the environment?   Should certain areas of science and technology be pursued because they promise to ease these problems, and others not pursued because they seem to be indifferent to them, or even to aggravate them?

Social Responsibility

What guidelines should Christians have who are called to a career in science? Is it possible that the day might come when Christians could not in good conscience participate in a branch of science or technology that is indifferent to or destructive of basic human values?

How many of these considerations should influence the Christian in business in an increasingly technologically involved situation?

To what extent is the Christian scientist or engineer personally responsible for the applications that are made of his or her work?

Summary

In this look at the issues we have raised many questions. Many other books have been devoted to suggesting answers to these specific questions. Our purpose here is more modest: (1) to suggest that the appropriate areas to compare are "science" and "Christian theology," and (2) to emphasize the importance of the way in which we relate insights from science and insights from Christian theology in order to come to some theoretical and some very practical conclusions.

Our first task in the next two chapters is to suggest definitions of "authentic science" and "authentic theology," which we can then apply in considering the various patterns of interaction.

Chapter 2

Authentic Science

We start with the assumption that it is possible to define what we mean by "authentic science" and to distinguish between this "authentic science" and other non-authentic science (or pseudoscience). It may be objected that science does not have such a well-defined definition and that many disagree on what form that definition should take. It is certainly true that the definition of "science" has changed over the last two millennia. But I believe that there is a core of agreement at least among all those actually involved in the practice of science, and it is this agreement that is presented here.

The Pattern of History [27]

The philosopher Aristotle explained natural events in terms of purpose. His concept was that objects fall to the ground when dropped because they seek their natural resting place. Explanations of this kind are called *teleological.* They are obviously quite different from the mechanistic descriptions of modern science. If the world is the creation of a purposeful God, then the working out of his purposes in the events of the natural world constitutes the ultimate explanation. Scientific theories following this approach are based upon the assumption of a "perfect" world. Questions about the shape of the planetary orbits are answered by the assurance that they must be circular because that is the perfect shape. The earth has to be the center of the universe for it is the stage upon which God's purposes are acted out. The very idea of experimenting to understand the natural world was an alien concept. As a consequence, the pronouncements of this kind of science were only as valid as the model of deductions based on a "perfect" universe could provide. It was commonly assumed then (as it sometimes still is today) that the question "What did God do?" is automatically answered by the question "What can God do?" The assumption is made that the character of God expressed in the second question necessarily ensures the answer to the first question, and that the answer to the second question is so well understood and defined that the answers to the first question are unambiguous.

Galileo (1564-1642) and his work are the symbols in history of the development of two new ingredients in human attempts to understand nature: the combination of mathematical reasoning with experimental observations. The perspective that these changes introduced differed greatly from that of Aristotle. Aristotle's view was that a swinging pendulum came to rest because rest was its natural state; Galileo's view was that the pendulum would continue to swing forever except for the effects of friction. Aristotle saw in the stopping pendulum the outworkings of a grand teleological pattern; Galileo saw rubbing on the axis. The shift in the nature of the explanation carried with it a logical shift in the nature of the questions to be asked by the new science. The ultimate teleological "why" questions were replaced by the immediate mechanistic "how" questions. Models to describe natural processes took the form of matter in motion; scientific explanations involve predominantly the categories of mass, energy, space, and time. The way was opened to finding out what God *did* do by actually looking at the effects of his action in the world, rather than by abstract deduction from the attributes that define what God *can* do. The approach of induction to understand the nature of the universe was given a place alongside the previously dominant approach of deduction.

None of this contradicted basic biblical theology in itself. The Judaeo-Christian doctrine of creation teaches that the creation is understandable by human beings, that it is a created order and not a direct manifestation of the divine itself, and that human stewardship over nature is part of the mandate given to humans by God. Science is based on the presupposition that the world is orderly and knowable and that the investigation of the world is a good pursuit to follow.

Nevertheless the basic change in the ways adopted to answer the fundamental question "What did God do?" had profound effects on the perceived relationships between science and theology. Many of these were excessive and unjustified. As a teleological mode of explanation (a mode based on the purpose of the action) gave way to a mechanistic mode, the concept of God as the Supreme Good was altered to that of the First Cause. Increases in mechanistic-type descriptions led to the picture of God as the Divine Clockmaker and ultimately to the deistic view of God as the vague, almost irrelevant, impulse behind the beginnings of things. The concept of a self-sufficient, law-abiding universe made any activity of God in the present apparently both difficult and unnecessary. It is essential that we realize that these excesses and overreactions are not demanded by science itself. Many of these excesses were identified as such through new scientific insights expressed through relativity and quantum mechanics, which themselves have been appropriated to defend philosophical and metaphysical extrapolations that constitute new excesses. They are the consequences of human beings with a philosophical ax to grind seeking to find in science the appropriate ax-grinder.

How then shall we define "authentic science" today? (1) We seek to understand what approaches or techniques give to scientific inquiry the kind of valid and trustworthy role that it plays in so much of our modern world. (2) We recognize the limitations of these approaches and techniques, so that we do not suppose that they enable us to answer all of the important questions in life, but only those that are accessible to the kind of approach that carries with it an inbuilt protection against human ignorance and perversity, the constant ability to check and test whether or not the latest descriptions really are adequate to describe physical reality.

Definition of Authentic Science

By the term "authentic science" we mean :

A particular way of knowing, based on descriptions of the world obtained through the human interpretation in natural categories, of publicly observable and reproducible sense data, obtained by sense interaction with the natural world.

This definition in no way rules out creative thinking or uninhibited speculation; it does demand that such efforts at interpretation be *testable* in the ways specified. To say that something is not included within this definition of science is *not* to say that it is not true, important, or meaningful. It is only to claim that such a concept or event is outside the domain of authentic science, which by itself describes only a part of reality, and that it cannot therefore claim whatever validating support authentic science might give. It is adherence to this definition of science that gives science integrity and value; once we begin to depart appreciably from such a definition, we have an enterprise that no longer shares in the reliability and trust appropriate to authentic science.

Each of the terms in the definition is significant.

(1) To say that <u>science is *a* particular way of knowing</u> is to deny that science is *the* (only) way of knowing. Other ways of knowing include (a) being told something by another person who knows and is worthy of trust, or in the Christian context being told something by God through the writers of the Bible; (b) interpersonal experiences, as in the shared experiences of two good friends or of husband and wife; and (c) intuition, to name a few examples.

The worldview based on the belief that science is *the* way of knowing is often called "Scientism;" it affirms that science is the only source of truth and that the scientific method is the only guide to truth. It is essential to maintain a sharp distinction between science, the outworking of a particular approach to understanding the natural world, and Scientism, the non-scientific developing of a philosophy or worldview that exalts the scientific approach above all others and draws consequent conclusions from such a position. Science can tell us something about how things work in the universe, but it does not provide us with knowledge of why the universe is ultimately the way it is, nor can it inform us about the purpose or meaning of its existence. [28]

One day a bright student in my seminar remarked, "I don't see how it's possible to say that you can know something if you can't prove it scientifically." Several other students in the class nodded in approval. "How do you know," I responded, "that it's not possible to know something that you can't prove scientifically." Can the basic presupposition of Scientism be proven scientifically? The student was taken by surprise. He was caught on the horns of a dilemma. So my student, and the many others like him, seek to develop an approach to life that is wholly scientific - but at the first step they find themselves cut off. They cannot scientifically choose an approach to life. Seeking to live a life based only on reason and not at all on faith, they must make a faith commitment as the very first step. Indeed to believe that science is the only source of truth is exactly that: a belief.

Any choice of an approach to life, a worldview, an ultimate perspective, a *Weltanschauung*, must be an act of faith. Nothing can be done until the faith commitment is made. Attempts to argue that some approaches to life are completely objective and scientific whereas others are entirely subjective and unscientific must all fail.

The claim that the scientific method is the only reliable guide to knowledge is not something that our modern scientific understanding demands. Indeed, if one accepts the presupposition that the scientific method is the only reliable guide to knowledge, he is involved in an inconsistent activity. By his own standard, the acceptance of this presupposition must be a subjective commitment with no more objective claim to truth than one's commitment to standards of artistic beauty or taste in foods.

To say that science is a way of knowing, is to affirm that there are other ways of knowing, that science is one way among several. What we wish to know determines which way of knowing is most relevant for us. This is another way of saying that deciding on the right questions is often a major step toward obtaining significant answers.

Science is concerned primarily with "how" questions. Such questions deal with the mechanisms of our physical universe. They are important questions, but they do not cover all the questions that we need to ask. It is important for us to try to understand not only how something happens, but in some ultimate sense why it happens and what its ultimate value is for the universe and its Creator.

Questions of meaning, purpose, and value cannot be answered by the scientific approach. These are the questions that are the most important for human life and fulfillment. We find their answers in other ways of knowing than that one way provided by science.

(2) <u>Science is a way of knowing</u>. By the pursuit of science we do indeed come to understand better the physical universe in which we live. Authentic science is not simply an esoteric game but a way to understand the world better. We construct scientific models that tell us partially about what the world is like. They do not tell us what the world is - but they are able to give us valid insights into some aspects of reality. This position is thus intermediate between the extremes of saying that science is the only way of knowing (scientism) on the one hand, and of saying that science does not provide us with a way of knowing at all (instrumentalism or operationalism).

(3) The question we need to ask is, "What kind of knowing is it?" The answer is that science provides us with <u>a way of knowing that arises from our ability to describe the world</u> to some degree of accuracy.

What we do is to construct a model (a picture, an analogy, a simile, a metaphor) of the unknown situation based upon our understanding of the known. A good model tells us what the world is like. It does not tell us what the world is. The result is that science provides us with partial knowledge - never with complete knowledge - but we have reason to believe that this partial knowledge is, within its own sphere, reliable knowledge.

It is often said that science provides us with explanations of the physical universe. This might be an acceptable statement if we understand it to mean that a good description is a partial explanation. Let us consider briefly the ways in which these two key terms are commonly used.

(3a) <u>Does Science Explain the Universe?</u> [29]   Typical of remarks that one may hear are: "Science has passed from the descriptive stage to the explanatory stage: from telling us what things look like to telling us what causes them to be the way they are." Or, "People used to believe mythological explanations for natural phenomena until science explained them. Now, of course, there is neither need nor room for supernatural categories."

Perhaps it is most helpful to realize that both of these words have meanings on two levels. Trying to match meanings of the two words from different levels always leads to confusion. Let us call the two levels, "soft" and "hard."

To describe in a "soft" way means essentially to catalogue. We note what meets the eye: the color and shape of objects, whether the objects be leaves, rocks, or animals. We tell what they look like "to the eye." We may make groupings such as large leaves, medium-sized leaves, and small leaves; magnetic rocks and non-magnetic rocks; animals that lay eggs and those that do not. We give "names" to the various kinds we see and we arrange these names in ordered sequences. It is the kind of activity found prominently in classical biology and botany, before biochemistry and genetics came on the scene. Science starts with "soft" descriptions, but it does not end there.

To describe in a "hard" way means to come up with a model or a picture of the thing or event being described, using phenomena with which we are familiar to describe phenomena with which we have not previously been familiar. It is the language of mathematics, simile and metaphor, of conceptual models that seek to produce properties that are similar to those that we see. We say that "an atom is like a miniature solar system with the electrons going around the nucleus like planets around the sun." There are profound differences, because the electrons are held by electromagnetic forces whereas the planets are held by gravitational forces. Then we ask, "If the atom can be modeled as a miniature solar system, what predictions can we make from our knowledge of the solar system that we might then test to see if their analog is exhibited by the electrons around an atom?" Later we find that the model of a miniature solar system is not adequate to quantitatively describe many of the properties of the atom that we can observe. We are led to try to come up with some other model that will be more completely consistent with known properties of the atom, and, if possible, be successful in predicting properties that we have not previously known. The model described by modern quantum mechanics supplies many of these additional insights into the nature of an atom. In the future, new models yet unthought of may do still better. In all of these activities science is fundamentally engaged in the process of "hard" as well as "soft" descriptions.

The "soft" use of "explain" arises from our ability to say the following: If we have come up with a reasonably reliable model (a "hard" description), then this model tells us accurately in a variety of ways what the thing or event is like and how it behaves. Whereas before the description we had no idea of "how it worked," now we have an idea of "how it works" - and hence, we have a kind of explanation (a "soft" explanation). Whereas at one time we did not know why an apple fell to the ground, now we can "explain" it by invoking the model of gravity. We are provided with immediate (sometimes called "proximate") mechanisms for how things work. Lunar eclipses are not totally mystical events that defy human understanding; we can "explain" them by noting the optical phenomena involved in the casting of the earth's shadow on the moon when the configuration of the earth, moon and sun are appropriate. In fact, we can with great precision predict future eclipses, since they depend rigorously on fairly simple geometrical properties of the solar system. Our "hard" description has provided us with a "soft" explanation.

A "hard" explanation seeks to go further - it claims that the knowledge of only immediate mechanisms ("proximate causes") is all that is meaningful, necessary or relevant, not only within science but for all of life. It denies that the concept of "ultimate cause" has any relevance. Once we have provided knowledge of a physical mechanism, then we have "explained *away* " any other interpretation. This use of the concept of "hard" explanations is based on the assumption that all meaningful answers are scientifically obtainable answers (the worldview of Scientism), and that therefore once a scientific answer has been obtained, there are no other relevant considerations. In this view the development of a "hard" explanation in terms of a mechanistic model that works does away with the meaning of any other kinds of "soft" explanations in terms of other models or categories of human experience.

Suppose again that we see an apple fall to the ground. In the absence of any scientific understanding, a person might argue that God is the direct cause of the apple falling to the ground. With an increase in scientific understanding, we may say that the apple falls to the ground because of gravity, a force between two bodies of matter depending on their respective masses and the distance between them. We have described the phenomenon by developing a model and can also observe its applicability to many other similar phenomena. We understand better than we did the mechanisms involved in falling bodies. We have provided a "soft" explanation of the falling apple.

Some might conclude that our scientific explanation has explained away any need to refer to God's activity at all. *Not at all!* What we have done is to obtain insight into the secondary or proximate causes of an apple falling; we have said nothing, nor can we say anything within science, about the primary or ultimate causes of an apple falling - why in fact there should be any such thing as an apple or masses in existence in the first place, or why, being in existence, they should exhibit the properties that they do.

Science, therefore, can tell us *how* things work in the universe, but it does not provide us with knowledge of *why* the universe is the way it is in an ultimate sense, nor can it inform us about the purpose or meaning of its existence, or of God's underlying sustaining activity.

To speak only of "soft" descriptions does not do justice to the nature of modern science in seeking for ever more sophisticated and representative models of the world – for "hard" descriptions. To speak of "hard" explanations is to introduce a faith commitment to Scientism that proximate causes are the only causes.

If we speak about science providing us with "explanations," we run the risk of being misunderstood by those who interpret what we say as referring to "hard" explanations rather than "soft" explanations. What science does is provide "hard" descriptions that serve as "soft" explanations.

(3b) Does Science Provide Proofs? [30] Another common assumption is that science can give us proof of its conclusions. The dictionary (31) defines "to prove" as "to establish the existence, truth, or validity of (as by evidence or logic)."

How do we respond when someone asks the traditional agnostic question, "Can you prove the existence of God?" Do we stammer and begin to talk about ontological, cosmological and teleological "proofs" for the existence of God? Or do we simply say, "No, and we shouldn't be surprised, because the kinds of things that can be 'proved' are very small indeed."

Few words are more often misused in discussions relating science and theology than the word "prove." This misuse reflects the equally common misuse of the word in everyday language. Following the dictionary definition, "to prove" means to *establish* the truth or validity of something by presenting evidence or by logic. Here the word "establish" is usually taken to imply absolute conviction, so that only a mentally incompetent or a willfully obstinate person could deny it.

The means of "establishing" in "proving" is the presentation of evidence or the application of logic, i.e., utilization of the scientific method. But a person who assumes that all significant dimensions of life or all insights into the truth, are ascertainable by the scientific method, has already made a fundamental faith assumption to Scientism.

We need also to recognize that major areas of life's most precious characteristics – the existence of God, the uniqueness of human nature, love, beauty, justice, courage, hope or any other topic with profound philosophical or theological significance – are simply not areas to which one can meaningfully apply the categories needed for "proof" to be considered.

But the appropriate understanding of "prove" is even more limited than this. Even within those areas in which it is appropriate to apply scientific methods, we are still severely limited in what we can adequately describe as "proof." The basic meaning of "to prove" – if interpreted rigorously - means (a) that it is not possible to prove *anything* without reference to some underlying assumptions that are chosen without prior "proof" (i.e., "on faith"), and (b) that even within the constraints of point (a) , it is still not possible strictly to prove anything except in the fields of mathematics and formal logic.

Here the dictionary definition may do us a disservice, for it implies that proof may occur equally well either by the presentation of evidence or the application of logic. If we take the definition of "to prove" as "to establish" in an unquestionable sense, then it follows that the presentation of evidence can never "prove" anything. The presentation of evidence may convince us that it is permissible and possibly even wise for us to believe something, but it cannot decisively establish "truth and validity."

Therefore, even within science itself, it is not strictly possible "to prove" our hypotheses. In science we do not prove; rather we accumulate and interpret evidence. If we are able to build up a sufficiently imposing set of experimental results consistent with a particular model or theory, that model or theory will be generally accepted - at least until a better or more complete one is suggested and tested.

There is, of course, a category of questions to which one might still insist that the label of "proof" is appropriate; questions of a relatively simple and factual nature for which the evidence is so overwhelming that indeed no one would disagree except the mentally deficient or the willfully obstinate. Can one not legitimately claim that it has been "proved" that the earth is round rather than flat, or that the earth moves around the sun rather than the sun around the earth, or that the universe is far more than 10,000 years old? These are indeed examples of situations where the accumulation of evidence is so great that no reasonable alternative can presently be envisioned. But this appears to be a "soft" use of "prove;" if we do use the word in this way, we need to stay alert so that its implications do not stray into other areas where it is not possible to speak of authentic proof.

It might also be claimed that whereas it is not usually appropriate to speak about "proving" the truth of a particular argument in science, it is appropriate at times to speak of "disproving" the truth of that argument. It is frequently said that all the evidence in the world cannot "prove" a theory true, but only one experiment can "prove" a theory false. In fact, the ability to be falsifiable is one of the criteria (a somewhat less stringent criterion than the ability to be testable) that has been used to ascertain whether a theory is really scientific or not. Although the case for this perspective may be overstated, and may not take sufficient account of the resilience of scientific orthodoxy and politics in the scientific community, it does come close to a valid case for the use of "prove" in a negative sense.

It is possible to prove some things within mathematics and formal logic - provided that we agree on the postulates which are assumed to permit the logical process to be carried out. In this procedure we do establish the truth of our mathematical and logical conclusions, provided that the postulates are true. But the truth of the postulates cannot be subjected to logic, and cannot themselves be proved from anything more fundamental.

(3c) <u>Determinism and Chance Descriptions in Science.</u> One of the most vital of all considerations concerning the type of descriptions that science gives involves the meaning and significance of such terms as "determinism" and "chance." Why is this so critical? It is critical because many people in many different lines of argument assume that one can draw philosophical or theological conclusions from the type of scientific description.   This is heard most often in statements such as, "Since science says that this is a chance process, this means that God has been ruled out." These considerations are so critical that we must take the time at this point to make absolutely clear what is and what is not involved in such statements. In various other parts of this book further on, we will need to refer back to these considerations - so common is the popular tendency to confuse "deterministic" and "chance" as scientific descriptions without theological implications, with "Determinism" and "Chance" as dominant worldviews with detailed theological commitments.

Our consideration starts with the basic realization that any scientific description must be one of two types. It must be able either to predict accurately the future state of a system from knowledge of its present state - such a description is called "deterministic"; or it may be able only to predict the probability of the future state of a system from knowledge of its present state - such a description is called "chance." *There is no other type of scientific description.* If you make a scientific description at all, it has to be of one type or the other. Dependence upon only one or the other of these completely can lead to some interesting paradoxes.

Consider, for example, the following curious paradox. What kind of scientific description of a human being is indicative of the ability of the person to act with some measure of personal responsibility? A deterministic scientific description appears to contradict such personal responsibility – for how can what is determined be an act for which one can be held personally responsible? But at the same time, a deterministic scientific description is needed. For how can a responsible choice exist without being describable in a definite cause (the basis for the choice) and effect (the result of the choice) framework?

By contrast, a chance (probabilistic) scientific description appears to make room for personal responsibility by removing the constraints of determinism; but how can a situation be considered to involve a responsible human choice if it corresponds to chance, a random and unpredictable action?

Now the situation is made infinitely worse if the mistake is made of supposing that deterministic scientific descriptions can be taken as the basis for a *worldview* of Determinism (note the capital "D") in which human beings are little more than genetic or environmental robots, or when chance scientific descriptions are believed to be the basis for a *worldview* of Chance (note the capital "C") in which existence is intrinsically meaningless. Determinism as a worldview is equivalent to Fatalism; Chance as a worldview is equivalent to Meaninglessness. *Neither* of these is consistent with a biblical worldview. If both Determinism and Chance do violence to the biblical view of the human being, therefore, and if *only* deterministic or chance descriptions are possible for science, how can we get out of this dilemma?

The first step is to realize that a deterministic scientific description does not demand a worldview of Determinism. Neither does a chance scientific description demand a worldview of Chance. In both cases a philosophical extrapolation has been made beyond the relevance of the scientific concepts to arrive at a worldview that is not demanded by the scientific concepts themselves.

In most major complex systems, there is an interaction between scientifically described deterministic (small "d") and chance (small "c") effects. An individual event, like the decay of a radioactive atom, may be scientifically described as a chance event since no known scientifically describable cause for the event exists; but the time for half of a large number of radioactive atoms to decay (their "half-life") can be predicted deterministically, since the application of probability to a large number of cases yields a well-defined value.

In a later chapter (Chapter 9, Pattern 6) when we consider some of the implications of quantum mechanics, we will consider other cases like this. As an example to look at now, consider the fact that the position and velocity of atomic particles can be described only within a scientific chance (probabilistic) framework, but the probability itself can be described deterministically (i.e., the variation of the probability with time can be described mathematically accurately).

A scientific description may be totally deterministic in form, but its future predictions may be largely controlled by particular " boundary conditions" (e.g., the exact values of specific quantities at a specific time) that may well be the result of scientifically described chance. What does this mean? It simply means that the boundary conditions cannot be scientifically determined. But what may in one framework be described scientifically by "chance," can within another framework be equally accurately described theologically as "Providence."

A deterministically describable process can be the instrument of design (as in the specific configuration of hydrogen and oxygen atoms in the water molecule), but so can a process scientifically describable as chance. If, for example, there are three different atomic or molecular configurations possible for a system, that configuration giving the lowest energy will be formed in equilibrium. The corresponding decrease in system energy is the cause of its formation. But if all three different configurations correspond to the same energy, then the one that is found in a given situation is by definition the result of (scientific) chance. This example corresponds to the creativity expressed in the multiplicity of human beings described scientifically through the chance assignment of DNA configurations.

This last observation is thought provoking: the activity by which unique individuals made in the image of God are formed in human reproduction is a process that is scientifically described as chance!

This is not an isolated occurrence but appears to be typical of the character of the natural world at a fundamental level.

It may be helpful to think of the relationship between chance in connection with natural processes and *coincidence* in connection with events. So many really decisive periods in a human's life can be associated with the presence of a coincidence. Consider the following typical scenario:

> I was going about my daily duties (in a way continuously describable as cause and effect) and she was going about her daily duties (also in a way continuously describable as cause and effect). Without any violation of these regularities, "it just so happened" that we sat down on the bus next to each other. We started a lifelong relationship of love and commitment, got married and raised a family. What happened that day on the bus has affected and shaped our lives to a tremendous extent ever since. It was all the result of that less than one-in-a-million coincidence of finding ourselves on the same bus in neighboring seats at the same time!

If described in scientific terms, the meeting was a totally *chance* occurrence. But would you conclude that we would be mistaken to also see it clearly as a *providential* action of God? Did God *intervene* in our lives from outside? Not in any perceivable way. Was what we were doing describable in a continuous cause and effect chain of events? Yes, apparently in every way. Did God bring about something new? Yes, he certainly did. Is there any reason, therefore, why something that we "scientifically" describe as "coincidence" cannot also be the expression of God's designing activity and purpose? Is the situation with scientific chance and God's genuine activity in the natural world really any different?

If there is a single thing that we learn from this consideration, it is the following:

> *Our affirmation of the genuine activity of God in creating and sustaining the physical universe is not dependent upon our using a particular kind of scientific description. A scientific description as "chance" is fully as compatible with the statement "God acts" as is a scientific description as "determinism." God creates and sustains the entire universe within which we carry out our deterministic or chance scientific descriptions.*

The failure to recognize this lies at the basis of many of the confusions in the attempt to relate scientific and theological descriptions.   We shall confront some of these in the following chapters.

As a kind of footnote to this discussion it is instructive to note that the development of science in the last few centuries has given the interaction between "determinism" and "chance" a new twist by the scientific recognition of a condition known as "chaos." In the popular mind, chaos is what one would expect in a completely random or chance-oriented environment.   In recent years, however, it has been realized that a state described as "chaos" can result from a strictly deterministic description in time if the final state is hypercritically dependent on the exact initial boundary conditions. Counter examples are also available that show how an orderly pattern or structure can be obtained from a large set of random (chance) events suitably limited by appropriate boundary conditions: the generation of order out of chaos. There is no necessary profound philosophical or theological implications in these results, but they warn us to avoid any simplistic dichotomies between deterministic and chance descriptions as we face interactions between science and theology.

(4) Science is an activity carried out by human beings. It is characterized by hard work, intuition, insight, guesswork, and serendipity as much as (and sometimes more than) the logical, step-by-step pursuit of closely interlocked deductions and inductions.

The actual doing of science is not free from the political, philosophical or religious convictions of the people engaged in doing it.   When it functions well, it behaves like a community of human beings with a common commitment and perspective.   When it functions badly, the ideological convictions of the people involved prevent them from being faithful to the openness and honesty required by authentic science and science's contributions wither.

(5) Science is based on the human interpretation of the evidences and observations made in the scientific pursuit of understanding. Sometimes science is described as if it consisted only of collecting and ordering facts.   Such a picture forgets that along with its experimental and empirical side, science is held together by its theoretical side.

Facts, at best, are only facts.   No fact ever provides us with its own interpretation: how it fits into the larger scheme of things, and which model is best for describing its occurrence and significance. We cannot work with any fact, put it into place in our total understanding of the universe, or decide on its intrinsic significance or meaning, without engaging in interpretation.   Interpretation is not some kind of undesirable limitation that we should avoid.   It is the necessary activity by which we go from data to significance, from experiment to theory, from principle to practice, from generalizations to specific applications. (Interpretation plays, as we will see, a similar role in theology.)

In some way every experimental "fact" is "theory-laden," and the scientist must strive to take into account the complexities of the interpretational task. He usually does this by constructing, in as neutral a mode as possible, experimental tests of a greater and greater demanding nature to test the hypotheses and theories being used. The ability to be open to "test" is a critical criterion for a scientific hypothesis. It is generally agreed that a hypothesis that cannot be tested (even if it should be true) cannot be considered as a *scientific* hypothesis. Examples of hypotheses that are not scientific are the following: (1) the universe instantaneously came into being five minutes ago, but with every possible sign and indication consistent with being much older (including the memory of every human being); (2) the investigation of a new property of matter is characterized by the behavior that it immediately disappears into an unmeasurable form whenever one attempts to measure it.

What we call scientific laws are the results of human interpretation of phenomena observed in the universe. They are our ways of tying things together. For this reason it is said that laws are descriptive and not prescriptive. Physical laws never cause anything to happen. Physical laws are human descriptions of the way that things usually do happen. For the Christian, therefore, physical laws are human descriptions of God's usual activity in creating and upholding the universe.

Some laws correspond to deterministic scientific descriptions (Newton's law: $F = m\,a$, relating the force F acting on a body of mass m and moving with acceleration a) ; whereas other laws correspond to chance scientific descriptions (Heisenberg's Indeterminacy relationship: $\Delta x\,\Delta p > h/2\pi$, relating the uncertainty in the position x of an electron and the uncertainty in the momentum p of that electron, where h is a basic physical constant known as Planck's constant). Either form of law, whether deterministic or chance, is a human description of God's activity. We may not understand fully everything that is involved in these considerations, but that is another story, a very common story for those working in science.

Our interpretations are constantly varying. For many years scientists spoke of the conservation of mass, arguing that in any interaction one of the quantities that had to be conserved was the total mass of the participating entities. It was for them a law of the physical universe: the Law of the Conservation of Mass. More recently we discovered that energy and mass can be converted back and forth from one form to the other under the proper circumstances. The energy released in nuclear reactions is the energy obtained from the conversion of some mass into energy. The conversion of a gamma-ray into an electron and a positron is an example of conversion of energy into mass. One could argue that this violates the Law of the Conservation of Mass, but it is far more appropriate to recognize that the Law of the Conservation of Mass was our description of what we experienced before we realized that mass could be converted into energy and that energy could be converted into mass. No immutable law has been violated; only our descriptions of the world have changed.

(6) Science is concerned <u>by definition with natural categories,</u> categories that can be described within the mechanistic perspective of science. Authentic science limits itself to a particular kind of description that is testable within a type of activity accessible to human beings in a reproducible way. It is precisely this limitation that also marks the strength of scientific descriptions and understandings. If we are going to deal with issues that transcend natural categories, we need other kinds of inputs and insights. We are free to embrace science gratefully for its great contributions within the sphere of activity where it is equipped to act, and we are free at the same time to embrace other contributions to understanding for their ability to supplement the insights of science with insights that science cannot provide.

Science does not limit itself to natural categories because of some prejudice against supernatural descriptions, but simply to limit the scope and the content of authentic science to a well defined and testable range. Science's emphasis on descriptions in natural categories is not the response to the question, "How must things happen if God is unable to act in the world?" But it is rather the response to the question, "If God chose to act in the world in a way that can be scientifically described (rather than in an unusual or miraculous way), how do we describe the proximate mechanisms that manifest his activity?"

We acquire a great freedom in understanding once we appreciate two closely related truths: (a) science does not, science should not, and science cannot provide answers to ultimate meaning, purpose, and primary causes; (b) there are insights into reality that cannot be obtained by scientific investigation, i.e., they are not scientifically-meaningful questions, but this in no way represents a negative judgment against the validity or value of such insights.

(7) Evidence acceptable as scientific must be <u>accessible to public and reproducible testing</u>. Private visions, insights and revelations do not provide the basis for a scientific description. A reported result that can be obtained only by a single experimenter is not accepted as scientifically significant.

(8) The kinds of information that scientists obtain involve the acquisition of sense data by interaction with the natural world. This part of the definition accentuates the experimental activities of science, just as the previous emphasis on human interpretation accentuated the theoretical activities of science. The two aspects of science fit closely together.

The subject matter of science, both theoretical and experimental, therefore, must be suitable for test by the acquisition of sense data in interaction with the world. These sense data must be able to be detected by one of the five human senses, or by an instrument (such as a microscope or a current meter) that makes accessible to the human senses quantitative information that they could not directly gather. The reliability of these instruments is by no means a trivial aspect of science.

Science is limited then to those kinds of questions and those areas of human experience that can be investigated by sense interactions. Thus we may say that science provides us with a partial knowledge of part of the world: a kind of partial, partial knowledge. This comprises an important set of categories for human life and experience, but it does not comprise all that human beings would like to know or need to know.

Characteristics of Authentic Science

As a consequence of this definition, science can be described as having various general characteristics. A few of the more prominent examples follow.

(1) *Presuppositional Foundations.* A Christian sees science as possible because it is a reasonable thing to step out in faith on the basis of the biblical doctrines of creation and providence. In order for the non-Christian to effectively do science, certain basic practical presuppositions must be shared with the Christian scientist, even if conscious personal assent to the theological basis for these presuppositions is absent.

It must be assumed that the world is understandable through rational processes of the human mind, that the human mind can conceive analogies and models that adequately describe the natural world. It must be assumed that natural phenomena are reproducible in some general and universal sense; if we fix a standard condition, it is possible to get the same results in the United States or Russia, under a Republican or a Socialist government, in South Africa by an African or at the North

Pole by an Eskimo. When one makes such assumptions and tests them, he finds in many cases that they are indeed justified and worthwhile. Nevertheless he had to assume them and act before he could know that they are reliable. He also has to assume that there are patterns of order than can be sought out and found. It is sometimes claimed that we force our concepts of order upon the universe; there may well be examples of this, but there are many examples where such a claim seems inappropriate (e.g., could the Periodic Table of the Elements be a figment of our imagination and not actually descriptive of atomic structure?).

Another striking experience is the way in which so often human minds working in abstract mathematics have developed a system of principles, postulates, theorems or the like, which then at some later time turns out quite independently to describe with remarkable accuracy the actual events taking place in the physical world. Is there not considerable wonder associated with the recognition that the Schroedinger equation (a simple differential equation) leads directly to the basic structure of the hydrogen atom on the condition only that its solutions not violate what is possible in the physical world (i.e., that they be mathematically well behaved)?

Why should these presuppositions be accepted? Why should we think that these presuppositions are valid and reasonable? The Christian answer is that they are reasonable because there is a given structure, there is an objective reality, there is subject matter for the pursuit of science. Furthermore we are made in the image of God and therefore have the possibility of understanding at least partially what this structure is like. No one can proceed successfully in science without tacitly accepting these presuppositions.

On the other hand, private presuppositions have no place in science. We cannot say, "I suppose that such and such must be found in a scientific investigation; therefore I will go out and find it. " As soon as that is said, as soon as we import some kind of philosophical or even religious presupposition and attempt to impose it upon science, then we may be doing something significant philosophically or religiously, but we have ceased to do science.

(2) *Revealer of Physical Reality.* In many different ways the pursuit of science in its basic and especially its applied forms forces upon us the realization of the objective reality of the world within which we live. We are constantly reminded that the structure and properties of this world, as expressions of God's continuing activity, encompass and rule us, and not we the structure.

If a person mistakenly believes that a description of reality in terms of gravity is something totally imposed upon the universe by human minds and hence not binding on himself, he is certain to suffer the consequences of violating the conditions of life in the context of that reality. If he believes that the attraction of gravity is available for subjective interpretation and that he has the individualistic freedom to walk off the top of a tall building in defiance of any objective reality to gravitational attraction ("Your reality may include gravitational attraction, but my reality doesn't"), he soon learns to his hurt that violation of the structure of the world defined by the continuing creative and sustaining activity of God cannot be made without paying the price.

If a person mistakenly believes that biochemistry and biology are such that taking a large dose of strychnine will have no affect on him, he soon learns that the structure of the world dictates according to God's intention what is poison for the human system and what is not. This dictate is not suspended by his attempt to ignore reality.

Engineering, technology, applied science – perhaps even more than basic science – bring home the necessity to conform one's design to the reality of the God-given structure of the world. The grandest idea, the noblest conception of the drafting room, the most elegant design conceived by the human mind, all must face the ultimate and intrinsic test of conformity with the natural world . A burning desire to design an airship in the shape of a giant octagon does not result in getting the craft off the ground unless the structure of the world that dictates the requirements of aerodynamic flight is heeded. Human beings can imagine what they will; their thoughts are confirmed only if they are consistent with that pattern of created structure that is given to them by God, which they did not form, and over which they have no ultimate control.

Certainly one of the major ecological lessons that we are learning today is the simple fact that we are constrained by the given structure of this world. We are not free to violate this structure endlessly and without limit; our forgetfulness of this limitation leads us to upset the balance of nature that is infinitely more complex and intricately interconnected as an expression of God's activity than we ever supposed before.

This revelation of the structure of reality through science also informs us about the nature of freedom. To live without due regard for existing structure is not the exercise of freedom; it is rather an invitation to loss of freedom both temporarily and possibly permanently.   The truly free person must recognize fully the constraints and limitations by which he is bounded; any attempt to act contrary to these constraints and limitations produces only loss of freedom.   Freedom can be experienced and developed only within the confines of existing structure. No amount of individual subjectivism enables one to violate the physical properties describing this structure in order to pursue some concept of absolute freedom.

And similarly we can press this point further to suggest that no amount of individual subjectivism enables one to violate the interpersonal, relational structures of life ordained by God in order to pursue some ideal of absolute personal freedom. Absolute freedom does not exist in this universe, because it fails to take into account the objective reality of both physical and interpersonal structures given to us and defined by God. Absolute freedom is characteristic only of chaos and is incompatible with order.   True freedom, freedom that is faithful to reality, operates within the framework of the given structure in both the physical world and in the world of interpersonal relationships.

(3) *Impersonal.*   By the human personality we mean such characteristics as rational thought, God-consciousness, appreciation of beauty, self-consciousness, the desire for understanding, insight, duty, faith, love, conscience - and most of all the ability to relate to other persons, including the most profound personal relationship to God.

This crucial distinction between the interaction of a person with a thing and with another person is developed at some length in Martin Buber's *I and Thou.* [32]   He distinguishes between an I-It relationship, a relationship between a person and a thing, and an I-Thou relationship, a relationship between two persons.   An I-It relationship has only one subject, the I; an I-Thou relationship has two subjects, both I and Thou. Although many of the activities of a human being involve I-It relationships, those that characterize the human state most often involve I-Thou relationships. It is science's necessary limitation to the realm of I-It that makes it unsuitable for an exclusive description of the life of the whole person.

In a scientific investigation, there is only one subject: the scientist himself.   All else is the object of the investigation.   This is clearly true when the physicist deals with the elements of the physical world, but it is no less true when the sociologist deals with society.   The object of the investigation is observed, measured, manipulated, tested, described and controlled.   The scientist succeeds as scientist to the extent that he maintains this impersonal relationship.   It is of course impossible for the scientist to prevent all interaction between himself and his experiment, and this necessary interaction forms one of the limitations of science, but it is the constant goal of science to minimize or at least to be able to take account of this interaction.

This restriction is desirable for science, but it makes it impossible for science to deal fully with the interpersonal dimensions of human life. It causes necessary distinctions to be made, for example, between research psychology and clinical psychology; the former follows a scientific (scientist/object) pattern, the latter incorporates a large measure of interpersonal interactions (scientist-as-person/person).

This necessary and desirable restriction of science to the impersonal, to the realm of I-It relationships, makes it intrinsically unable to deal fully with the personal, with the realm of I-Thou relationships. One of the saddest and most disastrous consequences of the worldview of Scientism is the attempt to reduce the richness of the I-Thou to the limited scope of the I-It. In this process, usually known as reductionism, the reality of the whole being is stripped down to the reality of the things that make up a whole being. The fatal error is made of equating events in the It-realm with events in the Thou-realm, concluding that Thou-statements are only coverups for ignorance about the real It-statements.

It has become increasingly realized that scientific reductionism does not produce the real person or the truth about a human being exclusively. Rather reductionism strips one of his personhood and leaves him only an animal or only a complex organic machine, depending on how far this reductionism is carried. Given the opportunity, the scientific reductionist will "solve" human problems by making the human into the sub-human. In a kind of self-fulfilling prophecy, the belief of scientific reductionism that the whole person is no more than physical, chemical, biological, psychological, or sociological, causes the treatment of the whole person in such a way that he becomes no more than these - that he becomes an It.

(4) *Ambivalent.* Since science provides a reliable basis for increasing knowledge, it is often assumed that science must therefore be capable of ultimately solving all human problems. There are several reasons why this line of reasoning is incorrect.

Knowledge is not self-motivating for good. To know the good is not to do the good. It is not enough to know what is right to do; it is necessary also to will to do it. Ignorance compounds the human dilemma, but does not cause it. Science has power, but human beings acting with this power are not purified by their possession of it. To change their fundamental motivations human beings need the special power that comes from God through a faith relationship in Jesus Christ.

Every valid insight of science can be used in a way that is good and beneficial, or in a way that is evil and dehumanizing. In the final analysis all knowledge in a world contaminated by sin is dangerous. Every time we increase our capability for good by increasing our knowledge, we simultaneously increase our capability for evil.

Do we now have the promise of unlimited supplies of energy through our ability to tap the power of the atom? So we also have the threat of civilization's destruction through the use of this same power. Can we now see in the invisible infrared portion of the spectrum so that we can aid medical diagnosis and analysis? So we also have the ability to see in the dark in order to kill more effectively. Do we have now vastly expanded abilities for mass communication through television and the media? So we also have the ability for controlling public thought and action in ways never before possible.

Even when scientists act from the best of motives and are successful in achieving their goals - even then the ambivalence of all human activity asserts itself. How well we know that we produce pollution along with enhanced travel and communication possibilities. We accentuate the population explosion by our successes in medicine. These consequences result because of the complexity of the universe in which we live; they are aggravated when we claim that the universe imposes no constraints upon our unlimited progress.

(5) *Ethical Silence* . Not only does science by itself not provide the motivation and the ability for doing good, but also science has no way of even defining what *is* good. A large part of a responsible person's concerns are with what *ought* to be done. It sometimes comes as a shock to realize that this "ought " cannot be scientifically derived.

Von Weiszaecker speaks meaningfully about this situation, [33]

> That scientific knowledge would supply us with the ethical greatness needed to bear this responsibility is a hope not warranted by the facts. I think it can be stated bluntly that scientism, if it rests its trust on the expectation that science by its own nature is enabled to give us sufficient guidance in human affairs, is a false religion. Its faith if going so far, is superstition; the role of the priest does not become the scientist, and good scientists know that; the scientific code of behavior needs a background of an ethics which science has not been able to provide.

Science has not been able to provide this basis for ethics for the simple reason that at its best science is capable of providing us only with a description of the way things are. Science tells us what is, not what ought to be. There is absolutely no way to go from a description of what is to a formulation of what ought to be except by the non-scientific route of declaring what is to be identical with what ought to be ("the is-ought fallacy"). This, in fact, is what every attempt at establishing a scientific basis for ethics amounts to. A scientific description can inform and guide intelligent exercise of the "oughts" of life, but can never form the basis for the initial formulation by any legitimate means.

The acceptance of what is as the guide to what ought to be is a faith commitment of the same type as the acceptance of scientism itself. It is no more objective than any other presupposition chosen as the guide to what ought to be. It is an attempt to form ethics by a kind of popular vote, an importation of democracy into ethics, a result of the conviction that all moral judgments are settled by local consensus.

(6) *Pseudoscience.* The mark of a counterfeit is that it closely resembles the authentic. Pseudoscience is an activity that looks like science, uses the terminology of science, claims the authority of science, but at a fundamental level violates the basic integrity of a scientific activity.

Pseudoscience can generally be traced to one of three major sources. (a) Some pseudo-science is simply bad science in which the person involved has neglected established scientific safeguards in order to arrive at his conclusions. (b) Some pseudoscience professes to achieve scientifically what science is incapable of achieving, as, for example, the development of an ethical system. And finally (c) some pseudoscience results when attempts are made to arrive at scientific conclusions as the result of pressure by some kind of philosophical, metaphysical, religious, or political ideology. Whenever ideology seeks to govern science, pseudoscience results.

An excellent description of pseudoscience from the point of view of a physicist has been given by William Pollard. [34]

> In my own field of physics it is a common experience to receive privately published papers which develop all kinds of strange and bizarre theories about everything from the electron to the universe as a whole. ... To the non-physicist they have as bona fide a ring as a paper in the *Physical Review.* But to physicists they are immediately recognized as fundamentally different. They constitute in the strict sense of the word unorthodox or heretical physics. In subtle ways impossible to describe clearly to the world at large, they violate everything which has given the physics community power to slowly and painfully acquire real and dependable insights into the nature of things. They are lone wolf enterprises unchecked by the discipline of the community and unsupported by an essential loyalty to the enterprise of physics as a whole. Most often the authors of these papers are completely oblivious to these elements and suffer from a deep sense of persecution. They cannot see why their theories have not been given an equal hearing with

those of accepted physicists. They cannot understand why the community consistently and repeatedly rejects them.

The experience of pseudoscience emphasizes the role played by objectivity in authentic science, as opposed to free individual subjectivism. Those engaged in pseudoscience generally fulfill the following criteria: (a) they are certain that they have found the truth; (b) this truth is generally unknown to the world at large, but is of extreme significance; (c) their case is built up on selected bits of evidence without a consideration of the picture as a whole; (d) they are bitter at the community because it will not listen to them, and they attribute the basest motives to the members of the community for this reaction; (e) they are generally neither able nor willing to react to genuine criticism of their work; and (f) they do not consider themselves to be, nor do others consider them to be, members of the scientific community.

In the next chapter we turn to note the similarities and differences between "authentic Christian theology" and "authentic science."

Chapter 3

Authentic Christian Theology

We have seen that science is a way of knowing that has definite potentialities as well as definite limitations. We turn next to a definition of Christian theology. If we take account of certain profound differences, we are able to apply many of the characteristics of a scientific description of the universe also to a theological description.

It may be objected that the definition of an authentic Christian theology is an impossible task. Christian theology is, after all, quite different from science. The major body of scientific understanding is held in common by scientists everywhere and it is only at the boundaries of advancing knowledge that temporary differences of opinion or conviction appear; the number of differentiable varieties of Christian theology is large in spite of 2000 years in which to sort out these differences. Disagreements in science can be, at least in principle and usually in practice, resolved in a relatively few years by carrying out direct experimental tests on the physical universe; disagreements in Christian theology can be discussed and debated, but there are no corresponding experimental tests that can resolve most issues in a short time.

In spite of these differences that we do not here seriously debate, we still contend that the basic methodology and the central content of authentic Christian theology can be defined with sufficient agreement among different sectors of the Christian community to constitute a meaningful activity. After this central content has been defined, there still remains the major task of deciding how to consistently apply the theological positions held in common to specific practical issues.

These are ongoing efforts that require continued use of the basic methodology and the opportunity for open discussion among Christians committed to this methodology.

Definition of Authentic Christian Theology

By the term "authentic Christian theology" we mean: *A particular way of knowing , based on descriptions of the world obtained through the human interpretation of the Bible and human experience.*

(1)   To say that Christian theology is *a way* of knowing is to affirm that it is not the only way of knowing. Few theologians hold that theology is the only way of knowing, although some come close to feeling that theology provides all that is truly important.   But we can hardly live in the modern, "scientific" world and consistently hold that all worthwhile knowledge on any subject must come to us through theology.

(2)   It is commonly said that to believe that theology is a way of knowing is nothing more than a matter of faith.   This assertion is acceptable if we recognize that it is a matter of faith to believe that any activity provides us with authentic knowledge (i.e., valid insights into the nature of reality), a judgment as true of science as it is of theology. Both rest upon presuppositions, both provide evidence, both require a faith commitment before genuine involvement is possible.

The main difference between science and theology is the kind of knowledge that each gives. The main differences are illustrated in Table 1 in an overly simplified way. As stated earlier, science primarily answers questions about' 'how" something happens, what mechanisms are acting in the universe for it to happen, and what are proximate causes for it.   Theology primarily answers questions about "why" something happens, what the purpose and meaning of the events are, and what the ultimate causes for it are.   Science can tell us to a degree what is happening, and what something is like, but only theology can provide us with the basis for the discernment of the meaning of a particular event, or with a standard against which to measure values and ethical imperatives.

The representation given in Table 1 should not be interpreted as indicating some kind of complete and simplistic separation between science and Christian theology, so that interpretation of the world never affects Christian theology, or that interpretation of the Bible and experience never affects science.   Scientific descriptions may be influenced by inputs from God's revelation in the Bible, and choices of scientific problems for research and development certainly will be

Table 1

GOD

	creates	speaks
Givens:	natural world	the Word of God: the Bible
Method:	human interpretation via scientific method	human interpretation via biblical hermeneutics
	scientific description	theological description

to know	understand theoretical human curiosity	to relate	understand theoretical human quest
to make	control technological human responsibility	to serve	service living human call

THINGS	PERSONS
mechanism	meaning
probability	purpose
what? how?	why?
I-It	I-Thou
evolution	creation
chance	providence
body	soul
brain	mind
animal	human being
machine	creation of God
temporal	eternal
physical	spiritual
secular	sacred
survival	salvation

! BUT THE SAME REALITY !

influenced by a scientist's theological convictions. Some theological descriptions are influenced by inputs from God's work in creation that guide us in understanding the majesty of God and in interpreting the Bible in terms of relevant models. Further discussion of these points is given in later chapters when considering some of the specific patterns developed for relating science and theology.

Science can provide us with information about the things that make up a person and the sociological characteristics of human society, but theology reveals to us the nature of interpersonal relationships and our relationship with God. Science establishes as wide a gap as possible between the observer and the observed, whereas theology deals with the realm of human experience in which we enter into relationships with other persons, making ourselves vulnerable in the process.

(3) Christian theology is based on <u>human</u> interpretation. It is God who made the world and inspired the Bible, but it is human beings who react with His revelation in the world to do science and with his revelation in the Bible to do theology. Theology is therefore also an activity of human beings, and so is subject to all the pitfalls and shortcomings characteristic of human beings influenced by their own personal prejudices and the biases of the culture in which they live. It is dangerous to elevate any particular codified theological system as being equivalent to the revelation of God, or as being the final expression of that revelation.

(4) Christian theology is based on human <u>interpretation.</u> Just as facts in science never provide their own interpretation, so Bible passages and experiences also do not provide the precise form of their interpretation either. To point out that we must interpret the Bible in order to obtain a knowledge of God's revelation to us is in no sense a downgrading of the inspiration, authority or trustworthiness of the biblical revelation. It is a simple statement of the situation that when communication passes, the transmission of the content of that communication requires interpretation by the one receiving it. The claim to believe only "what the Bible says" is, in fact, an impossibility; we are unable to believe anything except an interpretation (our own, the Bible writers', or someone else's) of what the Bible says. Nor does it imply that the meaning of the Bible and our experience are up-for-grabs, as though the Bible were a relativistic area in which anyone can make an equally valid judgment. Our desire is to interpret the Bible in a manner consistent with its own character and purpose so that we may truly receive God's revelation to us.

As pointed out earlier, when our scientific understanding and our theological understanding apparently conflict, it is not "Science vs. the

Bible," as if science required interpretation but the Bible does not, or as if the Bible required interpretation by science does not, but rather science (as a human interpretation following appropriate rules) vs. theology (another human interpretation following appropriate rules). The category equivalent to "the Bible" is "the physical universe." The physical universe cannot be in apparent conflict with the Bible, but our interpretation of the universe can appear to be in conflict with our interpretation of the Bible. If such conflict appears to occur, then our interpretation of the physical universe may be wrong, our interpretation of the Bible may be wrong, or they may both be wrong!

However we should not forget that we have spiritual resources available to us in interpreting the Bible. Our efforts to understand the revelation of God are aided by the working of the Holy Spirit in our lives. Without this relationship no authentic biblical interpretation is possible.

(5) Christian theology is based on human interpretation of the Bible. For a variety of evidences long summarized by theologians, we accept the Bible as a reliable guide to theological understanding. Here we do not debate this, but we consider what it means to affirm it.

Christians accept the Bible as a trustworthy source of God's revelation to us. Thus the Bible is more like a love letter from a friend than it is like a manual on how to make a machine. What do we want to know from the Bible? Presumably we want to know what God wishes to say to us. But the Bible is a collection of sixty-six books spanning hundreds of years, written by many authors in a variety of specific situations. We believe that by properly considering each of these authors and each of these situations we can learn something relevant for our own lives about the will of God and his relationships with human beings. Basically we want to know the purpose behind the giving of the revelation itself, so that we can determine the relevance of that revelation to us today. How do we do this?

Traditional guidelines on biblical interpretation involve three questions:

(1) What does the passage say?
(2) What did the passage mean when it was written?
(3) What does the passage mean to us today?

The first two questions are factual with scholarly content; the third is applicational with experiential content. To answer these questions a set of interpretational principles have been developed through the years by those committed to the Bible as the revelation of God, commonly called hermeneutics. To illustrate these principles, consider the following examples.

1. The recognition that the biblical revelation of God and his purposes in the world were given with increasing clarity over the period of the revelation is a fundamental one for interpreting it.   Therefore ultimate interpretation of the Old Testament should be guided by the New Testament, and ultimate interpretation of the Gospels should be guided by the Epistles. Similarly ultimate interpretation of symbolic passages should be guided by passages written specifically with a didactic purpose, and passages with less clear meaning should be interpreted using passages dealing with the same subject but with a clearer meaning.   General perspectives should be derived from passages with universal application rather than from passages with primarily a local application.

2.   The Bible is not a book of magic to be used as if each word or phrase had divine significance in isolation from the rest of the text, but all biblical statements must be understood in terms of the conditions under which they were originally written and of the purposes for which they were originally intended.   Proper interpretation does require some "scholarly" effort.   The more "theoretical" the theological question, the more scholarly effort is required in general to define its answer.

3. The Word of God comes to us in the words of men. Its language is the language of the people of that day.   Biblical authors used a wide variety of literary styles each with different rules for interpretation: prose, poetry, symbol, story, history.

4.   A full understanding of the biblical revelation comes from a treatment of it as a whole, not as a collection of mutually independent parts.

5.   Since God's revelation has only one divine source, authentic scientific interpretations of his work cannot ultimately contradict authentic theological interpretations of his word.   If scientific inquiry appears to discredit a fundamental assertion of the Bible (e.g., all human beings are sinners and need a savior), we are well advised to take a hard look at the validity of the science involved and its justifiable interpretations.   If biblical interpretation appears to discredit an assured finding of science (e.g., the earth revolves around the sun and not vice versa), we are well advised to take a hard look at the validity of our theological interpretation.

Another consideration is important. It may appear subtle at first, but often turns out to be crucial.   Differences between equally committed and biblically knowledgeable Christians often arise from the choice of a hermeneutical perspective: whether that of deduction of biblical truth from specific isolated passages, or induction of biblical truth from the Bible as a whole. If one of these two perspectives is chosen to the practical exclusion of the other, the conclusions of biblical interpretation are almost inevitable and predictable. [35]

Traditional Christian theology has often been based heavily on a deductive approach to the Bible. Such theology followed the pattern of science before Galileo and Newton. It emphasized specific passages in the Bible, which were assumed to give a clear and easily understood teaching; all other descriptions and events, whether biblical or extra-biblical, must then be interpreted to fit the deductions made from the selected passages.

Recognizing the essential role of induction in the development of modern science, Christian scientists in particular may be sensitive to the need for an inductive component to the approach to biblical interpretation. They recognize the value of the specific selected passages of the deductionists, but inductionists seek to fit these passages into the total context of descriptions and events with which they deal so that the overall meaning of the selected passages may be understood on their own terms.

Once again it is a version of the question: Is "what God could do" a reliable guide to "what God did do," or is it important to take a look at what God actually did do and how he did it? Must the orbits of the planets be circular in shape because God made them, and because a circle is God's perfect shape, or is it important to look at the orbits that God made and observe that they are in fact elliptical in form? Is it obvious that the planet Jupiter cannot have a moon because such a situation would suggest an imperfect creation, or is it important to take a telescope and look to see whether God created Jupiter with a moon or not? Can the full range of implications of the statement, "All Scripture is given by inspiration of God," be determined simply by reflecting on the character and omnipotence of God, or is it essential to look at the Scriptures themselves to see the form in which God's inspiration expressed itself through human authors?

(6) Authentic Christian theology is based on the interpretation of the Bible and __human experience__. Theology is not a scholarly investigation of esoteric problems in an ideal world, but is a practical application of biblical understanding to our actual world. Although experience may be highly subjective, we must think carefully about a proposed biblical interpretation that regularly violates human experience. In a probably apocryphal story, Martin Luther heard a booming voice proclaim, "I am the Lord God; $2 + 2 = 5$." According to the story, Luther replied, "Get behind me, Satan."

Theology, therefore, provides guidelines for experiences and events in the world today that are not covered specifically by the biblical revelation, by basing these guidelines on the biblical revelation. This is another area where the guidance of the Holy Spirit is vital.

Theology must also deal with the significance of the findings of modern science. The subject of "natural theology," the derivation of theological insights from a scientific understanding of the natural world, is dealt with in later chapters. The role played by events within science can be dealt with by scientific interpretation itself, but the meaning of events beyond science must be dealt with by theology. When scientists themselves claim to provide insights into ultimate meaning, they have stopped doing science and have entered into the practice of theology. The modern scientific paradigms such as relativity, quantum mechanics and cosmology all provide occasions for speculation in seeking to derive theological meaning from scientific theories. It is the task of theology to relate these insights to the biblical revelation.

Distinctives of Authentic Christian Theology [36]

In this section we attempt to outline some of the central characteristics of Christian theology, characteristics so basic that if they are not included in the theology being developed, severe doubt is cast on whether or not it can be classified as authentic Christian theology.

(1) *Creation.* The God of the Bible is the Creator of the universe. The God who loves is the God who creates. There is an essential unity between the God of Christian theology and the God of physical reality.

If God is the Creator of the universe, out of what did he create it? There are three formal possibilities: (a) he created it out of preexistent matter, (b) he created it out of himself, or (c) he created it freely, neither out of preexistent matter nor out of himself. The traditional Christian teaching that God created the world "out of nothing" is an affirmation of the last of these possibilities in order to deny the errors considered to be intrinsic to the first two possibilities. In maintaining that God did not create the world out of preexistent matter, Christian theology argues against the possibility of dualism, that is, that there is more than one ultimate basis for the world. It rejects the idea that creation means the imposition of form on eternal matter, and it rejects the possibility that good and evil are co-eternal characteristics of reality. The monotheism of the biblical revelation leaves no room for such manifestations of dualism. In maintaining that God did not create the world out of himself, Christian theology argues against the concept of pantheism, that is, that the created world is intrinsically divine, or that the sum total of the universe is identical with God.

To identify God as the Creator of the universe is to emphasize his transcendence over the natural order, his immanence in the natural order, and his complete freedom of action. Emphasizing God's transcendence upholds the fact that the universe is separate from God; emphasizing God's immanence upholds the fact that the universe is totally dependent upon God. It has sometimes been argued that these perspectives cannot be held within a biblical framework and that recourse must be had to another religious formulation; such a conclusion results from an insufficient understanding of the depth of the biblical revelation concerning the role of God in creation. Because he is the creator, his mode of existence is of necessity different from that of the finite spatio-temporal universe he makes, as well as being distinct from that of the universe. Because the universe is sustained moment by moment only by the continuing creative power of God, he is present in the natural order in the most profound sense. Because he is constrained neither by matter nor by any other power, he is free to act in accordance with his will.

Because God is the creator of the universe, the universe is intrinsically good. This means that the real evil and sin found in the world are not simply the result of the material, finite, or temporal nature of the world, but are rather aberrations on that good creation. This affirmation leads to several deeply significant conclusions. (1) It provides a basis for the scientist's presupposition that the world is indeed understandable by rational processes. Since the world is the product of divine wisdom and since human beings are also creatures brought into being by that same divine wisdom, it follows that the world itself is orderly and capable of being understood and that this process of understanding is a worthy enterprise for human beings. (2) It means that, in spite of the uncertainties and contingencies of finite human existence, still it is possible to maintain that such existence has the possibility of ultimate meaning, the more so as it is related to the divine purpose that underlies the creation and sustaining of the universe. (3) It declares that evil is not a necessary ingredient in the world but that it is an aberration on a good creation, an intruder into a world in which evil is intrinsically an outsider. Finally, (4) it affirms that the very real evil of daily existence can be challenged and at least partially overcome, and that human beings can be brought by the power of God to the realization of their potentialities as creatures made in the image of God. [37]

The concept of Creation is so fundamental that no discussion of the interaction between science and Christian theology could possibly be complete without including it.   It is of the utmost significance to realize that the theological significance of Creation, as outlined briefly above, has no necessary dependence upon *how* God actually created. For the Bible-believing Christian the fact of God's creation of the universe with all of its significance is established quite independently of any scientific knowledge or ignorance about the mechanisms involved in creation.   Unfortunately contemporary debates about Creation frequently obscure the issue by posing creation and evolution or continuous development as two mutually exclusive options, as though one must choose between a biblically sound faith that supports Creation and an atheistic Bible-contradicting position that supports continuous development. [38]   This issue will reappear several times as we consider the various patterns for relating science and Christian theology in this book.

Since God is the creator of the whole universe including the creatures in it, it also follows that there is an intended structure for relationships between different parts of the created order, a standard of values reflecting the character of God, and also expressed in interpersonal form as guidelines for human living such as are summarized in the Ten Commandments and the Sermon on the Mount. It is these that provide ultimate insight into the definition of "good" and "evil," "right" and "wrong," which have a definition in human relationships that transcends differences of time, culture or ethnic orientation.

(2) *Revelation.*   The God who made heaven and earth has not withdrawn himself from it. Both the biblical picture for the act of creating and the act of sustaining the world involves the speaking of a word by God.   God makes himself known to human beings through the revelation that he gives in the natural world, the events of history and their interpretations by prophets and apostles, and supremely in the person of Jesus Christ. The most significant record of this revelation for the Christian is that collection of books, biographies, poetry, and letters known as the Bible. This remarkable collection of writings, gathered and guarded by those who had experienced God in their lives, carries self-authenticating authority.

 Thus the Christian rests in the belief that God has not left human beings alone in the world, without a witness to the character and will of God, but that God has spoken and continues to speak today through the words of the Bible themselves and as made manifest in the lives of those who have committed themselves to him in Jesus Christ.

(3) *Evil* . The Christian sees real evil in the world, and he also sees human beings as participants in this evil because of their rejection of God and their exaltation of their own self-interests in an idolatrous act. To a considerable extent, self-centeredness encompasses much of what is usually termed "original sin." [39] Thus, although the existence of evil in an intrinsically good universe remains an aberration, the responsibility and potentiality of each person here and now are clearly set forth. Because evil and suffering in this world are not a necessary or proper aspect of reality, opposition to these forces is in accord with the divine will. Such opposition is to be expressed in the forms of self-sacrificing love and by responding to evil with good. [40] The dimensions of the problem of evil encompass moral responsibility on the part of human beings and are not simply inevitable consequences of metaphysical situations.

(4) *Redemption* . Because of human self-idolatry, human beings have separated themselves from God and are in effective rebellion against God in the ordering of their lives and goals. The power to overcome this separation and to restore them to the position they hold as creatures made in the image of God is not something human beings can do for themselves. It is something, however, that God has done for them. God has shown his love for human beings by acting on their behalf. What God has done is to become incarnate in Jesus of Nazareth, called Jesus Christ because of his unique identity as the Son of God. In the person of Jesus Christ, God himself made it possible for the separation between human beings and God to be ended, their idolatry to be forgiven, and the creation-ordained relationship to be reestablished. As human beings are moved to rely on the finished work of Jesus Christ and commit themselves to him, they enter into the new life of a restored and forgiven relationship with God, and into the process of sanctification in their lives through the ongoing work of the Holy Spirit.

How this work of redemption was accomplished through the life, death, and resurrection of Jesus Christ remains a marvel that has depths no human can reach. The authors of the Bible used many different approaches to attempt to spell out the significance of redemption. They spoke of salvation because the work of Christ brings healing to a spiritually sick human being; they spoke of redemption because the work of Christ is like buying an enslaved person from slavery in order to set that person free in new life; they spoke of reconciliation because the personal relationship between estranged humans and God was re-established; they spoke of victory because the resurrection of Jesus is the sign of the ultimate victory over the power of evil and death; and they spoke of sacrifice because Christ laid down his own life willingly in a demonstration of love that was both unique and an example to those who would follow him.

The work of redemption has significance for the individual in the present life here and now. The Christian looks in faith for a final redemption as well, in which the aberrations of evil and suffering that infect the present world will be cast off and the healing work begun in Christ and carried on in the lives of Christians will be completed in the fulfillment of the creation purpose.

Characteristics of Theology

As in the previous chapter we concluded our discussion of the definition of authentic science by summarizing some of the main characteristics of science that follow from this definition, so now in concluding our overview of theology, we consider a few adjectives that describe authentic theology.

(1) *Personal.* Theology is concerned primarily with relationships between human beings and God, between human beings and one another, and with the healing of broken relationships. It has to do with the possibility of a personal relationship between a human being and God, the giving of one person in trust and commitment to another, and to the forming of covenants between persons. Christian faith at its core is not a theology but a relationship, not a philosophy of life but the expression of love from God to a person and from a person to God, not a set of rules but a personal commitment that turns rules into joy and service into privilege. The fundamental act of a Christian, moved by the Holy Spirit, is to commit him/herself to God in an existential act of trusting faith in response to God's call to a relationship. This in itself is not theology, but theology then clarifies the significance of this commitment to living for God. Theology may be studied as if it were science, but it cannot be lived unless it is put into practice like marriage.

It is important to repeat again that simple intellectual assent to belief statements does not constitute Christian faith. Christian faith is based not only, nor even primarily, on faith *that* ...; it is based rather on trust and commitment *in* a Person - God in and through Jesus Christ. The only security in the Christian faith stems from the fact that God is trustworthy, that persons who have been moved to commit themselves to Jesus Christ as the Lord of their lives, enter into a new personal relationship with the living Christ. The vitality of the Christian faith arises from the power derived from this new personal relationship that informs and transforms every aspect of life. A living Christian faith without a changed and committed Christian life is a contradiction in terms.

(2) *Ambivalent.* More battles have been fought, more suffering inflicted, and more human misery caused by people who claimed allegiance to a particular theological system than can scarcely be imagined. The reason for this is that theology by itself is just as capable of being used for evil as for good, of being distorted and adapted for self-centered human needs as of being lived out for the glory of God and the welfare of human beings.

Theology is essential for a Christian life, but it is not from theology itself that the basis and strength for that life proceeds. The living out of theology as intended by the revelation of God in the Bible requires a personal relation of an individual to God, an involvement that recognizes how far one falls from the perfect holiness of God, and that responds in gratitude and love for the great love and grace of God shown to us in the life, death and resurrection of Jesus Christ.

(3) *The Basis of Ethics.* Any system of ethics requires the adoption by faith of a system of values. Theology finds the basis for ethics not in some human choice or in some misguided attempt to derive values from science, but in the character and will of God. Our knowledge of God, as given in his revelation to us, informs us of how we ought to live, and our relationship with God provides us with the strength and desire to do that.

Ethics are neither a subjective nor a relativistic matter. Ethics are not decided by popular vote, nor are conflicting ethical principles in different cultures defensible on the grounds that each culture must produce its own code of ethics. There are fundamental guidelines to what we "ought" to do given to us in the Bible; no matter how much Christians may disagree on the implications of these for specific issues today, still the goal should be to express in the clearest way possible the fundamental intention of the biblical revelation concerning the character and will of God. Such an expression may indeed take somewhat different forms in different cultures, but the central guidelines are the same for all.

(4) *Foundation for a Worldview and a Life .* We have described above four central elements of Christian theology. To these must be added the significance of theology for a way of life. For emphasis here we briefly summarize once more the central themes of this Christian worldview.

The God in whom the Christian trusts is the Creator of the entire space-time Universe. He called everything that exists into being, and by his moment-by-moment free activity maintains everything in being. He is active in the creation and sustaining of the universe at all times and at all places. He did not just create the universe and then step back to let it develop, nor does he occasionally step in to act directly in the shaping of the universe while leaving it to itself at other times, but he is constantly active and our descriptions of scientific processes are our descriptions of his activity. The God who made the universe is not an abstract principle or a hidden force upon which one can do no more than meditate, but one who speaks, communicates, and relates to the creation and to us who are part of it.

The evil that we see around us in the real world today is not an illusion, nor is it intrinsic because the creation is finite and temporal. It represents an aberration on the good creation planned by God and to be completed by Him in the future, an affliction partly caused by human self-centeredness and partly reflecting a condition of nature consistent with that turning away from God to worship idols.

The ability for self-centered human beings to be in relationship with a holy God, and to actually will to serve Him and do the good, is not something that human beings can achieve by their own efforts. But it is something that through his love for us and his grace toward us that God has made possible through the life, death and resurrection of His Son, Jesus Christ. We are not brought into this saving relationship with God through an act or process of natural creation, but by the cross of Calvary and God's act of redemption.

Finally, out of this new relationship with God, this spiritual "new creation" in Jesus Christ, comes the knowledge, the motivation and the strength to live a new life, following the example of Jesus Christ and overcoming the bonds of our self-idolatry. In this new life Christians seek to glorify God by what they say and do, and to demonstrate what it means to be citizens of God's kingdom while still being citizens of earth.

(5) *Pseudotheology*. There is also a parallel between pseudoscience, as described in the previous chapter, and its counterpart, *pseudotheology*. Practitioners of pseudotheology carry out an activity that looks like authentic theology, but violates the basic requirements of authentic theology; they have often been called apostates and heretics. Unfortunately the historical record also shows tragic cases where the practitioners of pseudotheology were in institutional power, and the officially declared apostates and heretics were advocating authentic theology to their own danger and suffering. This fact underlines the necessity to use responsible interpretation of the biblical record as the mark of authentic theology.

Pseudotheology, like pseudoscience, may simply be bad theology. Interpretations of the Bible, for example, obtained in violation of the guidelines of hermeneutics (e.g., taking poetic imagery as literal description), can easily lead to pseudotheology. Or pseudotheology, also like pseudoscience, may attempt to do things that authentic theology cannot do, whether this involves attempting to derive scientific mechanisms from theology, or using theology in the effort to establish or justify a particular philosophical or religious ideology.

Common Features of Science and Theology

Although there are critical differences between the methodology and general purposes of science and theology, it is also true that there are many common features that bind them together. Their differences have become such a publicly heralded aspect of modern society, that it is especially important to recognize the similarities between them. In fact, one might argue that a critical element in evaluating the relationship between science and theology is maintaining a balance between the false extreme of regarding them as totally different and mutually exclusive on one hand, and the other extreme of regarding them as essentially the same with a final destiny that will truly unite them into a single discipline on the other. Naturally, this will be the subject of several of our discussions of different patterns for relating science and theology in the following chapters.

We may summarize the common features of both science and theology as follows:

Both science and theology are based on faith commitments: a faith commitment to the intelligibility of the world and the "possibility" of doing science, on the one hand, and a faith commitment to God as most clearly revealed in the Person of Jesus Christ on the other. All fundamental human choices start with faith commitments; science and theology are not exceptions.

Both science and theology develop descriptions of reality based upon evidence. The evidence that each produces is usually obtained in a different way, but neither establishes conclusions as the result of proof. This evidence is obtained by sense interactions with the world in science, and by interacting with the biblical revelation and human experience, within the context of a personal relationship with God, in Christian theology.

Descriptions of reality produced by science are able to be tested by human sense interaction with the physical world. Descriptions of reality by theology are able to be tested to some extent by human experience both in historical context and in the present. Because science is the simpler, more completely defined, and more specifically restricted, it is generally easier to test scientific descriptions than theological descriptions. Proposed scientific models that cannot be tested even in principle are rejected as being non-scientific; a couple of examples were given in the previous chapter. Proposed theological models that have little effect on actual human living are usually regarded as being too theoretical to be considered as major theological issues. For example, it seems that a pre-millennial , a post-millennial or an a-millennial view of Christ's second coming has less consequences for the life of a Christian than one's fundamental faith and life based on the redemption of Jesus Christ, and one's faith in the fact of his second coming. Efforts to establish one of these millennialist views as authoritative over the other two have been attempted in the past, but none can be cited as the unquestionable position, nor does it seem that it can be said that one's view of a specific form of millennialism has a decisive effect on Christian living.

Both authentic science and authentic Christian theology provide us with partial descriptions of part of reality. Neither provides us with complete or absolute descriptions of reality. It is important to realize that a partial description may still convey true insights into reality. The argument that only a description capable of conveying the whole truth can be considered true in any sense, is a mistake. Insofar as the descriptions of science are compatible with the actual physical world, and insofar as the descriptions of theology are compatible with the biblical relationships that describe our life in and with God, both provide true and valid insights that need to be integrated. Each provides us with true insights into *what reality is like* .

In general these insights provide different kinds of information derived from the two different kinds of disciplines, yet dealing with the same reality. Since each description comes from a different type of interaction with reality, our knowledge about what reality *is like* is augmented by the attempt by individuals and the community to put these two insights together.

It is always important to realize that some questions may need to remain at any particular time simply "open questions." Judgment on these issues must be deferred until a possible time when clearer insights may become available. If an interpretation derived from authentic science appears to be in conflict with an interpretation derived from authentic theology, it may be necessary simply to leave the final resolution of the issue open without forsaking the valid insights that we do have from authentic science and theology. There are, of course, several possibilities: (1) our scientific interpretation may be incorrect; (2) our theological interpretation may be incorrect, (3) both our scientific and our theological interpretations may be incorrect, or (4) both scientific and theological interpretations may supply us with valid insights into the resolution of the problem without giving us the detailed descriptions needed to simply consider the issue closed forever. The willingness to accept the existence of "open questions" does involve the individual in a certain degree of tension. But being willing and able to live with such tension, which presents no danger or threat to our faith, may in some cases be an indication of Christian maturity.

The defense of authentic science is closely coupled to the defense of authentic theology. If one of these comes under serious attack or attempted drastic reformulation, the other suffers with it. This is because each is based, at least tacitly, on the belief that a universe exists, with which we interact and which we affect, but which has ultimate properties that do not depend upon us but rather upon the creative activity of God.   If it is assumed that there is no natural and interpersonal reality defined by God's creative activity, then both science and theology, as we have defined them, lose their validity.

Chapter 4

Pattern 1: Science Has Destroyed Christian Theology

Each of the patterns that we discuss in this book is based upon a specific set of assumptions or presuppositions. In an effort to clarify the distinctions between the different patterns, we will start each discussion with a brief summary of these major assumptions.   Pattern 1 is based on the following assumption:

Science and theology tell us the same kinds of things about the same things. When scientific and theological descriptions conflict, one must be right and the other wrong. In this encounter, science always proves to be the winner.

This is perhaps the most commonly held view of the interaction between science and Christian theology. It is a view that is part of the subconscious structure of our whole culture, the unspoken assumption of secular society around the world, our heritage from the age of the Enlightenment.   This pattern argues that Christian faith as expounded historically through what we have called authentic Christian theology has become meaningless in the present scientific day, a relic of a less knowledgeable past.   Science is the domain of empirical fact and theology is the domain of subjective fancy. The only role left for theology is to meet some of the psychological needs of those human beings incapable or unwilling to face the realities of a scientifically describable world.   Whether it is Freud claiming that God is only an anthropocentric projection, or Marx claiming that Christianity is an opiate of the people, the thrust is and has been for centuries the same:

no informed, modern person can possibly continue to accept the mythological claims of biblical Christianity.

A succinct statement of the case for Pattern 1 is given by V. Y. Frenkel [41], who argues that there is a simple and inevitable sequence of development.

(1) All religions start with fear of the unknown, in which the existence and activity of God or gods is invoked to allay communal fears concerning events and effects beyond their control. It follows that when the causes of the unknown become known through the development of science, there is subsequently no need to consider God's activity in the area of natural processes.

(2) After the divine category of ultimate Cause of natural phenomena has been lost, religion moves along to moral issues in an effort to develop a system of values that will define the do's and don'ts of a society.   The effort is made to produce a universal code of ethics that applies to all people in the world, based on some kind of divine sanction.   But it is sooner or later realized that the attempt to direct the moral sensitivities of a relativistic and pluralistic society is really neither effective nor ultimately possible.

(3) With God thus removed both from the natural world and from the area of moral values, religion then attempts survival by moving on to a cosmological stage in which the personal attributes of God are replaced by impersonal concepts such as the "spirit of the universe." God is no longer personal, one to whom prayer is possible, but becomes an abstract principle about which one may meditate. Much is made of the cosmological novelties of contemporary science with the claim that they provide now a new and scientifically-sanctioned basis for religion.

(4) Finally when this last attempt to sustain religion has run its course, proving by its abstract refinements to be unable to meet the religious needs of the everyday person, only atheism is left.

These remarks deserve at least two different kinds of response. One of the purposes of this chapter is to critique the claims expressed in the first of these objections, i.e., that faith in God has become superfluous, as well as to consider several other arguments advanced to support this Pattern.

But it is important to realize that there is a definite ring of validity to the above series of responses as a description of historical processes that have taken and are taking place.   In this sense, they should be kept in mind when we consider other patterns of relating science and theology that today can be interpreted as advocating moving along the progression outlined by Frenkel.

We consider five arguments from a much larger number that might be cited, which are advanced in various forms by advocates of Pattern 1

[42]. They are (1) modern scientific understanding has made God unnecessary, (2) belief in the supernatural has become outdated and intellectually impossible, (3) miracles violate our understanding of the world, (4) science has shown that Christianity is *only* ... , and (5) can one really regard the Bible as a source of God's revelation?

Modern Science Has Made God Unnecessary: The God-of-the-Gaps

In earlier days it was both possible and common to sustain a religious interpretation of the world by looking directly to God as the immediate Cause of those physical and biological events that human beings were then unable to describe or understand. In the historical context of growing scientific descriptions of the world, this religious interpretation became known as a belief in a *God-of-the-Gaps*. The practical consequence of the view that God's existence could be proved by human ignorance of certain key physical and biological mechanisms was that evidence for God's existence decreased as human scientific knowledge grew. In a curious paradox, the more human beings knew of the creation, the less reason they had to believe in the Creator.

Enough influential Christian apologists have espoused a God-of-the-Gaps, as we will consider in later chapters of this book, to require a careful appraisal of their position.   Such consideration involves both a re-evaluation of God's relationship to the physical world in the light of biblical insights, and an understanding of the nature of scientific and alternative descriptions. Earlier in this century the choice often seemed to be between God-in-Exile and God-of-the-Gaps; a viable alternative for biblical Christianity is to affirm that God-at-the Center best correlates with the totality of experience and revelation.

There can be no denying that human knowledge about the world and its inhabitants has continually increased over the years. There are three major ways to respond to this situation. Two of them, one commonly made by non-Christians and one commonly made by Christians, agree in accepting a God-of-the-Gaps.   The third view attempts to integrate modern scientific understanding with a biblical perspective on the relationship between God and the universe.

(1) The growth of human knowledge has freed human beings from the superstitions and rituals of past ignorance. Human beings have "come of age." When human beings were ignorant of what really was happening in the world, they readily fell victim to religious myths. Instead of exercising their reason, they were subjected to the ritual of priests. As a result, they had a false perception of reality. Our

understanding of scientific mechanisms has liberated mankind from the anthropomorphic projection of a cosmic deity.   Instead of being led astray and handicapped by subjective illusions, human beings are now able to stand on their own feet instead of relying upon some religious crutch. Human beings are finally responsible for what they do and for what happens in the world.   Such a response to the growth in human knowledge is common to many non-Christian interpreters who find a God-of-the-Gaps increasingly expendable as those gaps are closed by an extension of scientific understanding. For them, the consequence that modern knowledge banishes a God-of-the-Gaps is a cause for rejoicing.

(2)   The second response is to regard human increasing scientific understanding as a threat to faith in God. It is argued that there are aspects of life where only God has the power and the right to act; human encroachment on these areas recreates a modern Babel where human beings seek to exalt themselves and to bring God down. Christian faith rests, it is believed, upon the existence of areas of human ignorance and impotence, areas that can properly be described only as the direct intervention of God in the world, without involving any phenomena capable of natural description. It is essential that human beings shrink from further encroachment of this kind and, wherever possible, combat the impression that increases in scientific understanding are indeed firmly established. God is accepted as a God-of-the-Gaps; evidence for his existence is to be found primarily in human limitations. Here, the recognition that a God-of-the-Gaps is being squeezed out by modern knowledge is a cause for lamentation.

(3) The third response to human increasing understanding rejects the idea that God is a God-of-the-Gaps. It is God who has brought human beings to their new level of understanding, and it is God who can bring them the ability to make responsible decisions thrust upon them by this understanding. It is possible for Christians to accept responsibly their new position of knowledge and choice - but only with trembling, and as sustained by a vision of God as the Lord of all reality.   God is to be found at the center of life, as Dietrich Bonhoeffer declared: [43]

> Religious people speak of God when human knowledge ... has come to an end, or when human resources fail - in fact it is always the *deus ex machina* that they bring on to the scene, either for the apparent solution of insoluble problems, or as strength in human failure ... It always seem to me that we are trying anxiously in this way to reserve some place for God; I should like to speak of God not on the boundaries but at the center, not in weakness but in strength; and therefore not in death and guilt but in man's life and goodness.

In reading these words it is important to remember that Bonhoeffer draws a sharp distinction between religion in general and Christian commitment. He argues that human beings are intrinsically and incurably religious. Without a Christian commitment and the personal relationship of faith in Christ, humans will exploit religion to answer insoluble problems when they are in trouble, or they will exalt and deify religion itself when they are successful. Both responses are God-of-the-Gaps responses. Only commitment to Christ permits a person to escape from what amounts to a religious denial of God's reality in the world in order fully to participate in the world as a servant of Christ.

It is therefore right and appropriate that the God-of-the-Gaps has been dislodged by human increasing knowledge, for this "God" never was the God of the Bible. It is possible to rejoice, therefore, that the God-of-the-Gaps has been squeezed out, to refrain from attempts to restore this God-of-the-Gaps, and to seek to glorify the Lord of all created reality by placing him at the very center of life.

It is to a large extent the long history of Christian acceptance and use of the concept of a God-of-the-Gaps that has made the Christian position so vulnerable to the assertion of Pattern 1 that modern science has made God unnecessary. It is helpful to review a few aspects of this history in order to make more understandable the nature of this attack on the integrity of biblical theology and the reasons advanced for rejecting it. As mentioned above, such a choice ironically has allied the Christian with the non-Christian who also sees God as a God-of-the-Gaps, and has thus served to obscure the Christian witness to biblical theism.

The argument usually runs this way: Human beings may now know much about physics, chemistry, biology and the like, but certain key physical, chemical or biological mechanisms must forever elude them because such mechanisms do not in fact exist. These gaps in the description of natural events and processes can be filled only by recognizing that God acts in these gaps above and beyond any physical, chemical or biological mechanism. In this interpretation God remains the Great Mechanic, and his very existence and activity forever rule out the possibility of a complete, physical, chemical or biological description - even in principle.

The list of phenomena invoked by Christians to define the God-of-the-Gaps is very long and still with us. Newton invoked the God-of-the-Gaps when certain irregularities in the motion of the planets could not be explained by his theory of gravitation; subsequent analysis of the planetary system provided a natural explanation for these irregularities, and supposed evidence for the intervention of God was discredited. The healing of physical sicknesses continues to be an area of special interest, with a tendency to regard healing through the use of medicine or a doctor's action no longer as indicative of the activity of God as was healing and recovery in former days when the doctors were helpless. Weather patterns were formerly attributed to the supernatural intervention of God; now that we know that such weather patterns are meteorological phenomena, this evidence for a God-of-the-Gaps is gone. An attempt to reserve some place for the God-of-the-Gaps was made by those Christians who objected to human space travel on the grounds that earth was the proper domain for human beings, whereas the heavens were reserved for God and his angels.

No area has been more the focus of debate about the God-of-the-Gaps than the subject of origins: the origin of the known universe, the origin of life on earth, and the origin of the variety of living species including human beings. Consider, for example, the origin of life on earth. Somehow life originated. Those who hold to a God-of-the-Gaps object to any attempt to suggest that life may have originated in a way that can be described scientifically through specific physical mechanisms. For them, such a suggestion is equivalent to denying that God was active in the origin of life on earth. Any attempt to suggest possible continuous, scientifically describable mechanisms for these origins is an obvious threat to the God-of-the-Gaps who must act instantaneously and in a way absolutely indiscernible to scientific investigation.

Although some advocates of a God-of-the-Gaps appreciate to some extent the complete control that God holds over the universe at all times and in all ways, the emphasis normally placed on God's activity in the gaps often leads to the conviction that God's activity in any ongoing way is shown primarily, or even only, in the gaps in our understanding. It usually follows that human beings can never create life from non-living material, because that would violate their God-of-the-Gaps position. Yet the direction of experiments today seem to make it risky to insist that human beings can *never* create life. The possibility that laboratory scientists may someday construct a living creature from non-living substances is seen as forbidden by advocates of the God-of-the-Gaps, whose existence and activity demand that human beings be unable to accomplish this goal.

None of these remarks is meant to indicate that God *cannot* act in ways that are beyond our ability to describe scientifically , with the result being what we have traditionally called miracles, as we discuss further in a later section of this chapter. Physical laws are our descriptions of how God usually acts; if God chooses to act in a special way in accordance with his freedom, then the result may well be what we call miracles. We must be careful not to suppose, however, that

God always acts the way he *could* act and therefore insist on a simplistic God-of-the-Gaps explanation of unusual phenomena. If describing *how* God acts is our concern, we must investigate that question as directly as possible and not assume that we already know the answer. Once again it is a case of our seeking to determine, if we can, how God *does* act rather than simple assuming that God *must* act in a particular way simple because he *can* act in that way.

Sometimes adherence to a God-of-the-Gaps takes on really extreme forms as when people are willing to accept events and processes in the world as being the direct result of God's activity provided that these events and processes make no sense. If it can be demonstrated that a connection can be constructed tying various processes together so that these events and processes really "work" in the real world, then it is concluded that the evidence for God's activity in these events or processes has been destroyed. It is almost as if a person said, "I can believe that love is the power of God in the world provided that it doesn't work, but once it looks as if love in the world is a very practical expression, then I can't associate it with God anymore."

Before the recognition of the general principle of gravity, God the Mechanician was credited with the direct maintaining of the planets in their proper orbits. The answer to the question "What holds the planets in place?" was properly and completely, "God does." When it came to be realized that the general gravitational interaction between material bodies could be described in terms of a basic physical phenomenon, it was concluded that the view of God as Mechanician, directly holding the planets in space through a non-physical process, was no longer acceptable. This is really strange – surely the answer to the question, "What holds the planets in place? is still, "God does, but now we have more insight into how he acts to do it." Even more remarkable is the result that the recognition of a regularity of nature, an illustration of the efficacy of natural phenomena and evidence for God's activity in sustaining the universe, should thereby lead to the conclusion that it was *not* God who was holding the planets in place. Because the previous view of God the Mechanician needed to be reinterpreted, why should it follow that the place of God as Creator, Sustainer and Redeemer could all be summarily dismissed?

Isn't it strange that the recognition that God works well and in an orderly way (rather than in a chaotic and disorderly way) should have led so often to the conclusion that it is not God working?

For thousands of years, the Bible has proclaimed, "Do not steal." To some extent people refrained from stealing because they believed that God would be displeased with them if they stole. Then sociologists recognized the fact that actually "not stealing" was a beneficial characteristic of society . A society in which stealing took place was a worse place to live than a society in which stealing was prohibited. People recognized that the commandment of God was not an arbitrary dictum of a potentate-in-the-sky, but that the commandment of God *really worked.* It described the structure of life best fitted for improving the quality of life in human society . The remarkably strange aspect of this development is this: When people believed that the commandment "Do not steal" had only arbitrary authority, they freely attributed it to God. But when people realized that the commandment "Do not steal" actually described the conditions required for the good social life, they concluded that God was *not* responsible. Why is this? Should not the value of not stealing be considered direct evidence of the ordained system of a holy God?

Or to give one final example, consider the active field of sociobiology with its attempts to derive a scientific basis for human moral and ethical issues [44]. It seems that the argument is often made by some in this field that as long as moral and ethical values have no genuine correlation with the actual "stuff of life," then they can be attributed by naive people to the divine commandments of a god. But if it can be shown that life is preserved and improved by such ethical values, then somehow it must follow that these ethical values cannot be the expression of the character of God. It appears to many to be unthinkable that the purposes of God might actually be expressed and carried out in what we describe scientifically as biological processes!

Two quotations are helpful in setting the stage for what it means to rethink the God-of-the-Gaps and replace this concept with the biblical emphasis, thus countering this particular argument of Pattern 1 that God is rendered superfluous by modern science. The first is a statement by Malcolm Jeeves: "God, to the theist, while being the cause of everything, is scientifically the explanation of nothing." [45]   The second, somewhat enigmatic, statement is by Bonhoeffer, "Before God, and with God, we live without God." [46]

The thrust of Jeeves' remark is that God is to be conceived as the underlying cause of *all* created reality, not simply brought in occasionally to provide the mechanistic explanation for a few difficult cases.   Jeeves argues that one way to describe the world is in terms of natural science; in such a description God does not systematically enter at places where natural mechanisms are absent in order to provide a supernatural explanation . The God-of-the-Gaps is therefore avoided by Jeeves, not by giving up the witness for the activity of God in the world but by seeing this activity in the context of all of created reality - not simply in those aspects where we presently lack a scientific description.

Bonhoeffer's statement can perhaps be best understood by focusing on the meaning of the three prepositions he uses with respect to God: (1) *Before* - our life is lived in the created universe that God has called into being and sustains in being; we are constantly in the presence of God. (2) *With* - our lives are joined to God in constant fellowship in Jesus Christ, so that we are never alone but rest wholly in the arms of God. (3) *Without* - while recognizing the reality of God's activity in the world without us, we do not use this possibility as an excuse or stopgap for our own ignorance or apathy; instead we seek to serve God fully in all of life without constantly invoking him to deliver us from the need to serve him.

<u>Summary</u>   The claim that modern scientific understanding has made God unnecessary is true only if what is meant by "God" is a "God-of-the-Gaps." We can rejoice that modern scientific understanding has made unacceptable this caricature of a "God-of-the-Gaps." But at the same time we can be clear that this statement is a fundamentally mistaken view of the biblical revelation of the nature of God and his activity in the world, which sees God as active in all phenomena.

What is involved is our fundamental concept of the way in which God and the world are related. This is a theological question, and our answer must come from the biblical revelation that God himself has provided.

> By faith we understand that the world was created by the word of God, so that what is seen was made out of things which do not appear. (Heb. 11:3)
>
> He [Jesus] reflects the glory of God and bears the very stamp of his nature, upholding the universe by his word of power. (Heb. 1:3)
>
> He [Jesus] is before all things, and in him all things hold together. (Col. 2:17)
>
> In his hand is the life of every living thing and the breath of all mankind. (Job 12:10)
>
> In him we live and move and have our being. (Acts 17:28)
>
> There is one God, the Father, from whom are all things and for whom we exist, and one Lord, Jesus Christ, through whom are all things and through whom we exist. (I Cor. 8:6)

From these and many other passages it is clear that the Bible reveals that we depend moment by moment upon God for our very existence. There is nothing *natural* that can happen without God's free activity. To describe events in terms of natural categories is not to explain God's activity *away*; it is rather a fuller exposition of the ways in which we perceive this activity. It is not just the order of the universe, or the design of the universe, or the stability or moral character of the universe that depends on God's own existence and activity. He sustains the very *existence* of the universe on a moment-by-moment basis.

There is no event, either natural or supernatural, either physical or spiritual, either secular or sacred, described scientifically either as deterministic or as chance, which does not depend ultimately and completely upon the sustaining power of God.

The God-of-the-Gaps is a god who intervenes in the world in order to effect his purposes. However the God of the Bible does not *intervene* in the world. There is no world for him to intervene in except that world whose very being and character is constantly maintained and directed by his free activity.

Another response to the God-of-the-Gaps is the realization that a scientific description is only one of a number of possible types of descriptions of reality, each drawing on categories of experience different from the others. To argue that the discovery of scientific mechanisms makes God unnecessary is to make the faith commitment that scientific mechanisms are the totality of reality. But even if we could give a complete description of the universe using the categories of physics and chemistry, for example, (i.e., even if there were no gaps in our physical and chemical descriptions), we would still need other descriptions for dimensions of life not fully encompassed by the physical and chemical. We either accept the need for such other kinds of description, or we deny the need to describe experience in categories other than the physical and chemical; in the latter case, we choose to reduce a human being to an organic machine.

Reflection on this question shows that it is both possible and necessary to describe reality on several levels corresponding, for example, to the physical sciences, to biology, psychology, sociology and to theology. Every phenomenon that occurs in the world can, at least in principle, be described on every one of these levels. Furthermore, to be able to provide even an exhaustive description on one level (i.e., with no gaps *on that level*) does not rule out the necessity or utility of descriptions on other levels. Complete knowledge would require exhaustive descriptions on every level simultaneously.

An understanding of this rule of multilevel descriptions rescues one from many of the dilemmas that give rise to a defense of the God-of-the-Gaps. It plays a significant role in several of the Patterns to be described further in this book. The theologian, seeking to describe reality in terms of a relationship between human beings and God, need not reject scientific descriptions of the same aspects of reality in order to "leave room for God." Similarly, the scientist, seeking to describe reality in terms of natural categories, need not reject theological descriptions of the same aspects of reality in order to preserve intellectual integrity from supernatural mythology; having found a scientific description of a phenomenon or event (whether deterministic or chance), the scientist has neither the need nor the grounds to claim that this discovery in itself does away with evidence for the existence and activity of God.

Belief in the Supernatural Has Become Impossible

A second argument advanced to support the thesis that science has destroyed the possibility of acceptance of historic Christian theology is the claim that scientific understanding of natural phenomena has made belief in the "supernatural" impossible. [47] If a scientific description in natural categories is available, then a supernatural description is no longer acceptable. This is really just a slightly different aspect of the point that we have already covered: the claim is made that modern science has not only made God unnecessary, it has also made God incredible.

Once it was possible to believe in the supernatural. As little children are able to believe in fairies and Santa Claus, so in the infancy of the human race it was possible to see evidence of God and the supernatural everywhere, simply because so little was understood in natural terms. But now we ascertain truth according to the scientific method, and this guide to truth never tells us about the existence of God at all. Like the astronaut who returned from his space trip with his atheism confirmed because he didn't see God out there, modern people may be led to give up belief in God because God cannot be scientifically detected.

Now it is true that God cannot be scientifically detected. It is curious, however, that although science has been effective in preventing belief in the traditional supernatural, it has been remarkably ineffective in preventing belief in the avant-garde supernatural. People are always prone to believe all kinds of things. Even in our modern age, their gullibility is a constant marvel . It is almost as though this propensity of human nature were not to be denied. Convinced that science has made belief in the traditional supernatural impossible, people today manufacture their own new supernatural. In astrology, scientology, drugs, Zen, Satan worship, New Age variations, and a hundred other ways, they make perverted human attempts to inject a supernatural element into life. Any element of objectivity is welcome in such a morass of self-delusion. Authentic science can and should play the role of keeping people from believing nonsense; actually authentic Christian theology plays the same role.

Most of the misunderstanding arising from the use of the terms "natural" and "supernatural" can be traced to a misunderstanding as to what these terms actually mean. If the words are taken as being mutually exclusive, and "supernatural" means an act of God, then what does "natural" mean? A common conclusion is that "natural" means an event that is not an act of God.

As we have seen in our discussion of a God-of-the-Gaps, if our evidence for the existence and activity of God in the world is identified with specifically "supernatural" events, then every increase in our understanding that suggests a "natural" description of an event that previously had no such "natural" description appears to be a threat to our faith.

The dictionary [31] is not very helpful to us. It defines "supernatural" as "of or relating to an order of existence beyond the visible observable universe; departing from what is usual or normal, esp. so as to appear to transcend the laws of nature." And it defines "natural" as being in accordance with or determined by nature; occurring in conformity with the ordinary course of nature; not marvelous or "supernatural."   Thus the dictionary tells us that "natural " is "determined by nature," but as a matter of fact "nature" does not "determine" anything. It tells us that the "natural" occurs "in conformity with the ordinary course of nature," but what we mean by "the ordinary course of nature" depends at least as much on our current opinion of what that "ordinary course" is, as it does on what phenomena actually occur. It removes the "natural" from the domain deserving of awe or reverence by saying that the "natural" is not "marvelous."

The   dictionary definitions for "supernatural" are reasonably consistent with its definitions of "natural."   They make the "supernatural" and the "natural" refer to two quite separate realms.   If an event is "usual or normal," then it is "natural;" if it "appears to transcend the laws of nature," then it is "supernatural."   Thus it is not surprising that the common approach to "supernatural" and "natural" supposes that they represent mutually exclusive concepts. If an event is "natural," then it has no "supernatural" component;   similarly, if an event is "supernatural," it defies "natural" description. The consequence for our discussion appears to follow directly: since science provides a natural description of events, it excludes a supernatural description. Since "God" requires a supernatural description, science has excluded God.

The resolution of this apparent dilemma starts with the recognition that every event must be simultaneously considered in two ways, one expressed from a natural perspective and one from a supernatural perspective. This is consistent with the case suggested above for a multilevel description of reality.

One way is to ask: What is the description of this event in terms of natural cause and effect categories? This is equivalent to asking: What is the scientific description? To say that an event is "natural" is to affirm that it is susceptible to scientific investigation. To say that an event is susceptible to scientific investigation does not imply that a scientific description provides all of the information of value about the event, only that the event is such that some information can be obtained about it from a scientific investigation. To say that an event is intrinsically "supernatural," is to claim that no relevant scientific description can be given of it; we are dealing with a miracle, a specific issue that we discuss in the next section.

Another way is to ask: What is the meaning of this event? What is its purpose? How does this event relate to God, to his purposes, to the flow of history, and to ultimate reality? To consider such questions is to focus on a supernatural description for the event. It is a description that does not arise out of the event itself or its scientific description, but from a total context beyond it within which the event must be viewed.

It is essential, therefore, that it be realized that there are two distinguishable ways of treating these two terms, "natural" and "supernatural." In one way, they express whether or not a particular event is appropriate for description through scientific investigation. This is a categorization of the kind of event. The transformation of a caterpillar into a butterfly, a sunset seen from a mountain top, and the disappearance of electrical resistance of superconductors when the temperature is lowered sufficiently are all natural events. That they are marvelous, few would debate. They are seen as members of that set of events that can be meaningfully described by scientific investigation. The Resurrection of Jesus, on the other hand, and the many miracles he and his disciples performed to heal disease and demonstrate power over the forces in the world, are examples of supernatural events. As far as we know, it is not meaningful to seek to express scientific mechanisms for their occurrence.

But at the same time we must remember that whenever we speak of any event in this world, we are speaking of a manifestation of the power and activity of God. Thus, a natural event is never one that occurs without the activity of God, but rather is one that represents our perception of God's normal or regular activity. Every natural event must be interpreted within a supernatural context as well as a natural one. The coming of rain can be described in terms of air pressure and temperature gradients, but it can also be described in terms of an answer to prayer. A cow may be seen as an example of bovine biology, but how we treat the cow will depend on whether we see it as a creature made by God for specific purposes or not.

Summary. All events that take place in the created universe are manifestations of the free activity of God. A natural event is one that is susceptible to scientific description, but also to interpretation within the context of a larger supernatural perspective. An intrinsically supernatural event (a miracle) is one that is not susceptible to scientific description, but brings out of its own context a particular revelation of God and his purpose.

Once again it may be seen that if it is concluded that science has ruled out the possibility of supernatural descriptions, this is a direct result of the faith commitment to the principle that there is no reality except that susceptible to description in terms of natural categories. This is not a commitment that science demands of us, but rather one that may be imported into a person's worldview because of other philosophical or metaphysical commitments to Scientism. The resolution of the problem lies not in arguing that science should include supernatural as well as natural categories of description, but in recognizing the limits that characterize the endeavor known as "authentic science," and the relevance of seeing all natural phenomena within a supernatural context as well.

Miracles Violate Our Understanding of the World

Another direct facet of the two claims discussed above is the argument directed against the possibility of miracles. The assumption is often made that since belief in miracles is no longer possible and since belief in the supernatural is no longer possible, and since belief in God is closely coupled to belief in miracles and the supernatural, belief in God is also no longer possible. Indeed the rejection of miracles extends beyond this, being sometimes the concern of people who otherwise hold to the reality of God and the possibility of the supernatural. Mott, for example, has written: [48]

> I address this essay ... to those with a belief in God but who find repellent the idea that God should set aside his laws on special occasions. ... My assumption is that God relates to men and women who seek him, and that He works within natural law. This is an assumption I start with, believing that many scientists and others share it. It is – of course – an arbitrary assumption, and I can give no proof of it that would convince those who believe otherwise. I shall, however, hope to show that it is compatible with belief in the

supernatural and in God, and need not bring those who think in this way into conflict with the Christian Church – at any rate in its Anglican form.

It is certainly true that one of the points at which science and Christian theology seem most obviously to be at odds is the subject of miracles. As is often the case, a definition of a "miracle" is needed before we can discuss it further. In order to be called a miracle, an event must have the following characteristics: (1) it must either appear to be contrary to the normal phenomena of nature as they are currently known, or it must appear as an extremely improbable coincidence of diverse elements, and (2) it must have a deeper significance than simply being a rare and unusual event for the persons involved, usually related to their religious perspective.

A certain amount of skepticism before pronouncing that a particular event is a miracle is both reasonable and justified when one takes account of the subjective gullibility of the human species. But here we are concerned, not with whether every event that has been called a miracle was really a miracle, but rather with whether it is possible for any event that would be properly called a miracle to occur.

The claim is simply made that science has shown that miracles are impossible. What is really meant is that because the structure of a miracle does not fit the structure of scientific truth, it cannot therefore be true. Such an objection is based once more on the unjustified assumption (Scientism) that science is the only possible way to obtain knowledge and an insight into truth. Since miracles are events that by definition cannot be describable scientifically, then this perspective demands that they not be possible. Actually, since miracles are unique historical events, science can say nothing about them at all, one way or the other. The only judgment that science can bring fairly is to say, "I wouldn't expect one." But that, after all, is the very nature of a miracle and hardly constitutes an argument against its reality.

But the objection to miracles goes deeper, as is reflected in the comments of Mott cited above. Not only are miracles not possible, but the very thought of miracles is "repellent." Why is it so repellent? One of the most troublesome aspects of miracles is that they are often interpreted to call for God to intervene in a normally orderly and well-behaved world in order to pull off some kind of magic act that breaks his own natural laws. In this framework a miracle becomes an oddity, an affront to the work of creation, a meddling with a self-sufficient world that is operating well. If one believed that this were indeed the character of a miracle, it would be easy to understand why the concept should appear so repellent.

But, as we have discussed above, such a position is based on a faulty view of the relationship between God and the world. In a biblical view the world is not to be thought of as having been outfitted by God at some time in the past with the various physical laws that govern the behavior of matter, and as having continued since that time on the basis of God's initial momentum without his specific activity in the whole system (a Deist, not a biblical view).

The important correctives of a biblical view can be repeated here once more briefly. To achieve his purposes in the world, God does not *intervene* in the world as though he were normally absent and needed to make his presence felt in an independently existing reality. To perform a miracle God does not *break* his natural laws; such laws are our human descriptions of the normal way in which God's activity in the world manifests itself. Such laws are our inventions; they are descriptive and not prescriptive.

When it is realized that the very existence of the world from moment to moment depends upon the creative and sustaining power of God, that no natural law has any power of its own to continue, that no "expected" circumstance has any ability to bring itself into being, we come to the conclusion that God's activity in a miracle is not qualitatively different from God's activity in natural phenomena. In bringing to pass the natural phenomena that lead to our scientific description in the law of gravity or the laws of electromagnetic radiation, God acts freely and continuously. He is not constrained by these laws, as if he had to meddle with them to produce a different result. At rare times and in accordance with his specific purpose, he acts freely to produce what the world interprets as a miracle.

Consider once again the judgment of a scientist about miracles, "I wouldn't expect one." Why wouldn't he expect one? Because in the ordinary course of events his experience is that miracles do not happen. But no discussion of miracles ever suggests that they happen in the "ordinary course of events." When, however, miracles are recognized as a particular form in the outworking of God's purposes in the world, when they are associated with the preaching of God's Word, the spreading of the gospel of Jesus Christ, and the manifestation of God's witness in the world, they become clearly distinguished from the world of magic and sorcery. Then it becomes clear that miracles are not arbitrary violations of natural law to impress the people involved, but that they are appropriate evidences of God's free activity in making himself known.

Science Has Shown that Christianity is Only .....

In addition to the charges outlined above which claim that Christian theology has been made unnecessary, incredible and objectionable by our growing scientific understanding, there is also the charge that challenges the integrity of Christian theology as an authentic way of knowing. It is claimed that modern science has considered the phenomena associated with Christian theology and faith, and has successfully explained them *away* by revealing that actually they are not examples of objective reality at all, but only subjective illusions related to some other aspect of living. Thus it is claimed that science has shown that human beings are only complex machines, that Christian conversion is only a psychological experience, that the development of the Christian faith is not historically unique and that hence Christianity is only another human religion, that Christianity is only a sociological phenomenon retained by those in power to mollify the poor and downtrodden, or that Christianity is only a sociobiological phenomenon useful in evolutionary selective processes for survival.

One very simple response to such critiques is that science can *never* say that anything is *only* ..... As soon as the "only" appears a red flag goes up to indicate that what follows is an expression of the ideological convictions of the speaker, but not a necessary consequence of science itself. Human beings *are* "complex machines." That is an acceptable scientific statement. Human beings are *only* "complex machines." That is a subjective philosophical speculation not derivable from science. Such reasoning is another repetition of the old fallacy: if science shows us that human beings are complex machines, and if we can know nothing except what science tells us (Scientism) , then human beings are only complex machines. Christian conversion involves a psychological experience; it also involves a work of supernatural regeneration. The Christian faith is one of the religions on earth, but it is based on the supernatural revelation of the One who made heaven and earth, who became a man who lived and died – and then rose from the dead. The formulation of Christian faith has been colored by sociological influences and it has been misused by people who never knew what the name Christian means; but its content and its Lord are unique.

<u>Summary</u>. Every *only* is a subjective judgment of human beings. Science itself knows no *onlys*. The attempt to use the concept of *only* to discredit the Christian position is simply another restating of the faith commitment to Scientism: there are no valid insights except those given by science.

Can One Regard the Bible as God's Revelation?

A final charge often brought against the defense of Christian theology in this modern scientific day is the challenge to the integrity and authority of the Bible. Such a view of the Bible may seem on the surface to be hopelessly out of date with modern perspectives. In the old days people were instructed by those in authority, and accepted what they were told without appreciable questioning. The whole flavor of our scientific day, however, moves against this. Truth now is found by measuring and testing, not by listening to the words of learned authority. The premise of Scientism that all reliable information must come as the result of scientific investigation dominates our culture. How can a modern person today consider the Bible as an authoritative revelation of God? Can we really obtain from the revelation of the Bible as valid insights into the nature of reality as we can obtain from science?

One of the first steps in resolving these issues is to become particularly aware of the differences between the I-It relationships of science and the I-Thou interpersonal relationships of theology. Ordinarily, persons find out about things by scientific investigation, since things cannot reveal themselves except when probed by the scientist. On the other hand, persons find out about persons both by an extension of the same process of scientific investigation, but much more commonly and deeply by the mutual process of self-revelation. This is just another way of saying that if we wish to know a person, speaking and listening to that person is essential. Acceptance of the Bible as a reliable revelation of God to us, is our acceptance of his willingness and ability to speak to us through the writers of the Bible, and in particular through his son Jesus Christ whose life and teachings are reported and interpreted in the Bible. This acceptance, like every other fundamental choice we make, is a faith commitment based on the variety of evidences that we have of the Bible's reliability and trustworthiness and our own experiences in hearing God speak to us in the words of the Bible.

God's choice to reveal himself partially through the elements of this finite world - whether they be scientific phenomena, human characteristics, historical events, or human language - is in itself a task of revelation that no human being could hope to accomplish. God has taken the attributes of his being – his love, his mercy, his holiness, his justice, his power – and has translated them into a form that human beings can understand, believe, and respond to. He has done this through the course of history by meeting human beings where they are and revealing himself in a way, ever more clear with the passage of time, which makes use of the knowledge, culture, and understanding of the people at the time involved. The climax of God's revelation of himself is the person of Jesus Christ. In him the ultimate and the unconditional are wed to the transient and the conditioned in such a way that a human being can respond with his or her own personality .

Summary.   The worldview of Scientism, based on the faith commitment to science as the only source of valid insights into reality, is not demanded by science itself. It is far less consistent with the totality of our life and experience than a worldview based on the faith commitment to God who has revealed himself to us in the Bible.

Chapter 5

Pattern 2: Christian Theology in Spite of Science

In several ways, Pattern 2 shares the same presuppositions as Pattern 1, but then draws an exactly opposite set of conclusions. The basic assumptions of Pattern 2 can be summarized:

Science and theology tell us the same kind of things about the same things. When scientific and theological descriptions conflict, one must be right and the other wrong. In this encounter, the theological descriptions always have the priority.

Patterns 1 and 2 agree that both science and theology give us the same kind of information about the same things. They agree that if these two kinds of description conflict, one must be right and the other wrong. They agree that a God-of-the-Gaps is an important way to describe God. Advocates of Pattern 1 reject a God-of-the-Gaps because of increasing scientific understanding, and hence reject God. Advocates of Pattern 2 uphold a representation of God as a God-of-the-Gaps because of their theological interpretation of the Bible, and hence reject any apparently conflicting inputs from science.

Advocates of Pattern 1 are committed to the development of understanding through the scientific method, with only a peripheral nod to theology in areas of personal or subjective interest. Advocates of Pattern 2 are committed to the faithful interpretation of the Bible as they understand it, with only a peripheral nod to science in areas of impersonal or pragmatic interest.

Both invoke an "only" framework. Advocates of Pattern 1 see science as the only valid source of insights into the nature of reality, and theology as only a cultural and psychological phenomenon characterized by relativism. Advocates of Pattern 2 see theology as the only valid source of insights about anything that the biblical writers mention, and science as only an operational activity that allows us to do certain technological activities but contributes nothing on its own to any topics apparently covered by the biblical writers.

Advocates of Pattern 1 see the phrase "descriptions based on human interpretation in natural categories," in our definition for authentic science, in the light of their commitment to Scientism, leading to the conclusion that only those interpretations based on natural categories have any relevance or value. Advocates of Pattern 2, on the other hand, find this same phrase with its emphasis on "natural categories" as capitulation to "methodological naturalism" (a term equivalent to "scientism") , and therefore devote considerable effort to attempting to remove it or to involve theological inputs in the development of science. Curiously advocates of both Patterns 1 and 2 agree in the erroneous conclusion that "descriptions ... in natural categories" should be viewed within the context of Scientism.

Pattern 2 is one of the direct responses historically made by Christians against the apparent threat of increasing scientific understanding against the historic Christian faith. Such possible threats are warded off by holding up theology and its interpretations as the only relevant ones for a Christian in any area where theology and science seem to come into conflict. Its significance for Christians and Christian culture cannot be underestimated. It can be regularly found expounded in publications by various Christian institutions dedicated to a defense of the faith against the attacks of "anti-Christian science."

Those who feel that theology needs to be upheld over science in this modern scientific day frequently seek to find a scientific framework in which to make their case against the science that proves troublesome to them; such advocates are also found in another of the patterns, Pattern 4, to be described later (see Chapter 7). But there is a large Christian constituency that has very little interest in science itself, either apologetically or as an area worthy of extended interaction. This subdivision of Christians often adopts a fundamentally anti-intellectual stance with respect to its faith, and effectively seeks to separate itself and its society from the influences and temptations of a world dominated by science.

In this framework the important questions and issues of life have only supernatural answers, and meaningful scientific descriptions will never be found. If science appears to disagree with these theological interpretations, so much the worse for science, which is clearly either incompetent or more likely, deliberately anti-Christian.

The primary orientation of Pattern 2 is to ignore science and to discourage participation in science. Young people brought up in this environment are led to believe that a career in science is not something that a Christian should contemplate. The important things in life are spiritual and they have nothing in common with science and its earthly concerns.

When young people, brought up in a community where they have been consistently taught that one must always choose the insights of Christian theology over those of "anti-Christian science" whenever they appear to differ, do go on to higher education, they often find themselves in a difficult dilemma.   Having become aware of certain aspects of the universe in which a scientific description is not identical with a traditional theological description, they are now called upon to make a choice between science and theology.   If they can no longer simply reject the scientific input, they have little recourse except to reject their basic Christian theological commitment.   Considerable effort is required to enable them to see that this Pattern is not the only possible one.

Sometimes Christians involved in Pattern 2 do become involved with the interaction between science and Christian theology to the extent that efforts are made to make theology the ultimate guide for acceptable science (to develop a "theistic science").   The attempt is made to determine by theology which theories in science are consistent with Christian faith and which are not, or even to reformulate science so that its format can now be dictated by theology.   When this happens there is always the danger of sacrificing scientific integrity for the sake of apparent theological credibility, thus producing a pseudoscience.   We consider a few examples of this type also in this chapter.   This is, in a way, the inverse of Pattern 5 (see Chapter 8) in which the effort is made to formulate a theology on the basis of science (to develop a "scientific theology," with the corresponding danger of producing a pseudotheology).

Still it is not difficult to understand how Pattern 2 has arisen and continues to be supported. From the most positive outlook, defenders of Pattern 2 are seeking to ward off the attacks and threats of what is perceived to be anti-Christian science. Nor is this judgment necessarily mistaken, since there is no shortage of literature advancing the position that modern science has made Christian theology untenable, on the basis of scientism misrepresented as authentic science, as we have discussed in Pattern 1 (Chapter 4).

In a world in which the successes of science are established, it appears that Pattern 2 will not be able to survive very long except in isolated areas. Its demise may be accompanied by considerable loss of faith among its proponents. Those committed to it will find themselves squeezed into a smaller and smaller "God-of-the-Gaps" position, particularly if they seek to witness to the world around them.

Biblical Inerrancy

Advocates of Pattern 2 place the Bible and its interpretation, i.e., Christian theology, at the summit of the authority hierarchy in every area. Since the Bible is given to us as the revelation of God to human beings, the insights provided by God are more reliable and trustworthy than the apparent insights obtained through scientific interpretations, primarily by non- or anti-Christian scientists.

It is possible to invoke the following set of logical premises and conclusion: (1) God is Absolute Truth, (2) every word of God must be absolutely true, (3) the Bible consists of God's words, (4) therefore the Bible must be absolutely true. Any claim, therefore, that the Bible does not present the absolute truth about any subject with which the writers deal is to cast doubt on the credibility and trustworthiness of the Bible as a whole, and hence on the very integrity of God.

The position underlying this approach is expressed by Maatman [49]:

> Since the Bible is the inerrant Word of God and not to be criticized, it is its own authority. The Bible speaks on whatever it speaks, and whatever it says is true. If the Bible speaks on geology, it speaks true geology. Similarly, the Bible speaks truly of all other sciences if it discusses them: of cosmology, biology, geography, history, etc.

It is essential, therefore, that consideration be given to the concept of "inerrancy."[50] It is the purpose of this concept to uphold the reliability, authority, and trustworthiness -- the "truth" of the biblical revelation. It is reasonable to maintain that in order to be "true," the Bible must be free of all "error." In affirming that the Bible contains no errors, however, it becomes essential for us to define what we should mean by an "error," and how we would recognize an "error" in the Bible if we were to find one.

Does the Bible set forth a *true* description of reality? What constitutes a *true* description of reality is something that people have long debated. Some people argue that a true description is one that gives a trustworthy insight into the nature of reality. Other people argue that in order to be true a description must be literally correct. Others argue that in order to be true a description must be completely accurate no matter what criterion of accuracy is used to judge it. If these last two viewpoints are applied indiscriminately to the Bible, we obtain the conclusion that in order for the Bible to be called a true description of reality, it must be *literally* true in every place and *exhaustively* accurate in every way. No book meets these criteria. Perhaps a book in mathematics or formal logic might come close to satisfying them, but no book that attempts to treat the matters of deep significance for personal existence can consistently be literally true and/or exhaustively accurate; this is prohibited by the very use of human language and by the problems of communication.

What then do we mean when we affirm that the Bible presents a true description of reality? We mean that we may have complete confidence in the truth of the insights given to us by the Bible, provided that we derive these insights in the appropriate way. They must come from a contextual interpretation following authentic hermeneutics in the light of the purposes of the Bible, both generally and in local passages. These principles of interpretation will lead us to view some portions of the Bible as literal statements of fact, and some as symbolic presentations of truth in a universally understandable form.

A couple of commonly recognized examples will suffice to illustrate this point. We do not take the statement of Psalm 93:1a, "Yea, the world is established; it shall never be moved;" as a scientific description of planetary dynamics, but rather recognize it as an affirmation of the absolute reliability of God. We do not draw exact mathematical information from the genealogy of Matthew 1, summarized in Matthew 1:17; we realize that Matthew has deliberately omitted several generations (see I Chronicles 3:11, 12, 15, 19) in order to provide a symmetry to the genealogy. We recognize the limitations on expression imposed by the use of parables or poetry. We recognize anthropomorphisms, idiomatic language, and popular expressions (e.g., the sun rose). The disciples of Jesus were constantly making the mistake of taking literally what he intended for them to understand symbolically. We cannot, of course, go to the opposite extreme (how human beings love to go to extremes!); it is even more of a mistake to regard none of the biblical revelation as literal than to regard all of it as literal. Once again we are called by our Lord to be mature Christians with the guidance of his Holy Spirit as we seek to discern between biblical statements properly interpreted literally and other that would not serve the purposes of revelation if a strictly literal interpretation were demanded.

These principles will lead us to view some statements in the Bible as scientifically true today, and to view others as no longer scientifically accurate though they stated truths in terms of physical models of their own day. It was not information about scientific mechanisms that concerned the writers of the Bible, but the desire to use understandable thought forms and contemporary models to convey deeper and more profound truths. This perspective has been summarized succinctly by Ramm [51]:

> I think it is possible to teach the doctrine of creation from the point of view of the cosmological systems of Ptolemy, Newton or Einstein. I think the kinds of things Scripture wants to say can be said in the context of any of these three theories without dignifying the theories as such as revealed truth. ... A revelation couched in terms of perfected science as of the year 3000 A.D. would have been a meaningless and confusing revelation. Therefore it is valid to make a distinction between the structural or literary forms in which a revelation comes and what the revelation itself teaches.

The consequences of Pattern 2 are compounded by the fact that the advocate of Pattern 2 and the non-Christian with a scientific background may well agree with one another that the Bible must be literally and completely true whenever a scientific matter is mentioned in the text. If the advocate of Pattern 2 finds that scientific views appear to conflict with a literal interpretation of some portions of the Bible, on the basis of his conviction, he attacks science. The non-Christian with a scientific background may well agree that certain scientific views appear to conflict with a literal interpretation of some portions of the Bible. On the basis of his conviction, he rejects the Christian position. It is ironic that these two groups of people should agree on the wrong attitude toward the Bible, and then use their agreement to attempt to invalidate the other's position!

To clarify the situation, let us define a Type 1 Error as one involving an error with respect to the criterion of absolute truth, and a Type 2 Error as involving an error with respect to the criterion of the revelational purpose of the passage. Thus a statement is an error of Type 1 in any case where it does not accurately convey absolute truth; a statement is a Type 2 Error if it fails to convey accurately the revelational purpose for which the passage was written by inspiration of God. For example, the statement that "the sun rises" in the Bible is clearly a Type 1 Error, but it is not a Type 2 Error. The statement of

Matthew 1:17 in Matthew's chronology about the number of generations, or the statement (Matthew 13:32) about the mustard seed being the smallest of all seeds, are Type 1 Errors, but they are not Type 2 Errors.

A consistent position maintains that neither theoretically nor operationally are there Type 2 Errors in the Bible, but that if one insists on using the inappropriate criterion for Type 1 Errors, Type 1 Errors may well be found. Whenever an advocate of absolute inerrancy must face a biblical statement that is clearly and demonstrably not in correspondence with "absolute truth," he invariably argues that these should not be considered real errors, i.e., they may be Type 1 Errors but they are not Type 2 Errors. In order to defend inerrancy, it is inerrancy with respect to Type 2 Errors that must be defended. No other criterion for error can be biblically defended. Statements of contemporary culture and worldview, which would have to be judged as "errors" of Type 1 in any kind of absolute criterion for error, are seen not to constitute a revelational error of Type 2 because of the proper and effective role they play in conveying that revelation to us. Our understanding of the Bible (our authentic Christian theology) must be guided by a sense of the overall purposes of the revelation.

The Purposes of Biblical Revelation

Christians have traditionally confessed that the Bible is the Word of God, written in the words of human authors who were guided by the Holy Spirit so that they faithfully conveyed the purpose of God's revelation to human beings. Thus, when we inquire as to the content of the biblical revelation in terms of the purpose for which it was written, we are assured of a completely authoritative and trustworthy revelation.

Such a teaching of the nature of the Bible is consistent with the Bible's own testimony concerning the purposes for which it was written. These purposes can be conveniently summarized under three major categories: (1) to reveal Jesus Christ as Lord and Savior and through Him, God as Redeemer (e.g., John 20:31); (2) to confirm and strengthen the faith of believers (e.g., Luke 1:3,4); and (3) to provide a guide for Christian living (e.g., II Timothy 3:16) A reading of Paul's prayers also helps us understand the kinds of purpose for which the biblical writings were made (e.g., Ephesians 1:6, 18-20; 3:16-19; 4:12-14).

When the biblical writers use contemporary cultural terms or worldview perspectives, we do not automatically know whether that expression or perspective is indeed an accurate representation of the absolute reality of God's creation, or whether that expression or perspective is effective in conveying God's revelational content to us and people of all ages in spite of the fact that it does not present a totally accurate representation of absolute reality. The Bible is after all communication: communication between God and human beings, in which the language of the hearer must play as large a role as the content the speaker wishes to convey.

The recognition of the Bible as communication emphasizes to us the necessary role of interpretation in applying the revelational content of the Bible to ourselves in the development of theology. In the fundamental definitions of the nature of authentic science and authentic theology in Chapters 2 and 3, we have stressed that the understanding of information or revelation requires in both science and theology that we interpret its direct relevance and application in specific circumstances. The word *interpretation* here is not a negative term, but rather simply seeks to express that we have to make up our minds what something means for us (i.e., we have to interpret it to understand it and to apply it to our own lives.)

We may fully accept that we should "love our neighbor as ourselves," but then we have to enter into the process of interpretation in order to decide what specific attitudes or actions really constitute "loving our neighbor" in a particular situation. It is not a pejorative term that Christians should reject, but a simple statement of the necessities of communication. Fortunately the Christian is promised the assistance of the Holy Spirit in this task of interpretation.

This application can be done successfully only if we take account of the purpose of the biblical writings, as well as the historical and cultural context in which the various books were composed. We must be diligent in determining what is the proper interpretation from a careful examination of other aspects of the scriptural revelation on the same or similar material, and from a careful examination of other aspects of reality to which we may have access. We do not introduce this other extra-biblical material to see whether or there is an "error" in the Bible; we introduce it in order to make sure that we ourselves do not interpret falsely and so generate our own errors.

The partial and incomplete knowledge that we can obtain from our scientific interpretation of the natural world must be ultimately consistent with the partial and incomplete knowledge that we can obtain from our theological interpretation of the Bible. In most cases the biblical revelation must have priority over the natural revelation. This is because no interpretation of ultimate significance can be made without the biblical revelation, because the biblical revelation alone has the ability to let human beings see themselves as they are, because the biblical revelation alone has the ability to guide and judge the directions and motives of scientific research, and because the biblical revelation informs us of God's activity in history that we cannot deduce from scientific procedures alone.

There are portions of the biblical revelation, however, which deal with subjects for which the authors could not be eye-witnesses and which so deeply probe the significance of the future and of the past that their expression is given in a universally comprehensible form.   In those instances that deal with the vast patterns of the past or of the future, we may well expect to find true insight into reality set forth with a minimum of specific scientific mechanisms, so as to maintain the purpose for which it was written and its universal application.   To insist that every passage of the biblical revelation that seems to present a scientific mechanism *must* do so with absolute authority and finality, that the Bible *must* be literally and completely true whenever a scientific matter is apparently mentioned in the text, is to miss the kind of book the Bible is.   In a misguided effort to preserve and defend a "high view of inspiration," the very spirit of the book itself and its purpose may be misunderstood.

Ultimately truth alone must have the priority - and the truth is not a single-faceted thing.   What, for example is the true answer to the question, "Where did I come from?"

> Answer 1. God made me.
> Answer 2. The dust of the earth.
> Answer 3. My mother's womb.
> Answer 4. The union of my father's sperm and my mother's ovum.
> Answer 5. A middle-class family.
> Answer 6. Ancestors from Germany.
> Answer 7. The hospital where I was born.
> Answer 8. Providence, Rhode Island.

True answers to the question, "Where did you come from?" depend on our interpretation of the various words in the question and on the purpose for which we thought the question was asked. If I apply for a job and am asked this question, to reply, "God made me," would be both irrelevant and impertinent - just as irrelevant and impertinent as to remind my questioner of the biological origin of life. If the same question were asked in the midst of a profound discussion of matters of ultimate significance, to reply, "Providence, Rhode Island," would be equally irrelevant and impertinent.

Now if the scientific question of my origin is most appropriately answered in terms of the merger of sperm and ovum, and if the theological question of my origin is most appropriately answered in terms of the creative activity of God, is there any contradiction? Because the scientific answer does not mention God, do I condemn it as false?   Because the theological answer does not deal with the physiological mechanisms of conception, do I regard it as insignificant and of no relevance?   The theological answer does have much more ultimate content than the scientific answer; it is far more important to know that God made me than it is to know that I am the product of merger between sperm and ovum.

We may expect that the presentation of truth given in the biblical revelation takes into account the kind of knowledge the listeners possess and the concepts that will make sense for them. It starts where they are and works with them. It meets them where they stand and sets forth the truth about God, the world, and the nature of man in terms that are understandable and acceptable by people of all ages, all cultures, all degrees of scientific understanding. To accomplish this, the biblical revelation uses thought models and patterns common to the authors and their listeners and sets forth through them the timeless truths that we need to know.   The truths about origins and destinies revealed in the Bible far transcend in importance and significance any of the scientific mechanisms that may be discovered in the course of time. And yet this does not diminish the proper significance of the mechanisms nor the desirability of knowing and understanding them for a complete appreciation of the whole truth.

Science and Theology: Mutual Aids in Interpretation

Science can be a useful guide in deciding what degree of literalness is appropriate in interpreting certain biblical portions where scientific knowledge is applicable. Since the scientific view is never permanently established, but always subject to later findings, such an aid must be considered as subject to change and not the basis for dogmatic assertions. Nevertheless, it is evident that science has made valuable contributions to biblical understanding.

Scientific developments in astronomical understanding have drastically altered earlier accepted models placing the earth at the center of the solar system, or of a three-level cosmology with earth in the center level between hell below and heaven above.   Scientific estimates of the age of the universe and of human beings have affected our understanding of the models of the early chapters of Genesis and other portions of the Bible as well.   Enhanced scientific understanding of the biological and psychological aspects of human beings have informed the biblical view of human beings.   Increased appreciation for scientific mechanisms has emphasized that God's activity is commonly encountered in natural phenomena rather than overtly supernatural ones. Increased scientific awareness of the intricate web of interrelationships in the environment and their effect on ecological considerations has reminded us of the place that the human race occupies in the structure of creation.   Scientific understanding also guides in the application of biblical revelation to everyday life.   It acts as a bridge between the principles enunciated in the biblical revelation and the living out of those principles in contemporary society.

The biblical revelation in turn provides insight into human nature. It raises the much needed warning against the supposedly unprejudiced objective conclusions of scientists. It provides the basis for human dignity and worth essential for determining how human beings are to be treated scientifically.   It provides the guidelines to decide what kinds of scientific activities are to be given high priority and which are to be discouraged as much as possible. And it forms the foundation for the great number of ethical problems that modern science is encountering with ever greater frequency.

"Theistic Science"

The significance attributed to science in today's world is so great that there is to advocates of Pattern 2 an obvious problem in the insistence that scientific descriptions must by definition be given in natural categories.   It seems to them that God is being improperly excluded from the description of the physical world.   They do not think that God's creation and sustaining of the natural world can be upheld as long as God's actions are not included as being appropriate mechanisms for a scientific description.   They feel that if science is the dominant source of obtaining knowledge of reality, then science must include God's actions as mechanisms directly;   if science does not include God's actions, then they fear that God's actions are concluded to have no validity.

Out of the belief that the phrase "in natural categories," included in our definition of authentic science for the reasons presented there, represents an inappropriate exclusion of direct divine intervention from the discipline of science, a number of Christians have begun the call for what they have called "theistic science." [52-57]   Their claim is that direct divine action should be included in the categories used in scientific descriptions.   Moreland [53], for example, offers the following definition of "theistic science":

> In its broadest sense, theistic science is a research program that expresses a commitment to the idea that (1) God, conceived of as a personal agent of great power and intelligence, has through direct, primary agent causation and through indirect, secondary causation created and designed the world for a purpose and has directly intervened in the course of its development at various times (including prehistory , i.e., history prior to the arrival of human beings) and (2) the commitment expressed in proposition (1) can appropriately enter into the very fabric of the practice of science and the utilization of scientific methodology.

In the context of our own discussion here, there is clearly agreement with the contention that God "has through indirect, secondary causation created and designed the world for a purpose." There is some question about the contention that God "has through direct, primary agent causation ... created and designed the world for a purpose."   This question is not about what God *could* do, but about what God *did* do; certainly God could have exercised such direct primary agent causation, but it remains to be investigated whether or not that is what he actually did in any specific case.   The same comment can be made about the contention that God "has directly intervened in the course of its development at various times," a claim that is further obscured by the use of the term "intervened," the non-biblical inferences of which we have previously discussed. Finally, however, proposition 2 cannot be accepted in the framework we have been advancing for the simple reason that to impose beliefs about God's possible activity on science can lead only to a pseudoscience.

The approach of "theistic science" inevitably leads to a return to a position involving a God-of-the-Gaps. Moreland, for example, says [52],   "But the Bible implies that gaps do in fact exist in natural explanations, and the existence of such gaps is a part of the case for God." (p. 202)   In another place [53] he responds to the charge of endorsing a God-of-the-Gaps by claiming that it is not valid since "theistic science" does not call for a description in terms of God as direct primary agent without "good theological or philosophical reasons."   This may make it good sense, but it doesn't make it good science. If God were to create something from nothing instantaneously in front of a person today, the person could attribute what he observes scientifically only to "spontaneous generation." Then, as a human being reflecting on the situation, he may come to the faith conclusion that he has witnessed a direct primary creative act of God. This would be his personal holistic response to the experience, not the outcome of his science.

The practical implications of "theistic science" could be considerably greater and more damaging. Out of a disenchantment with the picture of the physical world given to us currently by relativity and quantum mechanics, Fraser [54] appeals to a biblical description that would be much clearer.

> Is this the kind of universe God would make for us?　.... The Bible does not leave us wondering about the properties of God's physical creation. It comments on such matters explicitly. ... Modern theoretical physics seems to want to change that clear picture. ... It seems clear that such a "scriptural physics" can be constructed and that it can offer us new insights and plausible alternatives to the difficult factual, theoretical, and scriptural problems embodied in the physics of this century.

We cannot let our puzzlement about the curvature of space, particle/wave duality, and the Heisenberg Indeterminacy Principle lead us to suppose that by imposing biblical ideas on science we will see the truth in a new and clarified way. It is not the purpose of God's revelation to give us insights into such mechanisms. We do not generally learn the detailed mechanisms describing how God acts in the physical world today except by examining the world itself.

It is absolutely crucial to realize that the debate here is not about what God could do, but about what God did (and does) do. The advocate of theistic science claims that unless God is admitted as a direct agent in scientific theories, then this is equivalent to saying that God cannot act as a primary cause directly. This is not true. If there were a case where God acted directly as a primary cause, the pursuit of authentic science (as we have defined it here) would lead to the conclusion that no scientific description was possible. It would then be appropriate to propose other possible situations such as the direct action of God as a primary cause. Such a proposal would always involve faith choices between simply concluding that not enough information was currently available to decide definitively that no scientific description was possible, or that enough information was available to allow a rational faith choice involving the direct action of God as primary cause.

Illustration: Creation and Evolution

Historically the debate about the relationship between creation and evolution has been a focal point for many of the issues described above. This debate illustrates many of the challenges and pitfalls of evaluating the different patterns for relating science and theology, and appears in several of our discussions.

On the one extreme we have the pseudotheological conclusions of Scientism, i.e., "evolution*ism*," the position which concludes that any reference to God's creative activity has been rendered superfluous by the development of the biological theory of evolution.   Evolution *explains* it all.   We have already considered the essential characteristics of this position in describing Pattern 1 in Chapter 4.   This position has no actual scientific foundations, but may mislead many who think that it does.

On the other extreme we have the unfortunate case of those Christians who agree with the advocates of evolution*ism*:   if evolution is true, then Christian theology is false.   This is one more case, like those enumerated above, in which Christians tragically agree with non-Christians on a fallacious perspective. They then proceed to attempt to advance their own cause by responding with pseudoscience, either by (1) promoting their own science or by (2) invoking God's direct action in theistic science.

The place to attack is the non-scientific conclusion that biological evolution must lead to philosophical evolution*ism*. Sadly in the debates about evolution this is often not realized.   Instead a frequent tactic is unsound meddling with the nature and results of authentic science. Van Till et al. [58] point out,

> The contemporary creation-evolution debate may be understood as a shouting match between two competing folk sciences.   As the debate is most commonly conducted, the two contenders are evolutionary naturalism and scientific creationism. Evolutionary naturalism is a folk science which seeks to employ the scientific concept of evolutionary development as a warrant for its nontheistic world view.   Scientific creationism is a folk science which claims scientific evidence for its scenario of a recent creation by divine fiat. The debate, therefore is not a contest between natural science and religious belief.   It is a confrontation of two folk sciences, each seeking to employ the results of scientific investigation in the support of its own world view. (p. 171)

An example of the first approach, the promoting of scientific arguments to contradict the findings that lead to the theory of biological evolution, is the attempt to develop a model in which all the evidences for the great age of the earth can be accounted for by the effects of the universal flood. [59] Christians trained in geology have considered these claims, [60, 61] and there are few, if any, professional geologists today, regardless of religious orientation, who would defend the scientific merits of flood geology as definitive.   Other similar attempts that have been advanced in what has become known as "scientific creationism" are summarized by Numbers. [62]

An example of the second approach, the argument for the necessity of God's *direct* intervention, is provided by the case presented by Johnson. [63] Here a good job is done of showing how atheistic evolution*ism* is the unjustified extrapolation of a non-Christian worldview, not the necessary consequence of scientific understanding. But underlying the argument is the inference that the limitation of science to descriptions in natural categories, and the theory of biological evolution itself, are the actual culprits [64]:

> What is Darwinism?   ... As a general theory of biological creation Darwinism is not empirical at all. Rather, it is a necessary implication of a philosophical doctrine called scientific naturalism, which is based on the *a priori* assumption that God was always absent from the realm of nature. ...   Another way to state the proposition is to say that Darwinism is the answer to a specific question that grows out of philosophical naturalism . To return to the game of Jeopardy with which we started, let us say that Darwinism is the answer. What, then, is the question? The question is: "How must creation have occurred if we assume that God had nothing to do with it?" Theistic evolutionists who try to Christianize the answer to a question like that are deceiving themselves.

According to the definition of Darwinism given, Darwinism *is* evolution*ism* and therefore is atheism by definition.   The philosophical position of scientific naturalism is defined as being based on the assumption that God is always absent from nature. This again comes very close to being simply a restatement of atheistic evolution*ism*..

But a critical mistake is made by identifying the implications of philosophical, scientific naturalism as the *necessary consequence* of the requirements of authentic science (see Chapter 2) that scientific descriptions must be given only in natural categories. The requirement that authentic scientific descriptions must be given in natural categories is a limitation on what can be legitimately called "scientific," not *in any sense* the result of believing that God is not active in the natural world.

The Christian *starts* with the conviction that God is active in creating and sustaining the natural world quite independent of any scientific inputs. When he asks, "*How* is God acting" he then seeks to arrive at a scientific description in natural categories as his legitimate scientific activity. If he is unable to arrive at such a description, he then declares either (a) the question must remain open for further evidence, and/or (b) there is a definite probability that a miracle has occurred, i.e., an instance of God's activity that is not describable scientifically. The question, "How must creation have occurred if we assume that God had nothing to do with it?" is not asked by authentic science in its pursuit of descriptions in natural categories.

The assumption "that God was always absent from the realm of nature" is characteristic neither of authentic science with its insistence on descriptions in natural categories, nor on the scientific theory of biological evolution. It is an assumption only of evolution*ism* .

Suppose that the origin of the universe, of life and of human beings all occurred by a process that is in principle describable in terms of natural mechanisms by science.   Such a result would have absolutely no effect on the fundamental theological statement that God was and is active in the creation.   If indeed it should be the case that God was active in a form that involved evolution, then we would conclude that our description of God's activity involved a continuous development. Whether a long period of development capable of being described scientifically was involved, or whether an instantaneous event or set of events occurred that are incapable of being described scientifically, does not affect in any way the basic theological conviction and consequences of believing and professing that God was and is active in creation.   To consider evolution as an historical development does *not* mean that we must reject God's activity in creation.

Now it may still be objected that acceptance of evolution is acceptance of chance, and it is commonly supposed that chance rules out the action of God.   Scientific chance (see Chapter 2) tells us about the kind of scientific descriptions that we are able or compelled at present to give: probabilistic ones.   Scientific chance does not necessarily lead to the philosophical position of Chance, a worldview denying the activity of God and the existence of meaning and purpose in the universe.   The presence of God's Design in the universe and our descriptions in terms of scientific chance are totally compatible.

Thus we have two illustrations of how not to respond to the fallacious extrapolation of biological evolution into evolution*ism*..
(1) One ought to challenge the false conclusions of evolution*ism*

directly by denying their actual foundation in the scientific theory of biological evolution, rather than attempting to find scientific problems in the theory of biological evolution. This is not to say that one should not continue to attempt to improve and extend our understanding of the possible mechanisms of development proposed to be active in theories of biological evolution, but it does emphasize that the fallacies of evolution*ism* do not necessarily arise from the scientific theory of evolution. Our arguments against evolution*ism* do not require us to invalidate the concept of biological development.

(2) One ought again to challenge the false conclusions of evolution*ism* directly, rather than by arguing that God's direct intervention should be included as elements of the scientific theory – thus producing a pseudoscience. This is not to say that God's direct acts may not have occurred in creation, but such a situation would manifest itself in our inability to describe the mechanisms of evolution scientifically, something that we ought to exercise patience and caution about before drawing a final conclusion.

When advocates of Pattern 2 face the issue of describing the origin of new properties and creatures in the world, they are led by their own presuppositions to move from the correct biblical premise that all new properties in the world must result from the free creative activity of God to argue that the origins of this novelty must be probably instantaneous supernatural acts, incapable of being continuously and scientifically describable. At the very least, such new properties must result from some "direct" action of God above and beyond phenomena capable of being scientifically described. The more dramatic and qualitative the degree of novelty involved, the more impelled is the Pattern 2 approach to insist on a supernatural "intervention" of God and to deny the possibility of any "natural" (usually falsely interpreted to imply "not related to God's activity") scientifically describable process.

If God's "direct" activity is not included among the mechanistic descriptions of the events, then it is concluded that God's activity of any kind has been denied. What is missed is at least the possibility that God's activity is far more grand than this, encompassing the existence, properties and continuous functioning of all of created reality, not simply as materials obeying laws established at the moment of creation, but as an immanent God acting in and with the materials he has created.

Therefore, particularly with respect to the origin of life and the origin of human life, Pattern 2 advocates find it essential to maintain that these were probably discontinuous and instantaneous, supernatural acts of God, impossible of description in scientific terms by their very nature. Any proposed scientific descriptions of these major qualitative changes are regarded as being the result of anti-Christian motivation and as constituting atheistic science that should be contested by Pattern 2 advocates. Paradoxically, Pattern 2 advocates find themselves often heavily engaged in the scientific effort to demonstrate that science is unreliable.

Genesis 1-3 provide profound insights into the basic structure of the world, the nature of God and human beings, and the relationship between God, humans and this created universe. These profound insights transcend in importance any possible theories of the age of the earth, cosmology or biology, by as much as the insight that love is foundational to a happy marriage transcends instruction in sexual mechanics. And, as instruction in sexual mechanics may be inappropriate in communication with a 5-year-old, so instruction in the details of "modern science" may be inappropriate in communication with people with varying degrees of personal, cultural and technological sophistication. For the individual person it is vastly more important to know *that* God created the world than to know when God created it, vastly more important to know *that* God created humans than to know how God created them . For the scientist, it is sufficient to know that if the world appears to be a certain age by scientific methods, then scientifically, according to current findings, it is that age; that if a person appears to be the product of developing processes according to scientific analysis, then scientifically evolutionary theory is a profitable guide to research. It is tragic when efforts to make the "when" and "how" of creation into items of Christian doctrine (on grounds that must be intrinsically uncertain) lead others to reject the very *fact* of Creation itself. We do not know how much of Genesis 1-3 should be taken as *literal* historical fact ; we must be open, however, at least to the probability that the principal purpose of these chapters lies elsewhere.

When one considers some of the major steps in understanding that have made in recent years in physics, cosmology, and biology, coupled with the tremendous advances in computers and computer programming made by human beings so very recently, are we not led to think, "What could God, much more capable than his creatures, have done, and what did he do?" Our scientific understanding of God's activity in the universe is always at a very elementary level. Hence, authentic science presents its understandings with the humble acknowledgment that the findings and interpretations of later generations may be far different and far more profound than current views. To continue to research and interpret in every field of science must certainly be legitimate and God-pleasing. We have here a lesson in humility for everyone, regardless of which view is espoused.

On this basis a comparison of the biblical record and of the general theory of evolution forces one to the conclusion that dogmatism must be ruled out. With all of its admitted difficulties, some form – not understood completely at present – of the general theory appears to be the best scientific interpretation of the data available from the natural world. As long as this is true, it is not possible nor is it necessary to force a dogmatic interpretation of the "how" of creation out of Genesis 1-3.

Advocates of a dogmatic acceptance of the general theory are embarrassed by scientific problems with the theory and gaps in the data. Advocates of a dogmatic rejection of the general theory in favor of divine instantaneous creationism are embarrassed by the negative stance vis-a-vis the general theory into which all of their scientific efforts must be directed, since instantaneous creationism itself would by definition be beyond the reach of scientific verification.

Finally, since the possibility of the "how" of God's creation being related to a developmental process need have no direct conflict with the revelational content of Genesis 1-3, it is far more productive to consider how general evolution might be interpreted in a biblical and Christian framework, than it is to insist that the general theory must be rejected because of the ways in which non-Christians have used it to advance their own non-Christian philosophies and goals. There are all too many historical examples of Christians refusing to accept some particular scientific interpretation until considerable damage had been done to their witness.

Chapter 6

Pattern 3: Science and Christian Theology are Unrelated

This pattern of compartmentalization represents the most extreme attempt to protect Christian theology from the perceived attacks of modern science. "Let science say what it will," goes the assertion, "nothing it says can have any effect whatsoever on Christian theology." Of course there is as usual the other side of the coin as well: "Let theology say what it will, nothing it says can have any effect whatsoever on science."

The defining statements concerning Pattern 3 are as follows:

Science and theology tell us different kinds of things about different things. There is no common ground between them. Science has absolutely nothing to say about theology, and theology has absolutely nothing to say about science. Conflict is impossible by definition.

Although this pattern probably needs the least space to describe, this does not mean that it has few advocates. It could even be argued that this is one of the most common of all the Patterns in everyday life. It is an attempt to eliminate the conflict that plays such a dominant role in Patterns 1 and 2. Science and theology are put into separate airtight compartments, so that no interaction between them is possible; such an approach is judged to be the safest way to handle the problem.

The Compartmentalization Solution

In the course of everyday life for many people, it has become convenient to think in a secular, cultural and scientifically-related way during most of the time, and then discontinuously to think in a religious and theologically-related way for the purposes of a worship service or gathering of those professing faith.

The frame of mind involved in Pattern 3 can be described as follows. This description may sound like a caricature, and possibly it is, but this does not detract from the core of accuracy that runs through it.   If the attitudes followed during most of a person's life contradict the attitudes held on special religious occasions, it does not matter.   In analogy with the situation where the person professing devout religious commitments and concerns in a theological context, can exercise the most unethical practices in unrelated business dealings the rest of the time, so during most of life we can talk as if the world were five billion years old, but in a religious environment we can also talk as if the world were actually only ten thousand years old.   Neither position has an actual claim on basic reality; each is an example only of unrelated statements.   We do not need to let these two apparently contradictory perspectives interact with one another at all, but simply hold them as two quite different and non-interacting pieces of information.

Scientifically inclined non-Christians regard theological descriptions as so much irrelevant speculation; indeed, some Christians unfortunately seem to ignore them part of the time.   Conversely, theologically inclined Christians regard scientific descriptions with suspicion, as inputs from an alien and unfriendly culture: one may have to live with these descriptions in the nitty gritty details of life, but it is certain that they contain no information of ultimate significance, and thus can easily be ignored.   Again Christians and non-Christians paradoxically agree: only one perspective is practically valid and significant. Not only can the other be safely ignored, or at least locked away in its own airtight compartment to be brought out only when appropriate, but it is safer and far simpler to neglect it.

In the compartmentalization approach of Pattern 3 it is quite possible to hold both scientific and theological interpretations of the world, but no interaction is allowed between them , even if to all intents and purposes they appear to conflict. Whenever a person separates the various concerns of life into such different non-interacting compartments, the almost inevitable consequence is that both types of description lose at least some of their life-shaping significance. When interpretations really matter, it is not possible to keep them so separate that interaction and conflict are impossible.

Because of this inherent instability in the compartmentalization approach, it frequently develops that one of the descriptions comes to take on primary practical significance, with the consequence that the other description is retained only as a useful fiction or as a cultural attachment. In many other cases the attempt to resolve the issue by schizophrenic reaction to scientific and theological descriptions leads to the situation where neither description is accorded much value, and personal commitment to a particular perspective no longer has the motivation that is required. In such a situation a commitment to either authentic science or authentic Christian theology is greatly weakened.

It is easy to slip from this Pattern either into Pattern 2 (Chapter 5), with the attempt to shape science by inputs from theology, or into Pattern 5 (Chapter 8), with the attempt to shape theology by inputs from science, or, perhaps even more likely, into an apathy concerning the significance of either science or theology for the important aspects of human living.

Natural Theology

Natural theology refers in general to the development of insights relevant to theology from an investigation of the properties of the natural world.   It clearly is not a contributor to Pattern 3, but we introduce it here to trace the various ways it is involved in the remaining Patterns.   It is evident from its definition that natural theology is ruled out by Pattern 3 and this exclusion has played a key role in what has been named "neo-orthodox theology."

In Pattern 4 (Chapter 7) natural theology is invoked to support Christian theology, in Pattern 5 (Chapter 8) it is invoked to formulate Christian theology, in Pattern 6 (Chapter 9) it is invoked to transform Christian theology, and in Pattern 7 (Chapter 10) it is invoked to inform Christian theology in a complementary fashion.

One example of the biblical foundation for the concept of natural theology is given in Romans 1:18-21,

> For the wrath of God is revealed from heaven against all ungodliness and wickedness of men who by their wickedness suppress the truth. For what can be known about God is plain to them, because God has shown it to them. Ever since the creation of the world his invisible nature, namely, his eternal power and deity, has been clearly perceived in the things that have been made. So they are without excuse; for although they knew God they did not

honor him as God or give thanks to him, but they became futile in their thinking and their senseless minds were darkened. (RSV)

This passage indicates that our experiences with the natural world do have the potential for conveying a fundamental revelation of God's reality and power to us, and that indeed when we reject this revelation of God we turn our backs on a deeply significant input.   Thus it is right and proper when we are inspired to think about the greatness of God as we contemplate a rainbow, watch the rushing waters over a mighty waterfall, or catch the reflection of the sun off the top of distant mountain peaks. It is right and proper when we reflect on the greatness of God as we learn of the vastness of the universe, the countless stars and galaxies, the indications of dark holes and anti-matter: for it is he who has made them.   We consider several other natural evidences that point to God through the eyes of science and faith in Pattern 4 (Chapter 7).

But natural theology is also silent on many of the most significant attributes of God with respect to human relationships. We cannot unambiguously learn that God is holy, just, merciful, gracious, loving or kind.   We cannot learn that God loved us so much that he gave his only Son to die for us and then to rise again to live with us today.

The relevance of this discussion for the present Pattern 3 in which science and theology are totally compartmentalized lies in the attitude toward natural theology taken by those theologians who became the advocates of what became known as neo-orthodoxy, of whom perhaps Karl Barth was the most outstanding. [65, 66]   Barth arrived at the conclusion of a necessary separation between science and faith from a relatively conservative theological position. Living in a period when the inroads of anti-Christian interpretations of modern science were growing rapidly, and disillusioned with the perspective of liberal theology which often tended to equate God with evolution*ism* (what we have called Pattern 5 in Chapter 8), Barth reacted with an extreme exaltation of special revelation and a categorical rejection of all natural theology. He argued that we can know nothing apart from the special revelation of God's Word. Thus science can contribute nothing of significance to theology.

Barbour comments on this situation as follows: [67]

In the twentieth century, Protestant *neo-orthodoxy* sought to recover the Reformation emphasis on the centrality of Christ and the primacy of revelation, while fully accepting the results of modern biblical scholarship and scientific research. ... According to Karl Barth and his followers, God can be known only as revealed in Christ and acknowledged in faith. God is the transcendent, the wholly other, unknowable except as self-disclosed. Natural theology is suspect because it relies on human reason. Religious faith depends entirely on divine initiative, not on human discovery of the kind occurring in science. The sphere of God's action is history, not nature. Scientists are free to carry out their work without interference from theology, and vice versa, since their methods and their subject matter are totally dissimilar. Here, then, is a clear contrast. Science is based on human observation and reason, while theology is based on divine revelation. In this view, the Bible must be taken seriously but not literally. Scripture is not itself revelation; it is a fallible human record witnessing to revelatory events.

Barth once stated that even if the Bible were found to be in error in every word, still by the grace and power of God it could provide a true revelation of God to us since the power of God in revelation transcended even the verbal communication modes.

Similarly Polkinghorne writes: [68]

For the Christian, the figure of Christ is the focal point for the meeting of the divine and the human, the one in relation to whom we will come to know God most fully. Yet if we feel we recognize in Jesus elements which for their proper appreciation call for the use of the language of divinity, then we already have some concept of God by which to make that identification (even if it is then expanded and corrected by the encounter with Christ). There is a theological tradition, associated in this century particularly with the name of Karl Barth, which denies that possibility. It states that God is known solely through his self-revelation in Christ; rational inquiry elsewhere has no role whatsoever to play in true encounter with the divine.

Although one can understand and even sympathize with the motivation that gave rise to this emphasis in the desire to overcome the undermining of the revelational aspects of the Christian faith through liberal approaches that claimed the support of modern science, still it appears to be an inadequate way to deal with the total insights available to us through both authentic science and authentic theology.

In a practical vein, it appears difficult to maintain a vital position in which the significance of science and theology for each other is totally denied. As such a Pattern is lived out, it is likely that indifference to the issues may well be the most common result.

Compartmentalization vs. Complementarity

It should be noted that the strict compartmentalization of science and theology advocated by Pattern 3 is an extreme attempt to give science and theology their proper relationship in human life. It is by no means the same as the complementarity of Pattern 7 (Chapter 10), which recognizes the legitimate differences between authentic science and authentic Christian theology, but argues then that an integrating interaction between them is the key ingredient in understanding the nature of the reality in which we live. This very significant difference is discussed in more detail in Chapter 10.

Cogent observations are offered by Berry: [69]

> If I draw one lesson from my experiences as a scientist and a Christian, it is that compartmentalization of life, thought or worship is damaging and potentially dangerous. ... Science and faith have different methodologies, but they are complementary, not contradictory; a faith without reason is as stultifying as a reason without faith.

Chapter 7

Pattern 4: Science Demands Christian Theology

In an age of science, there is a strong incentive for demonstrating that the values that a person holds true are scientifically defensible. This is a valuable and desirable activity, since it helps to counter the various caricatures of Christian theology (in Pattern 1, for example) as intrinsically irrational and subjective. The marshaling of evidences that support the reasonableness of the Christian faith and the trustworthiness of the biblical revelation is indeed a worthy attempt. It can be an effective witness to help those who have been led to believe that all of modern science contradicts Christianity, to see that this is simply not the case. The destruction of caricatures is always a valuable achievement.

This demonstration, however, may sometimes be extended to the attempt to show that the insights into reality provided by science make any religious choice except Christian theology rationally and logically unacceptable, i.e., to emphasize the rational foundation of Christian faith to the exclusion of the ultimate personal faith choice to accept God's grace in Christ. Pattern 4 often applies this kind of thinking to Christian apologetics.

The defining statements for this Pattern are: *Science and theology tell us the same kinds of things about the same things. An understanding of the scientific descriptions of the world provide us with such overwhelming evidence of the truth of the Bible and Christian theology that we have no defensible choice but to believe them.*

This Pattern joins Patterns 1 (Chapter 4) and 2 (Chapter 5) in starting with the premise that science and theology both provide us with the same kinds of information about the same kinds of things. Whereas Pattern 1 concludes that the things science tells us rules out the things that theology tells us, and Pattern 2 concludes that the things theology tells us must always take precedence over the things that science tells us, Pattern 4 concludes that the things that science tells us provide overwhelming evidence for the truth of a particular formulation of Christian theology that is very similar to that usually advocated by Pattern 2.

Pattern 4 claims to provide a kind of natural theology – a very special kind in which the conclusions of natural theology uphold and confirm the conclusions of Christian theology. Pattern 1 argues that science has destroyed Christian theology; Pattern 4 argues that science has established Christian theology.   Likewise Pattern 4 expresses a reaction against Pattern 2, with its non-rational and anti-intellectual emphases, and attempts instead to marshal all of the social prestige enjoyed by science in defense of the faith.

Pattern 4 is the approach of an appreciable subgroup of Christians who desire to bring to bear the most powerful elements of their modern armamentarium against the popular attacks on Christianity in the name of science. The emphasis is on a logical and systematic, intellectual defense of a particular Christian interpretation of the Bible, so compelling that non-Christians would be convinced on the basis of this evidence, almost alone, to become Christians.

If science has called the authenticity and the authority of the Bible into question, then the issue is dealt with by the attempt to show that the Bible can be scientifically defended, that the Bible revealed scientific truths long before they were scientifically discovered, and that the integrity of the Bible can be objectively demonstrated by showing how every apparent interaction with the descriptions of modern science can be harmonized with the biblical record. Although probably no one would openly claim that it was possible to prove the validity of the Christian faith by logical or scientific approaches, this Pattern sometimes comes close to such a claim.

Since there is a great temptation in this Pattern to go as far as possible in claiming that the insights of science "prove" the validity of a particular theological formulation, it is worthwhile to remind ourselves of the comments made about "proof" in our discussion of authentic science in Chapter 2. There we argued that in the normal pursuits of life and even of science, we never are able to "prove" anything, but instead what we do is put together evidence on the basis of which we finally make our decision. Insofar as advocates of Pattern 4 avoid the claim of "proof," they do make the claim for overwhelming evidence that demands only one legitimate response.

Faith and Evidence

An appropriate evaluation of the relationship between faith and evidence is essential for this discussion. To provide evidence for the truth of authentic Christian theology is a good thing and one to be endorsed. Earlier we made the claim that Christian faith was a rational faith, i.e., that it was a faith commitment made after a rational examination of the evidences.

Lest these two words – rational faith – seem to be mutually exclusive, let us consider what it means to act rationally. There are three terms that are relevant: rational, nonrational, and irrational. To act rationally in a given situation is to act upon a careful assessment of all the available evidence. To act rationally does not mean to take only those actions that are connected by a series of logically provable links; indeed, if this definition were to be assumed, it would mean that much of our life would be consigned to nonrational behavior which is simply behavior undertaken without due consideration of the evidence. To act irrationally then means to act contrary to or in spite of the results of a careful assessment of all the available evidence. To act meaningfully at all, whether in science or Christian experience, requires a rational act of faith.

Consider the following illustration of these ideas. Suppose that early in the morning the sky is dark, the wind is blowing, thunder and lightning are heard in the distance, and the weather report on the radio says that rain is due in about an hour. To believe that it will probably rain and hence to take one's umbrella for the day is to act on the basis of a rational faith. To put on one's best suit and to drive off in a convertible with the top down is to act irrationally. To believe that it might rain (or not rain) without looking out the windows or listening to the radio at all is to arrive at a conclusion by nonrational means.

Science becomes possible because of a rational faith in the ability of human beings to describe the world according to orderly patterns conceivable by the human mind. Christian theology becomes possible because of a rational faith based on the totality of biblical revelation, scientific understanding, historical events, and personal experience.

A Reasonable Faith: Statement for a Popular Audience [70]

To illustrate the fundamental nature of Christianity as a reasonable faith, I include at this point a brief statement made for television for a popular audience on this subject. In subsequent sections we consider some of these claims in more detail.

It is often thought that faith and reason are mutually exclusive, and in some cases they may be. But in most of life, experiences and events are the result of a complex interaction between faith and reason. Christianity involves a rational faith – a personal faith commitment to God in Jesus Christ, that is based on and is consistent with a rational assessment of the evidence. It is important to realize that this evidence does not *prove* the truth of Christianity. Instead it provides the basis for making a rational choice leading to what must ultimately be a faith commitment, a giving of self in trust into a personal relationship with God. What kind of evidence is there for making this life-important choice? Let us consider just some of the different types of evidence available.

When scientists explore the values of many of the basic physical constants that determine the properties of the universe, they find that these constants appear to be fine-tuned to allow the support of human life on the earth. Small deviations in any one of a number of these basic constants would lead to conditions in which human life on earth could not develop or be sustained. Such evidence is consistent with the biblical presentation of God as Creator, who designs and maintains the properties of the environment so that human life can exist.

When scientists attempt to describe a wide variety of intricate phenomena in the physical universe, they find that mathematical formulations invented in their own minds are able to give a surprisingly accurate description of what appears to be going on in the physical universe. Such an experience is consistent both with human beings as part of God's created order, and with human beings as special members of God's created order, created in his image to understand and care for his created world.

When we look at human interactions in the world, we recognize in our experience the basic role played by self-centeredness – which the Bible calls "original sin" – which leads human beings to respond in rebellion to God and their fellow humans. Such experiences are consistent with the need for a radical change in life such as is biblically described as "the new birth" in order for human beings to be delivered from this self-centeredness.

The biblical witness to Jesus Christ, his life, teachings, death and resurrection, and their effect on those who knew and interacted with him, provides evidence for the Christian answer to sin and to the power of God in human lives to help deliver them from it, and to enable them to live a life of witness to him in word and deed.

The evidence of changed lives can be seen again in the historical commitment of Christians to the education of children, the founding of hospitals to care for the sick, and the development of efforts to alleviate and help the poor.

Our personal experiences with those we know, with radical changes in life direction by people who commit themselves to Christ, give evidence for the vitality of Christian faith.

When all of the evidence of scientific description and living experience is sorted through, the Christian evaluation of the cause of our problems and the nature of the solution offered by God, rings true.

The issue to which such a statement addresses itself is this: Is Christian faith (a) reasonable (a rational faith), (b) something for which no evidence outside of the faith experience itself can be meaningfully given (a nonrational faith) , or (c) something that must be chosen by an existential act of faith in spite of much evidence that contradicts and invalidates it (an irrational faith)? The claim that Christian faith is indeed reasonable does not mean that reason can be used to prove the validity of the Christian faith. Nor does it mean that one enters into the Christian faith because of the rational evidence rather than through a personal existential relationship with God in Jesus Christ. Advocates of Pattern 4 tend to move in the direction of these last two approaches.

Classical Arguments for the Existence of God

When science developed among people who at least formally had a theological perspective, it was natural that they should attempt to deduce either from logic or from their understanding of the world a "proof" for the existence of God. Such a proof would settle the question of faith once and for all − or so it might be thought.

In *God and Other Minds* , Plantinga [71] argues that no logical proof can be given either for or against the existence of God. Logical proofs that have been proposed all have fatal flaws and constitute at best only part of the evidence to be considered. We include here a couple of examples of such classical "proofs".

One proposed logical "proof" is credited to Thomas Aquinas and is often referred to as the cosmological argument.

> There are at present contingent beings; whatever can fail to exist, does at some time fail to exist; so if all beings were contingent, then at one time there was nothing at all. But nothing could come into existence if there were nothing at all; so if all beings were contingent, there'd be nothing now; since there is something now, not all beings are contingent and there is at least one necessary being; this is God. [72]

Another logical "proof" is credited to Anselm and is often referred to as the ontological argument .

> By the word "God" we mean to refer to the being than which it is not possible that there be a greater. Now suppose God does not exist. Things that exist are greater than things that do not. So if God does not exist, then there is something greater than God – that is, there is something greater than the being than which it is not possible that there exist a greater. But that's impossible. So it's false that God does not exist; hence God exists. [73]

We shall not belabor these classical "proofs" for the existence of God further. They recur from time to time in discussions like this, but they are no longer the kinds of evidence that are invoked to provide evidence for the existence of God. They belong to an earlier day when what was called science proceeded primarily by deduction. In the day of experimental science with an emphasis on induction, different kinds of arguments have been devised. The very abstractness of these classical "proofs" seems to divorce them from the personal framework of Christian faith, and their logical flaws are enumerated by Plantinga. [71]

There are also pragmatic arguments advanced for accepting the Christian worldview that represent variations of Pascal's Wager. Montgomery [74], for example, says

> Given that we have a limited amount of time in this life to study religions, we can   dispense with those that offer us a second chance in the afterlife or which will reincarnate us if we make a mistake in this life, or which promise us that all will be well eventually no matter how we live now. Prudence dictates that we first ought to consider the claims of those religions which say that everything depends upon the decision made and lived by in this one life. (p. 175)

or again,

> Therefore, when considering biblical Christianity, the more appropriate rule to apply is: "The more severe the consequences, the less we should take risks." Even if biblical Christianity has less than a one-in-ten-million chance of being true, we should believe it and live in the light of it because of the possibility of an eternal hell is such a great torment.(p. 307)

This does not seem to be the basis upon which to build a sound defense of the Christian faith. The major question must always be, "Is it true?" Not, "Is it safe?"

In the following sections we consider some of the evidences for the existence of God that have been proposed on the basis of scientific investigations of the natural universe, together with some examples of the stronger claims of Christian advocates of Pattern 4. Moreland [52], for example, states as the purpose of *Scaling the Secular City: A Defense of Christianity,*:

> This book is an attempt to defend the thesis that the Christian God does in fact exist and that it is rational to believe that he does.. . In my view the evidence in this book contributes to making the Christian God exists at least permissible and, I would argue, obligatory.

And Montgomery [74] says of the authors of *Evidence for Faith: Deciding the God Question* ,

> Its authors .. became and remain Christians because the evidence for the truth of Christianity overwhelmingly outweighs competing religious claims and secular world views.

We make a few remarks as we go along to guide our evaluation of how effective these different evidences are toward achieving their goal, and at what points the proposed evidence may fall short of the claims made for it.

Evidence: The Universe Had a Beginning

A variety of evidence indicates that the universe has not always existed but came into being at a specific time and is so constituted that at least life in the universe will come to an ultimate end. One theory of cosmological origins is the Big Bang theory . It postulates the beginning of the universe in one spot at the beginning of time, from which all the matter of the universe has been subsequently expanding. The constant conversion of matter into energy, the finite amounts of radioactive materials found, and the general experience that the disorder in the universe as a whole is increasing with time (increasing entropy in a closed system, according to the Second Law of Thermodynamics), all argue for a universe that had a beginning and will have for all practical purposes an end.

If the universe had a beginning, then the universe must have a first cause – and that First Cause, advocates of Pattern 4 propose, can be identified with God. Moreland [74] goes further and asserts,

> The only way for the first event to arise spontaneously from a timeless, changeless, spaceless state of affairs, and at the same time be caused, is this – the event resulted from the free act of a person or agent. .. It is most reasonable to believe that the universe had a beginning which was caused by a timeless, immutable agent. This is not a proof that such a being is the God of the Bible, but it is a strong statement that the world had its beginning by the act of a person. (p. 42)

We have learned enough about the universe at least to be cautious before we say that something is the *only* way that it could have happened. From the biblical revelation we do know that God created and sustains the universe, but we do not know the many marvelous and apparently mysterious (to us) ways his action may appear.

Advocates of Pattern 4 emphasize that the very mystery of existence evokes a sense of religious awe. Why should it be that we exist, rather than that we should not exist? How should it be that matter, and space, and time – and you and I – are here at all? There must be a fundamental Cause, a fundamental Reason that can be identified with God. Even Hawking, who does not usually speak from a theistic perspective, comments: [75]

> Even if there is only one possible unified theory, it is just a set of rules and equations. What is it that breathes fire into the equations and makes a universe for them to describe? The usual approach of science of constructing a mathematical model cannot answer the questions of why there should be a universe for the model to describe. Why does the universe go to all the bother of existing? Is the unified theory so compelling that it brings about its own existence? Or does it need a creator, and, if so, does he have any other effect on the universe?

Evidence: Order in the Universe

The practice of science presupposes the existence of order in the universe, order that is ultimately objective, reproducible, and describable by human beings. The very fact that science is possible means that order exists in the natural world and that such an order is compatible with the concepts possible in the human mind. It does not mean that the form such order appears to take is obvious or immediately deducible from our everyday awareness of how things are.

The Periodic Table of the Elements is one great example of this order, which is objectively present in the world and cannot be ascribed to a particular perspective impressed on the world by the scientist. All the matter in the world is composed of the same set of slightly more than one hundred elements. These elements can be arranged in a periodic sequence indicating their constitution in terms of protons, neutrons, and electrons, each element differing from its neighbors by a difference of only one electron, one proton, and a small number of neutrons.

Order exists also among the variety of living plants and animals. In spite of the existence of millions of species of animals on earth, throughout nature there is a pervading similarity rather than a disorganized array of forms.

Often in connection with discussions of order in the universe, the subject of natural laws in the physical world is brought up.   There is then a strong tendency to describe such order as being governed by these physical laws, invoking the picture of God governing through these laws.

> Objects behave in accordance with the laws of nature. The paths of heavenly bodies follow regular temporal sequences in accordance with laws of gravity and motion. ...Simple natural laws govern almost all successions of events. (p. 45)   [74]

For consistency it is important to remember that "natural laws" are human inventions, that they are descriptive and not prescriptive, and that they are the not the cause of anything happening. "Natural laws" are nothing more nor less than *our* descriptions of God's normal mode of activity in creating and sustaining the orderly existence of the universe.

Pollard [76] quotes from the paper, "The Unreasonable Effectiveness of Mathematics in the Natural Sciences" by Eugene Wigner, Nobel laureate in physics. He points out the number of times in the history of science that a mathematical scheme, conceived originally as pure mathematical exercise in the mind of a mathematician, later turned out to apply exactly to a complex situation in the physical world. He writes,

> Since nature is certainly not itself a product of the human mind, the correspondence between the mathematical system and the structure of things in the natural world has a kind of miraculous quality about it. ..... It is impossible to appreciate the force of these considerations without having personally experienced the amazing ways in which the theories of mathematical physics apply to the natural world. I have a feeling that most physicists have become, through too much familiarity, insensitive to the really amazing and miraculous character of the correspondence which they live with and practice every day.

In my scientific textbook, *Electronic Properties of Crystalline Solids* [77] I included the following comments concerning the amazing success of the Schroedinger wave equation in describing the energy states of the hydrogen atom:

> The hydrogen atom is in one sense the simplest system in the atomic realm. Yet the properties of the atom, the distributions of charge, the various energy levels available, and so on are far from simple when looked at from the perspective of classical understanding. Still we find that by taking a simple second-order differential equation containing only an abstract function ψ and the specific form of the Coulomb potential energy, all of the basic properties of the hydrogen atom result only from the requirement that the solutions of this equation be suitable for use in the description of the physically real world, i.e., that they not become infinite. What does this mean? Certainly it is a remarkable occurrence, but it does not stand alone among many instances where the mathematical imaginations of man's mind have shown fantastically appropriate correspondence with the nature of the world around him. Can it be argued that this is a case where man has impressed the rationality of his own mind upon nature? Or is it perhaps more suggestive that the rationality of man's mind and the structure of the universe have a common source, that God who is the Creator of both?

Evidence: Purpose and Design in the Universe

The universe is not only found to be ordered; it is found to be dynamically ordered in such a way that design appears apparent and purpose seems inherent. Arguments along this line have often been called teleological arguments. A modern exponent of the teleological argument is Teilhard de Chardin, [78] who sought to combine his Christian faith with the theory of evolution by seeing in the evolutionary process the outworking of the purpose and design of God.

The teleological argument is based on such observations as the unique properties of the earth to sustain human life, the extraordinary properties of water that also contribute to human life and civilization, the marvels of human and animal physiology, and many examples drawn from the plant and animal world where the existence of each of two participants is completely dependent on the existence of the other. Arguments of this sort have been brought together in what has become known as "The Anthropic Principle." This is a sufficiently significant development that it is described separately in the following section.

Evidence: The Anthropic Principle

In recent years the continued development of understanding of the structure and properties of the natural world has revealed an enormous amount of evidence indicating that the properties of the universe are incredibly fine-tuned in such a way as to make the existence of conscious life possible.

The energy levels of carbon, the key element for life, are such that just a small change in their values would make the development of intelligent life in the universe impossible. The same kind of narrow range of possibilities applies to the "elementary particles" and other basic elements as well.

The rate of expansion of the universe appears to be critically tuned. If the rate of expansion were only slightly larger, then the galaxies would never have formed. If the rate of expansion were only slightly smaller, the universe would have long since collapsed back upon itself.

In many different ways, for which examples are given below, one could say that we can decide between different theories of the properties of the physical universe on the basis of whether they provide the appropriate circumstances for the development of intelligent life. Life is here; therefore appropriate circumstances for its development must have existed. We can rule out those circumstances that would not have been appropriate. The implications of this for the Christian today are striking. The implications that people have tried to draw from it to forecast the future provide a sharp illustration of the differences between secular and Christian attitudes toward the future.

In the face of this evidence many scientists have been led to propose what they have called "The Anthropic Principle." [79]   Based on the Greek word for man, *anthropos*, this Principle may in many ways be regarded as a secular "argument from design," although its scientific proposers usually deny any theological content in the Principle.

Forms of the Anthropic Principle.   What has come to be called "the Anthropic Principle" is actually a set of principles with claims increasing from what might be considered to be a simple restatement of the obvious to speculative claims for the future.

"Weak Anthropic Principle (WAP). *The observed values of all physical and cosmological quantities are not equally probable but they take on values restricted by the requirement that there exist sites where carbon-based life can evolve and by the requirement that the Universe be old enough for it to have already done so.*"

The following assumptions underlie this form of the Principle:

1. It is possible in principle for many different kinds of universes to exist, each with different values of defining parameters and interactions.

2. The fact that human beings (carbon-based living creatures) exist today and observe the universe, means that the defining parameters and interactions of the universe must be such as to allow the development and existence of human life.   This is commonly restated as: If the universe didn't have the properties it does, we wouldn't be here to observe it.

3. If carbon-based human beings came to be in this world through a process of evolution, then the properties of the universe must be such as to allow such evolution to take place, and the universe must be old enough to allow that process to have already been completed.

One implication of this appears to be that the size of the universe is a necessary condition for the existence of even a single site where carbon-based, living creatures could evolve.   [Note that if it is chosen to reject evolution as the process by which human beings actually came into existence historically, the data underlying the WAP still show that the universe has properties that would be necessary if living creatures had evolved.]

These same observations can be restated in "design language," by stating that the detailed properties and parameters of the universe appear to be designed for the origin of human life.   We must make a basic choice that is not dictated by the evidence.

(1) We may choose to believe that there can be and have been an infinite number of possible universes existing in the past, the present and the future, and that it just so happens that we exist and are aware of our universe because, of all the possible universes, it - perhaps alone –

had the unique combination of parameters and properties that would allow the emergence and sustenance of human beings.

Such a view is based on a worldview of Chance, not the descriptive scientific definition of chance, but an absolute, ultimately uncaused, non-theistic perspective, deliberately involving the faith choices characteristic of Scientism. It is clearly a rejection of the biblical view.

(2) Or we may (with equal justification from the scientific evidence alone) choose to believe that this one universe, which is so carefully arranged so as to bring forth human life, is the result of a creative design, the creating, shaping and sustaining activity and power of God on our behalf.

There is no compelling reason from the scientific data alone to guide us in which of these two choices we should make. If we choose to believe that there is no God, then of course we have at the same time chosen to accept the first position. If, for a variety of reasons not directly related to scientific evidence alone, we already have a faith in God, then the second position appears the more reasonable, and the evidence it offers is strongly consistent with a biblical view.

"Strong Anthropic Principle (SAP). *The Universe must have those properties which allow life to develop within it at some stage in its history.*"

This form of the Principle not only states the observation that the properties of the universe are restricted to narrow ranges compatible with the development of human life, but asserts in addition that this is a necessary state of affairs.

If one interprets the data as evidence for the designing purpose and activity of God as indicated by the biblical revelation, then the form of the SAP follows directly from God's intention. If it is God's revealed intention to bring forth a people for fellowship with himself, then the created universe clearly must have the properties that allow the development and/or existence of human life. There are, however, advocates of the SAP, who would dismiss this interpretation as "religious," and hence hardly worthy of consideration. Instead they seek for justification from certain speculative positions that they claim are derived from interpretations of modern quantum mechanics. Those who favor the speculative interpretation of quantum mechanics in which the "collapse of the wavefunction" by a measurement (i.e., the selection of one particular state of the system, out of the several different states each with finite probability of existing) is the result of participation of "observers," have argued that it is necessary for observers to exist in order to bring the universe into being. This is the context of the argument that the universe we observe is created by us, the observers, and does not exist independently of us. (See the more detailed discussion of these issues further in the treatment of Pattern 6 in Chapter 9.)

Others favoring the equally speculative "many-worlds" interpretation of quantum mechanics argue that there is an enormous number of real "universes" from which our life-sustaining universe is selected by an impersonal optimization.

These last two approaches illustrate the following: (a) It is extremely hazardous to attempt to arrive at philosophical (or theological) positions by extrapolation from currently-accepted scientific positions. (b) The search for and definition of such philosophical positions are driven by presuppositions already accepted by faith, rather than by any necessary implications of science itself.

If one accepts the SAP, particularly for the "non-religious" reasons cited above, then it has been proposed that a reasonable conclusion is the Final Anthropic Principle.

"The Final Anthropic Principle (FAP). *Intelligent information-processing must come into existence in the Universe, and once it comes into existence, it will never die out.*"

The FAP is a purely philosophical or quasi-religious speculation without any direct scientific support or necessity.

Teleological Descriptions. Classical theological arguments for the existence of God from design, as well as the positions represented by the Anthropic Principle, share the common characteristic that both are teleological arguments, arguments based on the assumption of purpose in the events or phenomena being described.

A radical shift that came about with the development of science in the last few centuries has been the departure from attempts to provide teleological descriptions, to attempts to provide descriptions in terms of "efficient causes," or physical mechanisms. Instead of seeking an understanding of physical phenomena by searching for some kind of purpose in their existence or characteristics, it has become far more acceptable to seek an understanding in terms of experimentally testable, quantitatively describable mechanisms.

It is therefore particularly interesting that the citation of the Anthropic Principle is an attempt to return to a teleological form of description, and even with the claim that it has had some striking successes when applied to global questions.

The first major use of an Anthropic Principle timescale argument occurred in connection with estimating the age of the earth. In a debate between biologists and physicists in the latter part of the 19th century, it was asserted that the age of the earth must be large enough so that evolutionary processes would have had the time required to bring about the development of human beings. Since this debate also involved the source of heat from the sun, the recognition of fusion reactions on the sun not being realized until some thirty years later, it may even be claimed that an Anthropic Principle argument was the first to predict nuclear sources of energy.

Examples of Fine-Tuning of the Universe's Properties. A slight deviation in any one of several possible crucial points would make any development and/or existence of intelligent life based on carbon impossible. Yet we find that the observable properties of the universe always satisfy the criteria needed for the development of intelligent life. One might respond by saying, "How could it be otherwise?" But that merely brings us back again to ask, "What does it mean?"

Atomic Level Coincidences. The synthesis of all the heavier elements essential for biology rests upon a nuclear reaction in which three helium atoms (He4) combine to form one carbon atom (C12), with an intermediate step in which two helium atoms first combine to form a beryllium atom (Be8) and then the relatively long-lived beryllium atom combines with the third helium atom to form one carbon atom.

The energy level in the carbon atom lies just 4% higher than the energy of beryllium plus helium, allowing the reaction to proceed. But if another helium atom were added to the carbon, it would form oxygen (O16) and the carbon would be rapidly depleted. The energy level of the oxygen, however, lies 0.6% below the total energy of carbon plus helium, and the reaction does not take place. Thus there is a remarkable set of "coincidences": the long-lived beryllium, the advantageously located energy level in carbon, and the disadvantageously located energy level in oxygen - all are essential for the development of any carbon-based life, and of our lives in particular.

We could trace these coincidences in energy level location back to the relative strengths of the nuclear and electromagnetic interactions active, as well as to the mass of electrons and nucleons, all of which must have finely-tuned values to provide the kind of coincidences observed at this single point.

Our Three-Dimensional World. If we examine the conditions required for atomic stability, and if we assume that the structure of the laws of physics do not change radically with changes in the number of dimensions, then stable atoms, chemistry and intelligent life can exist only if the number of dimensions is three or less. If the number of dimensions is four or greater, there are no stable atomic orbits.

Size and Life.   Many of the properties of the world essential for the development and existence of intelligent life can be related in a fairly simple way to the size of various components of the universe and the strength of the interactions between them.

The sizes of a variety of bodies, like stars, planets and people, are neither random nor the result of a selection process, but are a direct and natural consequence of the strength of different forces of interaction. The small sizes of atoms, the strength of the interaction between light and matter, why molecules are stable, and why biological life can function only within a narrow temperature range near what we call "room temperature," can all be related by a consideration of the relationship between size and strength of forces.

Two-Nucleon Bound States.   The simplest compound systems in the universe involve just two nucleons: the proton and the neutron. These may combine to form a deuteron (proton + neutron), a diproton (proton + proton), and a dineutron (neutron + neutron).

The overall evolution of the universe and the nuclear reactions occurring in stars are crucially dependent on whether or not certain two-nucleon systems represent stable bound states or not.   The deuteron is a stable bound state of the proton and neutron, but only barely; it has a very small binding energy.   On the other hand, neither the diproton nor the dineutron form stable bound systems, but again only barely. Thus the existence in the universe of stable deuterium, and the absence of the diproton depend critically on the precise strength of the nuclear force involved.   A decrease in a suitably defined parameter, equivalent to the fine structure constant for nuclear systems, by 9% would cause the deuteron not to form; an increase in this parameter by 3.4% would cause the diproton to form, and an increase by 0.3% would cause the dineutron to form.   If the deuteron did not exist as a stable system, or if the diproton existed as a stable system, we wouldn't!

The stability of higher mass elements can also be considered in a similar way and criteria defined that must be fulfilled if they are to be stable. The existence of living creatures based on carbon is the result of a striking "coincidence" between the strengths of the strong and the electromagnetic forces.   A 50% decrease in the strength of the nuclear forces would cause all of the elements essential for biological life to become unstable.

Origin of Light Elements.   The Big Bang Theory of the origin of the universe has been able to successfully predict the relative abundances of the lightest elements: hydrogen, helium, deuterium and lithium.   All of these can be made by fusion of protons and neutrons during the first few minutes of expansion. Nuclear reactions in the early universe are possible only within a narrow range of temperatures, which means only over a narrow time interval between about 0.04 and 500 seconds. It is only because the fine-structure constant is greater than the ratio of electron to proton mass that such nuclear reactions are possible.

Because of a delicate coincidence between the gravitational and weak nuclear interactions, the early universe gives rise to an abundance of He4 which is neither zero nor 100%. If this were not the case, we would have either 100% hydrogen coming from the Big Bang, or 100% helium; in the latter case the development of life would not have been possible.

Another contribution to this same coincidence arises from the fact that the difference between the mass of the proton and the neutron is approximately equal to the mass of an electron, equivalent to a 1 in 1000 coincidence. If the difference in mass between the proton and neutron were less than the mass of an electron, stars and planets could not exist.

<u>Initial Conditions for Big Bang Expansion</u>. The expansion of the universe after the Big Bang explosion can be described in terms of the ratio of the potential energy of the universe to the kinetic energy of expansion, Ω_0. The value of Ω_0 must lie within a narrow range in order for the presently observed universe to come into being (10^{-3} to 10); actually the present-day universe corresponds to the special case of $\Omega_0 \cong 1$, which is an optimal value for the formation of galaxies. If Ω_0 were too small, the expansion would occur so rapidly that matter would never be able to condense to form galaxies and stars. If Ω_0 were too large, the universe would have recollapsed after the initial expansion before stars could form or life could evolve.

<u>Properties of Water</u>. Many of the properties of water are uniquely different from other materials. Its specific heat, its surface tension, and many of its other physical properties are strikingly higher or lower than those of most other materials. The fact that ice (solid phase of water) is less dense than the liquid phase of water is almost totally unique. Water has a higher heat of vaporization than any other known material. These properties of water are critical for the development and sustenance of life; no other material can be substituted for water to achieve the same results.

Some Proposed Speculations Based on the Anthropic Principles. If the Anthropic Principles were taken seriously, it has been suggested that several speculations would follow.

<u>Argument Against Extraterrestrial Life.</u> The Anthropic Principle-related argument against extraterrestrial life can be simply stated. If intelligent extraterrestrial life existed with the technology for interstellar communication and travel, they would have by this time developed

interstellar travel and would be present in our solar system. They are not here, therefore they do not exist.

The conclusion that we are the only intelligent life in the universe willing and able to communicate is based only on the assumption that a species willing and able to communicate with us would evolve in less than five billion years and would initiate interstellar travel.

Common arguments in favor of the existence of extraterrestrial life can almost all be traced back to a very simple assumption: human beings on earth are nothing special, and we do not live in a time with any special characteristics. Like many other such assumptions, this is a philosophical, not a scientific, assumption.

Experimental evidence in favor of the Big Bang origin of the universe and in contradiction to the competing steady-state model in which the universe was conceived as eternal, appears to be a major step in establishing that we do live in a special time, even in terms of scientific thinking alone. It has been claimed that the Anthropic Principle rules out almost any kind of steady-state model of the universe.

The Future of the Universe. The reading of quasi-religious significance into the Anthropic Principle by those who have rejected the biblical perspective concerning God's purpose and design, is particularly evident in the attempt to prophesy the future. Perhaps this suggests that human beings must have some prophesies. If they are not biblically based, then they must be secularly based.

(1) Consideration of the future of this planet and human life on this planet shows without question that at some time in the future the ability of this planet to sustain human life will come to an end. If, however, intelligent life "must" continue, then it follows that such intelligent life must seek a home away from planet earth.

The true destiny of the universe may be realized only after intelligent life has colonized a substantial portion of it and affected its ongoing evolution. [We may note here the connection between space exploration and the quasi-religious desire for intelligent life to continue forever.]

(2) There is no question but that *Homo Sapiens* will become extinct. Although the human species is doomed, this need not mean that our civilization and values are doomed also. Advocates of this position argue not only for the development of sophisticated machines that can replace human beings as the source of intelligent life in the future, but also for the thesis that such intelligent machines can and should be regarded as "people" with all the rights of normal human persons. [This quasi-religious perspective tries to achieve the non-ending continuance of personal life by positing the extreme case of depersonalization: replacement of human by machine.]

(3) In keeping with its quasi-religious orientation, the exposition of the supposed implications of the Final Anthropic Principle leads to an enterprise suggestively named, "physical eschatology."   It identifies the program that runs the machine with the religious idea of "soul" for human beings, and then asks whether there will be material forms available in the distant future that will permit the construction of "computers" to carry on intelligent civilization, and whether there will be sufficient energy to run these programs.   Since it is posited that after about 10^{31} to 10^{33} years, the only matter remaining in existence will be a mixture of electrons and positrons, these are the physical materials that will be used for the indefinite extension of "intelligent life."

An elementary binary system could be set up using the orientation of spins of electron and positron in the positronium atom.   Within such a framework one might suppose that many of the properties of the universe that we are becoming aware of today do not have their form primarily because they were necessary to bring human life into existence, but because they will become necessary for the survival of "intelligent life" in the far future.

(4)   The extent of this quasi-religious perspective can best be illustrated by quoting the final words of *The Anthropic Cosmological Principle* [79]:

> If life evolves in all of the many universes in a quantum cosmology, and if life continues to exist in all of these universes, then all of these universes, which include all possible histories among them, will approach the Omega Point.   At the instant the Omega Point is reached, life will have gained control of all matter and forces not only in a single universe, but in all universes whose existence is logically possible; life will have spread into all spatial regions in all universes which could logically exist, and will have stored an infinite amount of information, including all bits of knowledge which it is logically possible to know.   And this is the end.   (pp. 676,677)

The contrast between this futuristic prediction and the Christian position is shown most clearly, perhaps, if we compare the quote in the final section above with another prophetic quotation:

> Then I saw a new heaven and a new earth; for the first heaven and the first earth had passed away ... and I heard a loud voice from the throne saying, "Behold, the dwelling of God is with men.   He will dwell with them, and they shall be his people, and God himself will be with them; he will wipe away every tear from their eyes, and death shall be no more, neither shall there be mourning nor crying

nor pain any more, for the former things have passed away.   ....
There shall no more be anything accursed, but the throne of God and
of the Lamb shall be in it, and his servants shall worship him; they
shall see his face, and his name shall be on their foreheads. And
night shall be no more; they need no light of lamp or sun, for the
Lord God will be their light , and they shall reign for ever and ever."
(Revelation 21:1 - 22:5, RSV)

Evidence: Human   Characteristics

The unique characteristics of human life call for the existence of a
source. Can it be believed that the application of random chance
processes over long period of time to inanimate and impersonal matter
could give rise to such human qualities as insight, rational thought,
courage, duty, faith, love, conscience, hope, awe, reverence, God-
consciousness, appreciation of beauty, self-consciousness, the desire for
understanding, in brief, to human personality?

Note that the assumption behind this use of the phrase "random
chance processes" is the worldview of Chance which declares that there
is no meaning or purpose present in the universe. The question asked
is essentially: "Can it be believed that human qualities could have come
into being in a universe that is intrinsically meaningless, purposeless,
and impersonal?"   The answer would be: "That would be hard to
believe."   But we must be careful to distinguish it from the statement
that our scientific description of the development of human qualities is
a chance description in a scientific, not a worldview, sense. The
corresponding question would be: "Can it be believed that
developments that we at present describe in terms of scientific chance
have come into being because of the activity of God in the universe?"
The answer to this question would be: "Yes that can be readily
believed." A worldview of Chance rules out God; a scientific chance
description does not.   There is nothing incompatible between a
scientific description as chance (meaning only that it must be described
probabilistically, not deterministically) and a biblical view that the
process itself is the activity of God.

Moreland [74] seeks to make a case on the basis of what he calls
"substance dualism," and comments,

> Though some theists have denied it recently, the historic
> Christian view has been substance dualism. The mind, distinct from
> the body, is a real substance which can cause things to happen by
> acting and which can exist when the body ceases to function.

He then goes on to make an argument for the existence of God from the evidence of such substance dualism, claiming effectively that the only choices are (a) an absolute physicalism in which mind is superfluous, (b) epiphenomenalism in which mind is a non-interacting consequence of physical processes, or (c) substance dualism in which body and mind are different substances.

But there is another option that seems to be completely consistent both with the insights gained from modern science and from the biblical revelation. This is the possibility of "emergent properties" that arise from the appropriate, dynamically patterned interaction of physical parts in consistence with the creating and sustaining activity of God. It is not true that one must choose between "either the origin of the mind from nothing or its emergence from potentiality in matter" [74] (p. 103) Mind is viewed as an actual dynamic entity (a property of the whole), that does not exist by itself without the interacting parts, and that interacts on the parts through feedback mechanisms as well as being interacted on by the parts. This is not the same as epiphenomenalism that sees the mind, for example, as only subjective phenomena occurring parallel to the physical brain, rather than an objective, dynamic reality that occurs as a result of the interactions taking place in the body. The marvelous achievement of human mind (and soulfulness, spirituality) by such patterned interaction of appropriate biological parts is still itself, of course, evidence for God the dynamic designer and creator, but to try to base such evidence on "substance dualism" seems inadvisable.

Since the existence and properties of human personality is a fundamental focus for arguments concerning evidence for the existence and activity of God, it is appropriate to take a particular look at this subject at this point. Effective evidence does not arise from models or thought patterns that do not correspond to the actual created reality. We enlarge the subject somewhat by considering the broader question of "How do new properties arise in the world?"

Descriptions of Human Personhood: the Origin of New Properties [80]. We consider here the occurrence of new properties associated with different patterns of interaction in different structures of matter. For example, atoms have certain atomic properties like atomic number, valence state, number of electrons etc. When atoms are arranged to interact in a variety of ways they form molecules that may exhibit the properties of solids, liquids or gases. When atoms are arranged in an ordered pattern to form a crystal, a whole host of new properties come into being too numerous to even begin to mention: electrical, optical, and magnetic properties. Appropriate atoms arranged in appropriate patterns of interaction give rise to the property of being alive. The question being raised here is: where do these new properties come from? Here we give just an introduction to this subject; a more complete and detailed discussion of the issue is given later in connection with Pattern 7 in Chapter 10. If this present summary should leave the reader with serious unanswered questions, please refer to the later discussion for possible clarification.

Within the context of secular scientism, the question of the origin of new properties has received a single answer: Chance, purposeless and meaningless Chance. Note that we have here capitalized "Chance" to emphasize once more its significance as an atheistic worldview, and to distinguish it from "chance" (small "c"), one of the only two possible types of scientific description.

Within the context of historic Christianity, this question has received two types of answer: (1) new properties arise from the direct and frequently instantaneous creative activity of God, without the possibility of continuous scientific description; and (2) new properties arise as the result of a particular patterned interaction of the material parts in ways that can, at least in principle, be described scientifically (sometimes deterministically and sometimes as chance) and which are our description of God's immanent and continuing activity. Note that this second answer recognizes that a scientific chance description may be fully consistent with a theological description in terms of God's activity producing design.

The first Christian answer demands some kind of *direct* divine activity, in which God's "intervention" into the natural order is seen as essential for the origin of new properties. As we have seen, such an approach has frequently become a case of the God-of-the-gaps. God must add to the material system something from *outside* the material system in such a way that no scientific description of the event as continuous development is possible. For such an apologetic to have force, it is necessary to maintain both that God *did* act directly in historical time (the fact that God might have acted directly is insufficient), and that no scientific description in natural categories is possible. The argument is made that God *must* have acted in this way in order for the new properties to come into being. It is precisely these contentions that seem to be receiving increasingly suggestive answers. Although we certainly do not wish to claim that God does not have the ability to act in such a direct way, or even to dogmatically assert that God did not indeed act in such a direct way at some times and in some places, it is our desire as usual to learn how God *did* act rather than simply how God *could have* acted.

As we learn more about the structure of created reality, it seems more and more likely that it is indeed possible to provide a continuous scientific description for many of these origins. Being alive does not require the presence of some externally added entity, a vital essence, but can most probably be correctly regarded as a property of the patterned interaction of the created matter become alive. Being human does not require the presence of some externally added entity, a soul and/or spirit, but can most probably be correctly regarded as a property of the patterned interaction of the living creature become human, with strong support from the general biblical perspective as we show in our discussion of Pattern 7 in Chapter 10.

Three types of explanatory contexts have been advanced to deal with the origin of new properties in the world if that origin is indeed in principle describable scientifically by continuous process: reductionism, "preductionism," and "hierarchical emergence."

Reductionism considers all new properties to be the inevitable consequence of the laws of nature as these are applied to situations brought into being by uncaused chance (according to the worldview of Scientism and Chance).   All phenomena, whether conventionally described in terms of biology, psychology, sociology, anthropology, or theology, find their only true and complete description in the physical and chemical description of the behavior of matter.   Theology must be reduced to anthropology, psychology to biology, and biology to physics and chemistry, which are the only *real* entities. Reductionism advocates the position that the whole is no more than the sum of its parts. If the parts are known, then the whole is known. Not content with providing an authentic scientific description of reality, reductionism presses further into Scientism and insists that a scientific description is the only meaningful description of reality that can be given. This is the perspective we encountered in Pattern 1.

Preductionism (a play on words that I have made) takes complete issue with reductionism by effectively standing it "on its head." If reductionism claims that the properties of the whole are only illusory because they are not explicitly in the parts, preductionism claims that the properties of the whole are authentic because they are indeed implicit in the parts. If reductionism claims that there is no such thing as "spirit" because that is not a category used in physical and chemical descriptions, preductionism claims that the reality of "spirit" is made known by its presence in all of matter.   We shall refer to this perspective again in treating Pattern 6 in Chapter 9.   A principal difficulty with this perspective is that there is no real evidence in its favor. It is an *ad hoc*, semi-poetic construction of a mind in search of a solution for a perceived dilemma. Furthermore, it requires only the subtlest of shifts to become identified with a modern form of animism, with some type of pantheism, or with the characteristic monism of Eastern religions. Both reductionism and preductionism agree in dehumanizing the human person by insisting that the person has no more value than the matter present in the person; reductionism reduces the person to matter, while preductionism elevates matter to personhood. If both reductionism and preductionism are to be rejected, the advocate of Pattern 4 is quick to offer a *direct* and totally supernatural act of God as the only possible alternative, and then to use this fact as part of the evidence for the existence of God. There is, however, another alternative, which provides evidence for the existence of God in another way possibly more faithful to the way that God actually acts.

Full faithfulness to both the understanding of modern science and the biblical revelation, without subjecting one to the other, appears to demand that the answer to the question concerning the origin of novelty must maintain the following perspectives on the relationship between matter and personhood: (1) both matter and the characteristic properties of personhood are created; (2) matter is matter and is not characterized intrinsically by personhood; (3) the attributes characteristic of personhood are real and not an illusion; (4) in the earthly world of our experience persons do not exist without the matter that composes them.

An approach that deals faithfully with the problem within these boundary conditions is the one that may be called "hierarchical emergence." The elements of the world are viewed as being described by a hierarchical model, of which the most obvious levels correspond to (1) material but not living, (2) material and living but not human, and (3) material, living and human. Such a structure, of which further details might be spelled out at considerably greater length, [81] (see the discussion in Pattern 7 in Chapter 10) consists of parts and wholes, such that wholes at a higher level depend upon and yet transcend the parts at a lower level (e.g., biological life and physical "particles") in such a way that the unique properties of the wholes are not present even implicitly in the parts but emerge when the parts participate in a particular, suitable pattern of interactions. It is the pattern of interaction that is responsible for the real properties of the whole, a pattern that is not demanded by the properties of the parts but shapes and focuses their interaction in the way that boundary conditions shape and focus the solutions to a differential equation. To be alive is a systems property of a particular type of material system composed of suitable parts arranged in a suitable pattern of interactions. To be human is a systems property of a particular type of living material system composed of suitable parts arranged in a suitable pattern of interactions.

The Christian can see evidence for the existence and activity of God in this marvelous and somewhat mysterious system, but not, as is so often maintained by advocates of Pattern 4, because it is impossible for life to arise from non-living matter, or human beings from non-human creatures, without the direct "intervention" of God in an act that is not scientifically describable. Again it is not argued that God *could not* have acted in this way, but only that the evidence indicates that he probably *did not* so act.

Evidence: the Bible is Scientifically Defensible

In their pursuit of evidence that would "decide the God question," Montgomery et al. [74] concentrate on showing that the Bible stands up to a test of its scientific accuracy and reliability. They seek to demonstrate that (1) the Bible contains "history written in advance," (2) accurate statements are found in the Bible "demonstrating scientific knowledge and concepts far before mankind had developed the technological base necessary for discovering that knowledge or those concepts," (3) historical assertions in the Bible are verified by continuing historical scholarship, (4) statements about people and places are made in the Bible that are verified by ongoing archeological research, and (5) the Bible contains "well-developed common themes and is internally consistent,...even though written piecemeal over thousands of years."

Most of these arguments can well be advanced positively to demonstrate that Christian faith is indeed a rational faith. We should expect the Bible to present a trustworthy account of people, events, places, and historical developments, as they express the purposes of the biblical writings.

But Montgomery and his fellow authors wish to do more: to set forth such "objective evidence" in such a convincing way that faith itself almost becomes unnecessary. Rightly set as they are to show the weakness of "blind faith," they often appear to step over the boundary into a position based on and made credible by science and by an intellectual approach alone to the Bible. They state that there is no "scriptural basis for believing any inner feeling, conviction, or sense of peace is the voice of God." (p. 34) There appears to be little place for a personal response to Christ's love, only an intellectual response to scientifically testable evidence. So great is the prestige of science in our day that even the details of the Bible must be subjected to it, quite independently of the purpose for which they were written or the revelation that they were intended to convey.

Perhaps the most questionable of the evidences advanced in such a treatment is the existence of "prescience" in the Bible. Almost everything we know about the nature of the biblical revelation as developed from its own character and purposes, almost everything we understand from the relevance of revelation expanding over time, almost everything we would ascribe to the actual purpose and meaning of the Bible argue against hidden prescientific insights *as the result of special revelation* thousand of years ago. This resembles more an argument from mysticism or magic, which the authors would certainly denounce, than it is a faithful understanding of the nature of communication between God and human beings. It appears to be quite inappropriate to cite Mosaic divisions of animals into clean and unclean, for example, *as the result of prescientific special revelation* about the effects of these foods on health (what happened to Peter in his vision before going to visit with Cornelius in Acts when this same distinction was discredited?), or to argue that Mosaic prohibition of eating the fat on the meat was actually prescientific understanding of the effects of cholesterol.

Summary

All of these evidences for the existence of God from the natural world are indeed just that: evidences. They can all be accepted by rebellious human beings as meaningless statements of the way things are. One grand meaningless product of chance, a long shot with all the odds against it, just happened to lead to us and our world. The mystery of existence, indications of order and design, and even the apparently unique characteristics of human beings themselves can all be dismissed with one mighty exercise of existential doubt in the attitude that such things must simply be accepted. Beyond that they have no meaning. The rejection of these evidences does not argue for the mental incapacity of those who reject them. As to what is implied concerning the willful and arbitrary motives behind their rejection, only they can judge. This is a point at which Christian faith does have a comment to make. According to the words of Paul in Romans 1:19-22, previously quoted, the perspective of Christian faith questions the mask of detached objectivity and inquires, "Did you reject these evidences because they were so unconvincing – or because you wanted to?"

One other deficiency of too extreme an emphasis on these kinds of evidence, sometimes characteristic of advocates of Pattern 4, is that they point to only a very few of the attributes of God. If a natural theology is constructed on their basis alone, the result is likely to resemble deism more than Christian theology. The quotation from Paul in Romans indicates that natural theology can reveal only the power and existence of God. Natural theology alone suggests as models for God such concepts as the Great Mathematician, Machinist, Lawgiver, or Designer. That God is love, that he cares for you and me, that he is righteous and holy – these attributes of his are not revealed by the natural universe. Only his own special revelation through the words of the Bible is able to convey them to us.

The methodology of Pattern 4 is troublesome for two fundamental reasons. First of all, it makes science the ultimate judge and arbiter of truth and reliability in an area where such a position for science is not justified. There is a strong desire to set forth "objective evidence" in such a convincing way that a faith commitment itself almost becomes unnecessary. There appears to be little place for a personal response to Christ's love, only an intellectual response to scientifically testable evidence. So strong is the commitment to "science" that proponents of this position frequently argue that miraculous events should be properly considered as part of a scientific description, sometimes siding with advocates of "theistic science" in Pattern 2 (Chapter 5), and sometimes arguing for a change in the definition of authentic science and its inbuilt limitations with similarities to advocates for Pattern 6 (Chapter 9).

Secondly, this approach to Pattern 4 gives far too little significance to the nature of the biblical revelation that is actually given to us in the Bible, choosing to assume instead that it is the same type of communication that we might expect to obtain by reading a daily newspaper or textbook today. Such an approach comes to a focus in claims for the existence of "prescience" in the Bible, information provided by divine revelation that anticipates the later findings of science.

Advocates of Pattern 4 frequently miss the importance of the "human interpretation" element in both science and theology. Instead of recognizing that there are no "self--interpreting facts," they often argue the contrary. Montgomery, for example, writes, [74] "Theological presuppositionalists.. tell us that there are no self-interpreting facts, .. We profoundly disagree. .. the very nature of legal argument ... rests on the ability of facts to speak for themselves." (pp. 334, 335)

But any student of the philosophy of science (rather than the quite different way that words like "prove" and "fact" are used in legal settings) knows that facts do not provide their own meaning, that many facts can be interpreted according to several different models, and that every experiment is itself "theory laden." To fail to recognize this is to reject the very qualities that characterize authentic science as human interpretation of observations. But then such arguments also commonly misunderstand the essential role of human interpretation played in biblical interpretation to develop authentic theology.

Chapter 8

Pattern 5: Science Redefines Christian Theology

Advocates of Pattern 5 focus their emphasis on the claim that the findings of modern science have made, are making, and will make in the future, major substantive changes in Christian theology. They are concerned with the effects of changes in scientific thinking over the past 2000 years on corresponding changes in theological thinking.

The statement of this Pattern can be summarized as follows: *Science and theology tell us the same kinds of things about the same things. Traditional biblical theology must be thoroughly redefined and rewritten in order to be consistent with the developments of modern science.*

It is interesting to note that Patterns 1, 2, 4, and 5 (including Pattern 6, as well, as we will see in Chapter 9) all agree in the assumption that science and theology both tell us the same kinds of things about the same things. Whereas Pattern 4 was aimed at justifying a traditional Christian theological interpretation by showing that it was really scientifically defensible, Pattern 5 is aimed at arguing for a new definition of theology to become consistent with the results of modern science. It is the general position of a considerable number of Christians, well versed in science, who feel the need to alter traditional theological positions to bring them more into harmony with the philosophical implications suggested to them by modern science.

One might argue that in Pattern 4 scientific reasoning was put into the service of theological convictions, whereas in Pattern 5 new theological formulations are proposed in order that they might be consistent with an interpretation of the results of modern science. This approach is based on the effort to reconstruct Christian theology in categories that are acceptable to a modern scientific worldview, or to argue for a major new insight and revelation of God coming to us through the models and descriptions of modern science. There is often only a thin line that separates Pattern 5 from Pattern 6, which calls for a radical revision of both science and theology in the future to form one common view.

One of the issues that relates to several of the Patterns described in this book is "natural theology," the attempt to derive theological concepts from observation and scientific investigation of the natural world, which we have described briefly in connection with Pattern 3 in Chapter 6. Since for some, as in Patterns 2 and 3, natural theology was seen to constitute a threat by science to theology, the thrust of theological apologetics was to deny any validity to natural theology. The opposite extreme in which scientific descriptions are used to defend traditional theological conclusions characterized the arguments of Pattern 4.   In Patterns 5 and 6 scientific descriptions are seen as providing the basis for a theological revolution, and arguments are heavily based on natural theology.   This is, of course, a risky course of action since later revisions of scientific findings and theories may well force a change of theology, an all too common event in the past even when unintended, as in the case of the church in the time of Galileo. Finally in Pattern 7 in Chapter 10 the effort is made to avoid the extremes of the poles of such responses to natural theology and to integrate insights from both authentic science and authentic theology.

Historical Background

Over the last few centuries science has been interpreted by many to lead to Scientism, which is now the major "religious" worldview in many parts of the world. [82, 83] This worldview claims to be based on empirical knowledge and has been perceived by both non-scientists and scientists alike to be inadequate for the full description of human life. Modern disenchantment with traditional science perceived as leading inevitably to the ultimate worldview of Scientism leads to increasing emphasis on alternative worldviews in which elements of science and religion are blended, which appear to offer new dimensions of personal influence and freedom.   The nature of these alternative worldviews is often such that they are simultaneously more appealing to the scientific mindset than the traditional Christian worldview, and at the same time are equally as inimical to biblical theology as were the former views of Scientism. They offer a subtle blend of science with pseudoscience, and of theology with pseudotheology, with a sophistication that may mislead the unwary into believing that major breakthroughs beyond traditional science and historical Christianity are about to be achieved.

It is essential for Christians, and particularly Christian men and women of science, to understand these alternative worldviews as thoroughly as possible so that they are able to serve as guides, both to scientists who for the first time are considering Christianity, and to Christians who for the first time are considering scientific inputs to their theology.

Changes in Theology Due to Science

If by theology one means the whole framework of concepts, models, metaphors etc. which have been used to convey the message of authentic Christian theology, it would be foolish to deny that major changes have occurred, particularly in the last few hundred years.

Early theological pictures of the world and universe in which we live were naturally framed in terms of the models of that world and universe known to the people for whom the Bible was written and for whom the revelation was intended. Now we know that many of those models are not good representations of the universe and we do not use them to convey theological insights. We know that the earth is a planetary body in space, rotating on its axis and revolving around the sun in our galaxy, one of many other galaxies that exist in the universe. We no longer use the model of a three-level universe, with earth midway between hell and heaven. We know that the universe is vastly larger than we had ever thought earlier, and that it is characterized by black holes and perplexing properties beyond our current understanding. We no longer use the model of God living beyond the atmosphere of earth, or of heaven as a place in our universe outside our atmosphere.

Because of our new perspectives on the physical structure and interactions of the universe brought to us through such modern theories as relativity and quantum mechanics, we no longer use models of simple determinism or of the universe as a simple machine. We recognize some of the complexities of four-dimensional space-time, and the intrinsic indeterminacies (scientific chance descriptions) of the world made manifest at the atomic level. When we speak about God's activity made manifest in the events of the universe, we try to use models that are consistent with our apparent scientific descriptions of this activity.

By observing the way in which God seems to have acted in the history of the universe, we are impressed with the importance of development over time in his pattern of activity, rather than attempting to view the universe as static, unchanging, and variable only by direct, usually instantaneous "intervention" by God. We are impressed by how new properties and new potentialities can come into being through continuous process over time as the expressions of God's activity, involving interactions that scientifically are described by both chance and determinism. And we again adapt our models to be consistent with these apparent realities.

All of these changes in our understanding of the universe impress on us what we should have realized all along: our God is far greater than we could ever imagine. Our simplistic ways of thinking about him prove inadequate time after time. Scientific research shows us with ever more wonders the fantastic ways in which God acts in the universe.

But as we learn more and more about the ways in which God acts, we do not learn anything that necessarily challenges the basic revelation of God as the loving Father of our Lord Jesus Christ, who died for our sins on the cross. Nor does this increased scientific knowledge make any significant differences in the meaning or our expression of the fundamental characteristics of the Christian life: love, joy, peace, patience, kindness, goodness, faith, gentleness, self-control, mercy, compassion, forgiveness, redemption and regeneration.

One of the difficulties of assessing advocates of Pattern 5 is the determination of whether they intend their rhetoric to be taken literally, or whether it is only a form of poetic overstatement; in more extreme cases of the former type, there could even be considerable overlap with Pattern 6. We examine several different examples in this chapter. Are advocates of Pattern 5 only reacting to the increase in our scientific understanding with excessive language that proclaims the greatness of God? Or are they really proposing that Christian theology needs to be totally revolutionized and changed because of these increases in scientific understanding, both with regard to models of redemption as well as models of creation, as their language often indicates?

Visionary Rhetoric or Serious Confusion?

In order to give the flavor of the some of the comments of those who appear to be advocates of Pattern 5, we consider here a few illustrations of these comments made in serious writing on the relationship between science and theology. They are written largely by Christians who have experienced some of the insights made available through modern science and interpret these insights as a genuine contribution to authentic theology. Their comments are often difficult to analyze because they are so non-specific .

Several examples can be found in *The God Who Would Be Known: Revelations of the Divine in Contemporary Science* by Templeton and Herrmann. [84] An opening statement appears to fit reasonably well with the themes we have been developing,

> Indeed, many in science now see the limitations of scientific description and do not presume that scientific descriptions are ultimate truth. For some there is the added conviction that the Creator is revealing himself through science, so that the results of science serve as signs pointing to a larger Reality. But people cannot learn all about God by studying nature, because nature is only a contingent and partial manifestation of God. So we look to theology, particularly as it opens itself to the discoveries of science, to extend our knowledge of God. And so the sphere of the spirit will spread and energize new creative dimensions of understanding for future humankind. (p. 5)

Still one might wonder how the results of science point to a larger Reality, how theology will extend our knowledge of God by being open to the discoveries of science, and what is really meant by "the sphere of the spirit." Later, in language reminiscent of Teilhard de Chardin, the authors tell us more about the "sphere of the spirit." They describe a series of evolutionary-developing spheres: of life, then of intellect, and finally of spirit.

> We are beginning to see evidence of a new sphere outside the sphere of intellect, which may be called the sphere of the spirit. This suggests that the things we see, hear, and touch are only appearances. They are only manifestations of some underlying forces, and those underlying forces are spiritual. Evidence of this is not based on study of the Bible or other ancient scriptures, but on recent discoveries of modern science. (p. 33)

It is certainly true that science has been showing us that everyday, common experience, macroscopic expectations are often not fulfilled in the worlds of the very small or the very fast. But to conclude that this knowledge leads to the conclusion that the "underlying forces are spiritual" appears to have no scientific basis. To go beyond this with the claim that "science itself, for decades a bastion of unbelief, has once again become the source for humankind's assurance of intimate divine concern in its affairs" appears to be simply a visionary invention of people with a particular religious worldview living in a scientifically dominated time, and not a statement that corresponds necessarily to the interpretation of scientific discoveries.

For another example consider the dramatic words of Russell [85, 86]:

> I believe we stand at the brink of a new Reformation, one in which virtually all of our theology will be rethought in new terms. We must begin to make sense of our cherished traditions in terms of contemporary science if we are to enter a new period of theological discovery and vitality. [85]

These words have a brave and visionary sound. Are they to be taken literally? What does it mean to "rethink" all of our theology? Is the intention of statements like this simply to call for a broader recognition of the changes that scientific understanding have brought to our theological models of creation, as summarized in the last section above, or do they really envision fundamental changes in the basic structure of Christian theology in all respects including redemption, as the findings of modern science are appreciated and applied?

A third illustration of an approach that fits at least approximately in Pattern 5 is that described by Capra et al. in *Belonging to the Universe*. [87] They list five fundamental paradigm shifts that have been experienced by both science and theology in recent years. Such shifts as, for example, from "structure" to "process" in science, and from "revelation as timeless truth" to "revelation as historical manifestation" in theology need raise no real problems if read in an appropriate perspective. Pointing to the resurrection of Jesus as evidence for his deity, however, is disclaimed as "old-paradigm" thought, no longer viable today. In new-paradigm theology, it is concluded that "the cosmos, God, and humans are all interrelated ... you cannot speak about God except in the context of cosmos and humans." The world is seen to be a living system with its own intelligence, its own mind. In the "new-paradigm" there is a switch from salvation-centered theology to creation-centered theology. It is evident that these particular advocates of Pattern 5 (or Pattern 6?) claim that the revolutions in Christian theology brought about by recent insights in modern science affect every aspect of that theology.

A switch from salvation-centered theology to creation-centered theology appears to be a common feature of efforts to develop any science-reformulated theology. Such efforts seem to be consistently lacking when it comes to meaningful reformulations for such significant theological concepts as holiness, sin, salvation, and regeneration. Meaningful development of the human being is described in terms of the ongoing changes of evolution, not in terms of a new birth through faith in Jesus Christ. At best "salvation" is treated under the results of "creation," not under the effects of "redemption." If these are among the classical conceptions that are going to be changed by the new science/theology breakthrough, then whether we have anything "Christian" left seems open to question.

Scientific Theology [88]

One advocate of Pattern 5 who has written extensively in favor of the development of a "scientific theology" is Ralph Wendell Burhoe. [89, 90] There is no doubt about the extent of the changes that he envisions as necessary and desirable. Some of the conclusions that he draws include the following: it may not be necessary to ascribe "personhood" to God, or better to *god* (Burhoe's choice of expression), which is a term for the whole cosmic ecosystem, not a being beyond nature; the revelation of *god* occurs through genetic and cultural evolution; and

> the religious reformation now ... will be a theological adaptation of traditional religious beliefs and rituals to the modern sciences. The new religious and theological language will be as high above that of five centuries ago as contemporary cosmology is above the Ptolemaic, as contemporary medicine, agriculture, communications and transportation concepts are above those of the fifteenth century. ... I prophesy human salvation through a reformation and revitalization of religion at a level superior to any reformation in earlier histories. (p.328) [89]

It is Burhoe's purpose to achieve a synthesis of science and religion and thereby to demonstrate that the prominence of religion in the future is not incompatible with the rationality of science or of basic freedom. He seeks to do this by developing a scientific theology with only superficial resemblance to biblical theology. Scientific theology is an eclectic system, a universal and natural religion, based presumably upon the major insights available to us through modern science, essentially the insights derived from an interpretation of human evolution.

According to Scientific Theology, religious beliefs are the product of an evolutionary development, leading from primitive ritual, to primitive beliefs or myths, to theology, and finally to scientific theology. We are currently at the breakthrough, Burhoe argues, between theology and scientific theology at the present day. Although old religious systems have wisdom in them, this wisdom cannot be utilized in a new social context until the symbols of this wisdom in the old cognitive scheme are translated into appropriate symbols in the new cognitive scheme. The new religion rests upon the revelations of modern science, the insights of which will be incorporated in old belief systems to revitalize them and provide a scientific basis for moral and religious problems.

"Scientific theology" may be summarized as follows. It is based on the presupposition that the modern scientific mind cannot accept truth in the form of the biblical categories, that religious beliefs are wholly human products, that in the final analysis it is knowledge and understanding that save, that adherence to the traditional biblical position inevitably leads to a defense of a God-of-the Gaps, and that individual life will not be preserved as individual life beyond this world.

In view of these presuppositions, the attempt to reinterpret biblical categories into scientific ones results in an eclectic universalistic religion in which Nature is *god*, the natural system is the Kingdom of *god*, the supernatural is anything not covered by common sense, science is truth, evil means non-viable or incomplete, and salvation is the human quest for survival. Optimism in the future rests on the hope that increasing knowledge will lead us to do what we must to save ourselves.

The God who calls, empowers, forgives, loves and acts is no longer there; only the impersonal silence of the total ecosystem remains. There is no mention of Jesus Christ, of love, or of prayer. There is no moral rebellion, no personal fellowship with God, no Body of Christ. The individual person is submerged in mankind as a species; salvation and eternal life are not applicable to individuals who live here and now, but only to the total human race. Authentic theology has not been reformulated; it has been demolished. Only pseudotheology remains.

Summary: Are We Saved by Creation or Redemption? [91]

Consideration of Pattern 5 raises some fundamental questions that we have touched on in the above discussion. In concluding this section, we consider the general question raised by the effects of "scientific theology."

What is our ultimate hope? Do we expect deliverance from the evils of the present day through the outworking of God's activity in creation, or do we have special need of His work in redemption? This is a critical issue for Christians as we face the future.

One of the consequences of our dependence on science is a growing tendency to translate theological concepts into scientific ones. When this is done, it follows that salvation/survival is linked to events in the physical universe. Survival follows from some future pattern in the way that the universe develops, and sight tends to be lost of the central Christian teaching on salvation of the whole person from sin by redemption. In the final analysis, are we saved by creation or redemption?

There is no biblical disjunction between Creation and Redemption, between the God who creates and the God who saves. The Bible clearly answers the question: "Who is this God who saves?" with the answer, "The Father Almighty, Maker of Heaven and Earth" (Isaiah 44:24; Psalm 89:11-15; John 1:1-12; and Colossians 1:16-20). How then can there be tension in preserving the integration of Creation and Redemption?

It has been argued [92] that Greek and Hebraic understandings of "creation" are quite different. The Greeks saw "creation" as concerned with the mechanisms of the origin of the world, with the type of concerns that characterize a scientific view. The Hebrews saw "creation" as the inauguration of salvation history – a mighty work of God inseparably tied to the more transcendent aspects of salvation and redemption. It can be argued in the same way that Greek and Hebrew readings of the meaning of "salvation" also differ appreciably. The Greeks saw "salvation" as a journey out of this world, and "redemption" as perfection. The Hebrews, on the other hand, saw "salvation" as a re-creation of this world, and "redemption" as liberation for the oppressed. Considering the strong philosophical blending of Greek with Hebraic thought that underlies our own theological understanding of these concepts, it is not surprising that extreme positions can easily develop, extremes that break the biblical perspectives on Creation with Redemption.

Elevating Creation over Redemption. The Creation/Redemption tension is a reflection of the traditional Science/Theology tension. To elevate Creation over Redemption often takes the form, therefore, of attempting to establish a scientific theology, which since it is scientific, is devoid of all traditional revelational aspects. The motivation for this reformation of theology is to allow the benefits of "religion" to become available to the modern mind, saturated with scientific and skeptical perspectives. Since the realm of the applicability of science is the natural world, it inevitably follows that biblical revelation is rejected and only a very naturalistic religion results.

Since there is no personal God, there is no holy God, there is no sin against moral standards, no need for atonement from sin, no biblical remnant of the concept of Redemption left, and of course no need for a

Savior. Jesus Christ is curiously absent from such "scientific
theology."

Elevating Redemption over Creation . There is also the reverse
emphasis: to elevate Redemption over Creation by elevating theology
over science and attributing little or no value to the present world
because it will pass away at the return of Christ and the new creation of
the world to come.   This is the strong thrust of much that has been
called "fundamentalist," particularly of the dispensational variety, in
recent years, but it also has an historic root in Christian asceticism and
monasticism.

It is indeed acknowledged that God did create – and in fact dogmatic
insistence on anti-scientific views of the mechanism of that creation
fairly generally characterize this position – but since the curses that
followed the Fall were leveled against this creation, it is a dying and
corrupted thing, suitable only to be set aside or tolerated for the present
in view of the demands of eternity.   The return of Christ is to be
expected at any moment. The devotion of considerable thought and
effort in the attempt to live responsibly in the real world by dealing
with its real problems are often condemned as a waste of time: "When a
great ship is sinking, one doesn't try to bale out the water with a bucket
or plug the holes; one tries to save the living" – by which is meant the
preaching of the Gospel to save souls exclusively.

One of the great tensions faced by Christians, who take seriously the
commands of Christ to follow his example in responsible stewardship
and the apparent thrust of biblical revelation concerning the ultimate
disposition of the future, is the effort to work daily for the preservation
and righteousness of a world that is destined for destruction.   It has
always been a central theme of biblical teaching that Christians are
called to be faithful in the deeds of today, following the commands of
Christ in this business of day-to-day living, without allowing these
contemporary concerns to be displaced by hopes or fears for the future.

The biblical teaching of the imminence of Christ's return has always
been seen as both a comfort and a warning, with nothing clearer than
that no one knows the day or the time.   When concern with the future
calls for a withdrawal from human responsibilities, it ceases to be based
on biblical theology and instead becomes cultic. Watching and waiting
for Christ's return must always be coupled with our call to be salt and
light today. A probably apocryphal story relates how someone asked
Martin Luther what he would do if he were sure that Christ were
returning the next day. "Why," Luther is reported as replying, "I would
plant an apple tree today." Today is the day for planting even if
tomorrow is the day for ending (or beginning!). Each day is to be lived
as if Christ were indeed returning tomorrow, but with that responsible

planning and concern that would characterize the case if Christ were to delay for a thousand years.

Equating Creation with Redemption. Of the three distortions of the Creation/Redemption tension we are considering here, this is perhaps the most difficult to evaluate. Since both Creation and Redemption in some sense are expounded as central concepts, the subtleties that lead to the confession, "Creation is Redemption" are more difficult to judge fairly and without error.

One of the standard ways of maintaining that "Creation is Redemption" is to invoke the process of evolution as the means by which this works itself out in time. Teilhard de Chardin [78], paleontologist and Catholic priest, is an outstanding example. He saw the unfolding of the world under the power of the love of God, finally to be characterized by a period of convergence that would bring all to Christ. Teilhard assigned characteristic names to each of the three major transition points in the development of life on earth. The evolution of non-living matter, he called "cosmogenesis;" the evolution of living creatures he called "biogenesis;" and the evolution of human beings he called "noogenesis." He saw the emergence of higher-level properties arising out of the interaction of the parts making up the whole, as the pattern of these interactions took on increased complexity.

But, at this point Teilhard deviated from a biblical perspective, in that he saw evolution finally reversing its diverging trend to unite all in Christ at the Omega point by Christogenesis. In the final analysis, evolution as scientific process was to be the means by which individuals would be united with Christ. In this framework, however, evil and sin are simply byproducts of the process of evolution, and have nothing to do with the central issues of life. Either all human beings will arrive at Omega in Christ or none will. Although the name of Christ is named, it is not Jesus the Christ who lived, died and rose again, of whom Teilhard speaks, but rather a kind of universal "Christ symbol." If Creation is Redemption, then God redeems through creative activity, and not through the death of Jesus Christ on the cross. Human beings participate in the work of creation and hence of redemption: we become co-creators with God and high priests of God's creation.

An Alternative Approach. Teilhard de Chardin was motivated by a supreme desire to integrate his scientific perspective with the valuable insights of Christianity as he knew them. It is possible to move toward this goal in a way that does not violate the biblical tension between Creation and Redemption, but retains the authentic inputs from both. I suggest here a scenario with inputs from science and the biblical revelation, not as the necessarily correct picture, but as a possible picture with scientific and theological integrity.

We start with God's purpose in creation: to bring forth a people for himself. To achieve this purpose God called into being from nothing this universe in embryonic form and sent its various parts hurtling through space (according to the Big Bang Theory of the origin of the universe), establishing the immense universe in which we live. All of the elements heavier than hydrogen and helium are believed to have been synthesized in cataclysmic supernovae explosions much earlier in the history of the universe. We are made of the ashes of the supernovae. It has been suggested that one meaning of the universe is to bring forth life. Without 100 billion galaxies, life would never appear!

To achieve his purpose of bringing forth a people to Himself, God brought into being the solar system in our galaxy that we call the Milky Way. In that solar system he brought forth the earth as the environment suitable for a people that he would call. As he worked in activity that we might call "cosmogenesis" (the birth of the universe and our earth), so he continued to work in activity that we might call "biogenesis," bringing forth on this earth living creatures in the seas, on the land and in the air. When the time was ripe, when the cosmic "temperature" of creation was at white heat, a new reality burst forth that we might call "noogenesis," the birth of self-conscious human life.

But this new humanity endowed with the ability of choice is self-centered and unwilling with its newly given self-consciousness to recognize the lordship of its Creator. Made in many ways like the animals, but called to transcend the other animals as that unique creature enabled to have personal fellowship with God Himself, these human beings choose to forsake this humanity for their lower nature. For animals to be self-centered is natural and not sinful; for human beings made in the image of God to be self-centered is sinful. Thus the characteristic of "original sin" as innate self-centeredness leading to rebellion against God, is recognized. Sin enters the world through the disobedience of the first people. The living, sinful human creature needs one more transformation to complete the purpose of God.

Before the origin of life, God's changes functioned in the physical stuff of the universe. When living creatures emerged, the focus of change shifted from the physical stuff to the living creatures, from the physical realm to the biological realm, as cosmological evolution, having arrived at the bringing forth of life, gave way to biological development. In its turn biological development gave rise to self-conscious human beings made for fellowship with God . But this self-centered, sinful creature needs a final transformation - needs another shift in fundamental development – a transformation now adequate for the thinking, self-conscious world brought into being with noogenesis.

What transformation is adequate for the task of creating new spiritual life in a human being, of completing the calling and purpose of God by providing a new creation in the realm of the spiritual? To ask the question of authentic Christian theology is to answer it: the new birth in Christ, the regeneration of the Holy Spirit – this is what is needed to complete God's call and purpose; this is the final earthly stage in the great drama that God has been working out over the life of the universe, to be followed only by the end and consummation of that drama at the end of this age.

Here, then, is at least a possible scenario that is consistent with current understandings of evolutionary description and with the essential themes of the biblical teaching. Furthermore it leads in a direct and continuous way into the essence of the Christian Gospel, without making sin any less real or less serious than it is, without invoking self-salvation or cosmic salvation, without reducing moral human beings to metaphysical animals, and without being universalistic. God's work in both Creation and Redemption are clearly defined, are seen to interrelate, and yet need not be confused with each other. The significance of the universe and the significance of the Cross are both retained. Our existence we owe to God's creative and sustaining activity, our salvation to the work of the Cross, both expressions of the love and graciousness of a holy God.

Temptations for Christians. Christians in science find the equating of Creation with Redemption particularly seductive. Sometimes it seems as if Christians have either crossed over into the "Creation is Redemption" camp, or at least speak in such a way as to leave their position ambiguous. In their zeal to obtain scientific support for their theological convictions, Christians sometimes speak glowingly of new developments that are causing a major new synthesis of science and theology, so that these two disciplines that previously have been quite diverse, now are merging into one new discipline of the future. Such a major "synthesis" of science and theology carries with it all the dangers of forsaking what is authentic in science and what is authentic in theology. This pattern is discussed further in the next chapter.

Chapter 9

Pattern 6: A New Synthesis of Science and Christian Theology

One of the recurring visions for the future is that science and religion will become one discipline. Does our hope for the future really lie in a synthesis of science and religion? Or does such a proposed synthesis involve dangers that we should constantly be on the alert against?

We may spell out the defining description for Pattern 6 as follows: *Science and theology should tell us the same kind of things about the same things, but the present status of science and theology makes this impossible. What is needed, therefore, is a radical transformation of both science and theology into new approaches compatible with one another and a new understanding of reality.*

Pattern 6 is one more variation on the theme that science and theology do or should tell us about the same things, which it shares with Patterns 1, 2, 4, and 5. It also shares the visionary properties of Pattern 5, but goes beyond even them to envisioning a time when both science and theology will have been reformulated into a new worldview, a new paradigm, a new synthesis of science and faith.

Listen to a few of the prophets of this diverse movement as they join in predicting the Utopian world of the future.

And what would a science of the spirit be? Quite simply, it would be a commonly held higher level of knowing in which the nonphysical becomes objectified, empirical, and publicly demonstrable. It would answer our questions about the physics of paranormal phenomena in a way which integrates our intellectual knowledge with our deepest feelings and most honored values in a life-supporting, life-enhancing manner. And in doing so, it would help bring about a new social order which various spiritual and esoteric traditions envision: the New Age. [93]

We are on the threshold of a revolution. A revolution so vast, much more vast than this world has ever seen, even in the days of the Greeks.   We are talking about a revolution of scientific understanding, vast new technologies growing out of that understanding, knowledge of man's relationships with himself, between himself and his brothers.   ... As we learn the true meaning of mind and thought and put them to work we will grow to a potential far, far beyond what, presently, we manifest; and we can make of this earth a rather fantastic place. [94]

To evolve in a spirit of peace and blessed coexistence, human beings must understand quantum physics and its application to their mind and their consciousness.   There may be no other way for this kind of conscious evolution.
Through this understanding, which I have only begun to investigate, and which I feel is inevitable, human beings will realize a vast potential for a true spiritual evolution.   .... Each of us follows a path. At each step of the path an infinite number of branches into the future are seen from the pathfinder's viewpoint. With billions of forks in the road, each pathfinder must choose the path he/she follows.   The only guarantee each pilgrim has is that all paths lead to the same Designer. If this isn't God, then I don't know what God is. [95]

Having become disillusioned with the continuing apparent conflicts between science and theology, Pattern 6 concludes that a major part of the fault lies with the presently understood structures of science and theology, and looks with visionary hope toward the time when both science and theology will have grown into one coherent discipline. Then science will bring validation to religion, and religion will bring transcendence to science. A wide range of advocates can be found from moderate to extreme, extending from variations on sound Christian positions to extremes of New Age.
At its most constructive this pattern envisions a growing awareness of the similarities between scientific and theological descriptions while

continuing to recognize their legitimate differences. At its most destructive it calls for a radical change in both science and theology, thus denying the characteristics of both authentic science and authentic theology with their corresponding effectiveness and trustworthiness.

A mystical convergence of science and theology in the future does not necessarily speak of the fulfillment of authentic science and authentic Christian theology. If such a convergence does occur, it may well be because we have lost both authentic science and authentic Christian theology. Nowhere is this more evident and more challenging than in those cases where pseudoscience and pseudotheology have been joined together in the effort to synthesize a new relationship between science and theology, a great new transformation in the not-too-distant future spoken of in glowing terms: a transformation in which science and theology will join together, their conflicts will end, and the two will become one marvelous and mystic celebration of spiritual dimensions. Such a movement sometimes claims the authority of science, but actually rests upon a particular philosophical or religious interpretation of science not actually derived from authentic science itself. While promising New Age consciousness, it often delivers only Old Age illusions. A detailed analysis is given by Mangalwadi. [96] Bright, new revolutionary insights are seen to be only ancient heresies redressed and outfitted in modern terminology.

The case for this new revolution in thinking, this new paradigm that calls for a thorough rethinking of all of our theology in the light of modern science, together with our redefinition of science in order to accommodate dimensions of life not previously included in our definition of authentic science, abounds in poetic language and dramatic claims. Much of this language is indistinguishable from an uncritical embracing of a western version of Monism: the position that all reality is essentially one, that everything in existence is part of everything else in existence, that we are all God, and that God is us.

It is important, therefore, to appreciate the great temptation that such New Age thinking poses for modern people immersed in a scientific world but looking for a means of religious expression. The subtlety of language, the ease of shifting from one perspective to another, the harm of incorporating new visions constructed from pseudoscience and pseudotheology, are all very much a part of the challenge that faces Christians today. When we read in the Christian literature such phrases as the development of the sphere of the spirit expanded by modern science, a new order in which science will enrich our spiritual understanding, a new understanding of spiritual truths based upon discoveries of modern science, or a revitalization of science by appreciation of the spiritual qualities of all of life including the earth itself, we ought to reflect on the similarity between these words and those of New Age advocates. Christians will wish to be very careful that statements of theirs that may sound like these will not be misunderstood to be the same kind of statements being made to support New Age thinking. They will wish to be very careful in maintaining clearly the definitions of authentic scientific and spiritual thinking.

Many of the claims advanced in support of Pattern 6 are supposed to be based on insights gained from the "new science," by which usually relativity and quantum mechanics are intended, as its scientific basis, but in reality they are often little more than *ad hoc* constructions. They speak in mystic terms about the findings of modern science showing the reality of an intrinsic "spirit" in all reality . But as a matter of fact scientific descriptions have not shown any such thing; by their very nature they are intrinsically incapable of giving information about the existence or non-existence of "spirit." In fact, consideration of the effects on human society that have been brought into prominence by scientific and technological developments strongly suggests that the trend is toward depersonalization of human beings, not toward recognition of a non-material spiritual quality.

We examine some specific examples of these claims in the remainder of this chapter. Contrary to frequently-heard claims, physicists, for example, are not telling us that there is an innate "intelligence" present in each atom of matter. There may well be people saying such things, but they are philosophers or theologians (or people who work in physics who are acting as if they were philosophers or theologians) who are mistakenly seeking some kind of apparent foundation in science for their own preconceived faith commitments. They are attempting a grand synthesis of pseudoscience and pseudotheology. Its strongest advocates have adopted the viewpoint of Monism and have then sought to find support in particular interpretations of modern science.

Historic Examples of the Synthesis of Pseudoscience and Pseudotheology

Examples of specific attempts at uniting pseudoscience and pseudotheology are characterized by attitudes that have been expressed in various forms in the past and will undoubtedly reappear in new forms in the future.

Sampling the Universe: Forms of Fatalism. Adherents sample the universe for guidance, a practice as ancient as human records. They claim that it is possible to hold any religious or philosophical position at the same time that one is a faithful adherent of their perspective.

Followers believe that the disposition of our lives is partially or totally determined by forces beyond our control, but that the fate determined by these forces can be known to us through apparently unrelated observations. By knowing our proper place in the universe, we may then take what advantage is possible of this special knowledge to improve our lives and situations in the world.

The forces beyond our control may be wholly impersonal, such as those revealed by astrology, palmistry, reading tea leaves, casting sticks, or coins in I Ching, or various forms of the ancient arts of discerning the future by inspection of the entrails of birds or the livers of animals (hepatoscopy). Or these forces may have aspects of personality as spiritualism, witchcraft and Satanism, which involve religious expressions of their own.

Astrology is an ancient and currently repopularized expression of this type. For most devotees, astrology assumes the form of both a pseudoscience and a pseudotheology. Certainly the biblical assessment of astrology is negative in that historical context (e.g., Daniel 2:27; Isaiah 47:13,14). To argue that the planets have dominant effects on our personality, metabolism, and health, not to mention our success, wealth, sex-life, wish-fulfillment etc., and to couple this argument with the admission that we really don't know how they have this effect, adds up to a position that can be accepted only on faith with little regard for any objective evidence.

Not only is the position non-rational, but it is basically irrational since its conclusions frequently contradict other available evidence. Its popularity is correlatable with an infatuation for the irrational as a reaction against excessive rationalism. When the irrationality of astrology is coupled with the admitted uselessness of daily newspaper horoscopes and the realization of the vast business potential in the astrology area, the conclusion appears inescapable that astrology is a pseudoscience.

When, in addition, the subtle ways are recognized by which faith in astrology replaces faith in the living and loving God, it is also justified to regard it as a pseudoreligion as well as a pseudoscience. Actually, an investigation into the religious perspectives of astrologers usually reveals a dimension of pantheism or mysticism regarding the Unity of all things, of which the planetary motions may be only a relatively unimportant manifestation.

The Key to Health and Success: Neo-Gnosticism. Gnosticism is a philosophic-religious movement that pre-dated Christian times but has continued on in a variety of forms. The main conviction is that "salvation" or "emancipation" comes through knowledge (Greek, *gnosis*) that is able to deliver the special possessor of this knowledge from the constraints of matter.

Adherents claim that their particular founder had insights that prove to be the key to a healthy and successful life. Several well-known groups may be considered to be modern examples of gnosticism. In each case the founder has lived in the past 200 years and has written prolifically. Each stresses in its own way that "salvation" comes through knowledge; particularly knowledge of that arcane key which had been hidden and is hidden still from all who do not participate in the group.

L. Ron Hubbard (1911-) discovered the principles of "dianetics" and his discovery has grown into the Church of Scientology. The teachings and beliefs of Jehovah's Witnesses are based to a large extent on the writings of Charles T. Russell (1851-1916) and his style of biblical interpretation and extrapolation. Christian Science is founded on the book by Mary Baker Eddy (1821-1910), *Science and Health, with Key to the Scriptures*, which dominates Christian Science throughout. Mormonism came into being with Joseph Smith (1805-1844) who claimed to translate the golden plates delivered to him by an angel and produced the "keys" of the Latter Day Saints: *The Book of Mormon, The Doctrine and Covenants*, and *The Pearl of Great Price*.

All of these four groups maintain fairly closed communities and are usually not open to genuine scholarly interchange or debate with either the scientific community or the Christian community. They involve many sincere and well-intentioned people who are desperately seeking for some source of security and assurance in our tension-ridden day. Insistence on the uniqueness of the "key" and the community unfortunately makes it virtually impossible for its adherents to appreciate authentic science and theology rather than their pseudo-counterparts. The obvious hard work of many dedicated devotees can be associated with the conviction that human work is the basis for a person's ultimate position, both in this life and in the life to come.

Becoming One with the Universe: Monism. Since the Eastern religions in their classical forms make little pretense at being scientific, it may not seem appropriate to include them in a discussion centering around pseudoscience, or it may seem presumptuous to treat such religions with their long history and millions of adherents under the category of pseudotheology. On the other hand, there are strong influences of Eastern religious thought on astrology, Scientology, Christian Science and New Age. We are also living in a day in which interest in the Eastern religions is at a new high in the Western world, and many forms do manifest aspects of pseudoscience and pseudotheology.

Not only do the Eastern religions agree with other groups in rejecting the Trinity, the deity of Jesus Christ, and the biblical revelation of reconciliation with a personal God by grace through faith, but they reject even the biblical doctrine of Creation, which is the implicit basis for much of Western thought. Unless this rejection of the doctrine of Creation is recognized, any understanding of Eastern religious thought is impossible. Eastern thought regards acceptance of the reality of matter as the cause of evil, and the effort to preserve the individual as the cause of moral failure. Human beings do evil according to Eastern thought because they are finite, limited, individual and conscious of self as reality. They can be delivered from this bondage only by withdrawing from finiteness, limitations of space and time, handicapping illusions of individuality, and destructive self-consciousness into the great Unity of unindividuated reality. The method of withdrawal usually involves some form of meditation and obedience to discipline: to the acquisition of knowledge, not by the Western method of "study," but by the Eastern method of "satori," sudden nonrational enlightenment.

The biblical doctrine of creation takes seriously the pronouncement of God that the universe, according to His creation purpose, is good, and that the real evil which we see around us today is not caused by our faulty perception, nor is it the inevitable consequence of the structure of the created universe (with its finite, limited, self-conscious individuals) but is the result of human moral rebellion against God. Moral rebellion has little meaning within Eastern thought: unless we perceive that God is us, and that we are God – that all is God and that we are all, we are blinded by the limitations of appearance and fail to grasp the Unity of reality.

Considerable interest has developed in recent years on the borderline between pseudo-science and authentic science with interest in parapsychology, paramedicine, extrasensory perception, clairvoyance, psychokinesis and related phenomena. Although these areas could be investigated purely in terms of natural science (and should be so investigated), they are most frequently tied to a mode of thought derived from the Eastern religions. While disagreeing in detail, they agree in general with the claims of Scientology and Christian Science that a person in full tune with the universe (a "clear," or one united to the divine Principle) has within himself the ability to transcend the limitations of space and time, to burst the bonds of finiteness and individuality, and to propel himself into the All with the ability to exercise the powers thereof. Thus the Christian Scientist argues that only failure to achieve the ultimate apprehension of reality causes Christian Scientists to experience death.

Advocates of these positions often speak of the scientific demonstration of the validity of a spiritual nature to human beings. Although this may sound like good news for the Christian, it is usually a dangerous pitfall. For what the advocates of these positions mean is a spiritual nature of the human being constructed according to human expectations and not in accord with the biblical revelation.   These combinations of pseudoscience and pseudotheology, like the others, are an attempt to construct a religious view over which human beings have control, rather than encountering the religious reality over which God has control.   Christians must be aware, as the biblical record makes clear from the magicians of the court of Pharaoh (Exodus 7:11,22; 8:7) to the Beast of Revelation (Revelation 13:13-15) that simple performance of an extraordinary feat does not authenticate the philosophy and theology of those who perform it.

Other Contexts. Pseudoscience or pseudotheology can arise also in other contexts. Those who profess an authentic Christian position can be entrapped in pseudoscience in order to justify their theology; those who are engaged in authentic science can be entrapped in pseudotheology in order to justify their scientific philosophy.

The Christian, therefore, needs also to be aware that an orthodox theological position does not automatically establish an orthodox scientific understanding, any more than an authentic practice of science guarantees an authentic theological interpretation.   Discrimination is essential.

To attack one engaged in pseudotheology and authentic science (e.g., one who advocates atheistic Evolution*ism* because he is working on biological evolution) by attacking his science is disastrous. So also is the attack on one engaged in pseudoscience and authentic theology (e.g., one who advocates creation-science because he believes in the biblical doctrine of Creation) by attacking his theology.   Christians have frequently been guilty of the former, and non-Christians have often been guilty of the latter.   Hopefully Christians will learn from the past not to fall into the same kind of pitfalls as non-Christians in this matter.

New Age Consciousness

Disillusionment with the failure of science to solve all human problems and a growing awareness of the magnitude of the problems facing the human race in the future, have led in recent years to an outbreak of mysticism. People have tried to find religious comfort in an impersonal world, to establish individual freedom in a world of increasing collective limitations, and to prepare the foundation for that great Utopia of human making, which is always around the corner and never at hand.

Although this move toward mysticism can be viewed as a reaction against scientific rationalism, it often seeks in spite of itself to establish its validity on scientific grounds. In its various forms it presents itself as a grand harmonization of science and religion, a final unification of the whole person. It has a unique appeal to scientists dissatisfied with the fruits of their labors, and to those who are seeking some objective evidence for the validity of their religious faith.

This general movement toward mysticism may well present at one and the same time, therefore, a major move toward the breakdown of the dichotomy between science and Christianity, and a major move toward the denial of every basic concept that Christians hold dear. It seems to offer "the answer." In fact, it is only once more "the problem," an ancient heresy with a modern veneer. It poses a major challenge to Christians in the encounter for human minds in the future.

Such worldviews and perspectives often claim to be new discoveries of the modern age, a new consciousness developing at the present time, or the first step of a bright new future. The dawning of the Age of Aquarius that promised all of these blessings in the '60's has already been forgotten. Advocates of a New Age today speak of the same ideas and the same longing for a universal "harmonic convergence."

Sire [82] gives a good assessment of these movements. He offers three principal critiques. (1) They share with naturalism and pantheistic monism the concept of a closed universe. Ethical issues are therefore largely ignored. If the self is truly in control of the universe, why is anything required except the satisfaction of the self? (2) They reverse the process of desacralization of nature that Christianity accomplished, by once again calling into being the spirit inhabitants of the "inner spaces of the mind."

> While spirit activity has been constant in areas where Christianity has barely penetrated, it has been little reported in the West from the time of Jesus. Christ is said to have driven the spirits from field and stream, and when Christianity permeates a society the spirit world seems to disappear or go into hiding. It is only in the last few decades that the spirits of the woods and rivers, the air and the darkness have been invited back by those who have rejected the claims of Christianity and the God of Abraham, Isaac and Jacob.

(3) They have no inner test for truth, only for patterns of coherence. "Every system is equally valid; it must only pass the test of experience

152   *Putting It All Together*

and experience is private. Taken to its logical conclusion this notion is
a form of epistemological nihilism." A thorough analysis
of New Age concepts is given by Mangalwadi. [96]

With antecedents in such movements as Spiritualism, Theosophy,
and Christian Science, the various aspects of the New Age movement
emphasize the power of mind over matter. Most include the basic
assumption that the world perceived in normal human fashion through
the senses is much less real and certainly less significant than the world
that can be perceived through arriving at altered states of consciousness.
By combining modern psychotherapy with inputs from Eastern
religions, the New Age movement turns inward upon the individual in
order to produce harmony between the individual and his own true self,
nature around him, and finally the cosmic forces of the universe.

Most forms of the movement assume the innate goodness of human
beings, the inevitability of human progress, and the inherent alterability
of human nature. Here finally is a way to change human nature, a way
at the control of each individual and justified by its scientific validity,
rather than a way based upon the authoritarian edict of an ancient
religion.

The field of "psychoenergetics" [94] gives a further illustration of the
underlying concepts of this kind of perspective. (1) Energies exist in
the universe different from any known to date. (2) The aspect of
reality we perceive with our senses is quite limited. Our human view
of reality is an effective jailer, limiting our perspective. Other
dimensions of reality exist beyond those detectable by our five senses,
but human beings have within themselves latent systems for contacting
these other dimensions. (3) The universe can be likened to one great
organism, just becoming aware of itself. At some level of reality
everything is interrelated. We are all part of that one organism. (4)
Time, space and matter can all be changed by human beings. One can
perceive events out of time and out of their locations in space, and
matter can be de-materialized and re-materialized. (5) The world that we
perceive is not an objective world with existence independent of us.
Rather it is a world altered by our intentions. We cannot perceive
reality. (6) We are at the present time developing the final stages of a
new sensory system which will enable us to couple into other
dimensions of the universe.

In his treatment of the meeting of science and spirit in the New Age,
White [93] offers a whole host of "scientific" topics such as
enlightenment, pole shift update, firewalking, UFOs and the search for
higher consciousness, the physics of paranormal phenomena, karma and
reincarnation, Yoga, kundalini, and toward a science of consciousness.

Corresponding "spiritual" topics include the sparkle of the spirit, channeling, gurus, the paranormal in Judaeo-Christian tradition, enlightenment and the martial arts, the Judaeo-Christian tradition and the New Age, the New Age and the second coming of Christ, and the meaning of the Christ.   Still, White represents himself as a moderate, turning away from the more esoteric aspects of New Age.

> In its worst aspect, the movement is a grab bag of superficial, trivial, irrational, and even menacing ideas, attitudes, beliefs, products, and services, all of which amount to a sad caricature and prostitution of the real thing. There is a dark side to the New Age movement . .. crystal healing, aura cleansing, the Bermuda Triangle, gods from outer space, the hollow Earth theory, chakrabalancing, the Harmonic Convergence, financial "abundance" games, and pyramid prophecies.

His total revision of Christian theology, however, is part of his overall worldview.   Although Jesus was an historical person, Christ is a transpersonal condition to which we must all someday come. The witness of Christian theology "that Jesus was the only Son of God, that he incarnated as a human in order to die on the Cross in a substitutionary act as a penalty for our sins, and thereby save the world ... is a sad caricature, a pale reflection of the true story." "The Second Coming is a false concept and an unwarranted doctrine."

> So although Jesus of Nazareth is popularly called the Christ, it is more accurate to say that *the Christ was Jesus*, just as the Christ was also Gautama, Krishna, Lao Tzu, and other avatars, sages and saviors of humanity who realized their true Self. None of them, I dare say, would claim to be the Christ exclusively.

Such a New Age approach leaves us with very little of either authentic science or authentic Christian theology.

The Influence of Modern Physics

Philosophically minded scientists trained in modern physics often seek to find in interpretations of physics a clue to the worldview that leads to New Age consciousness. This connection does not receive much public exposure, except almost at the level of caricature, because it is difficult to discuss on a popular level.   On the other hand, it is this aspect of the subject that has considerable appeal for scientists with a bent toward believing in paranormal phenomena.

Influence of Human Consciousness?   One starting point is a paper by the distinguished physicist Eugene P. Wigner, [97, 98] who addresses himself to a basic problem in the interpretation of quantum mechanics. He concludes that not only does the body influence the mind, as is generally conceded, but also that the mind influences the body. In a day when psychosomatic illnesses are generally accepted, this statement is not very revolutionary, but it is coupled with another by Wigner, "The second argument supporting the existence of an influence of the consciousness on the physical world is based on the observation that we do not know of any phenomenon in which one object is influenced by another without exerting an influence thereon." Wigner therefore urges a search for instances in which it is observed that consciousness alters the laws of nature.

What lies behind Wigner's paper is a problem in the interpretation of the mathematical formalism of quantum mechanics. In conventional quantum mechanics the total state function of a system is represented as a combination of possible state functions for the system. The act of measurement somehow selects one of these states as the result of the measurement.   The question is: how does the act of measurement select one of the possible states and make it the observed state?

As a specific illustration of these somewhat abstract concepts, consider the famous case of "Schroedinger's cat." Imagine a living cat in a cage together with a device that can release poisonous gas as the result of a chance process The total state function of the system for future time (according to quantum mechanics) consists of a function describing the state of a living cat plus a second function describing the state of a dead cat.   Each of these two functions expresses the probability of the state being described depending on a variety of local conditions. Sometime later we make a measurement: we look in the cage.   We see either a living cat or a dead cat.   We conclude that the act of measurement has "somehow" selected just one of the possible states in the total state function.

In the "traditional" interpretation of von Neumann [99], the act of measurement causes the state function to collapse to the single state given by the measurement. The state function itself does not represent reality but only provides a means of making statistical predictions about reality.   Wigner, on the other hand, proposed that it is the entry of the measurement signal into the human consciousness of the observer that selects one of the many possible outcomes.

The Scientist as Part of the Experiment.   Another effect of modern physics has been to demolish the classical separation between the observer and the observed. The Heisenberg Indeterminacy Principle states that a scientist cannot simultaneously determine, for example, the position and the velocity of an electron. This conclusion arises from quantum mechanics itself and not only from some experimental limitation on the measurement. It is not always possible to view the scientist as an independent observer, whose observation of the system leaves it unaffected. Rather it has become necessary to incorporate the scientist and his observation into the total system being considered; the scientist has become an integral part of the experiment which he is performing.

If this is true, then why is it that we are able to live our ordinary, everyday lives without paying attention to it? The answer appears to be that the forces that control the physical world are so different in magnitude and range that there is very little overlap between the domain of one force and that of another. For the motion of the planets, gravitational forces dominate; for the chemical behavior of atoms, forces between atoms dominate; for the properties of the nucleus, nuclear forces dominate. It is this separation of physical forces into regions of influence that permits formulation of physical laws in such simple forms. A remote body in the universe does exert a finite gravitational attraction on my body, but the magnitude of that attraction is so small that it is totally negligible compared to the effects of other forces.

Philosophical Monism. .Physicists speak of four major forces: the gravitational, the weak, the electromagnetic, and the strong, in order of increasing strength. Both the gravitational force and the electromagnetic force are in principle of infinite range. Both the weak and the strong forces arise from studies of the nucleus; the strong force has a range of 10^{-13} cm, and the weak force has an even shorter range by about a factor of 100. One of the challenges of modern physics has been to develop a unified theory that would encompass all four of these forces.

Physicists speculate that at a sufficiently small scale three of these forces may be the same: the electromagnetic, weak and strong forces. When the universe is perceived as being describable by a series of different forces with different ranges, then separation between phenomena is a natural philosophical correlate. But when the universe is perceived as being describable by one basic set of forces, then support of philosophical monism can be claimed. At its most profound level, the universe is a unity of interaction, occurring among all levels through a fundamental interrelatedness that our classical view of physics with its domains of different forces has obscured until the present time.

Add to this the additional concept of "mind" as a kind of "cosmic force" operable at a fundamental level, and then it becomes "obvious" how mind can control matter by operating at this fundamental level to change gravitational, weak, electromagnetic and strong forces of "everyday" physics.

Link with Eastern Religion. Several authors [100, 101] have drawn conclusions from thinking like this to argue that it is possible to produce an interpretation of modern physics through the concepts of Eastern religions, in fact that it is only the Eastern religions that are adequate to such a task.

Arguing from the unity and interrelatedness of all phenomena and the intrinsically dynamic nature of the universe, Capra [100] suggests that "quantum theory forces us to see the universe not as a collection of physical objects, but rather as a complicated set of relations between various parts of a unified whole." This monistic conclusion seems to Capra to fit beautifully with the views of Eastern philosophers. The concept of the universe in ceaseless motion that comes out of modern physics, Capra sees as similar to that symbolized by the dance of Shiva, revered by Hindus.

An Assessment. Perhaps it is possible to see a parallel between the historical development of the theory of evolution and this modern twist arising from physics. Evolutionary theory can also be interpreted as a striving toward "monism" – a common origin for all things, in contrast to a series of unrelated multiple origins. If a series of unrelated origins is considered philosophically essential for harmonization with the biblical account of creation, then evolution with its thrust toward monism becomes a threat to Christianity. But there appears to be no reason why such a threat should exist.

So in this present development, if a monistic view of the phenomena of the natural world is viewed as being intrinsically anti-biblical and anti-Christian, it will cause profound difficulties in attempts to treat scientific and biblical thought in an integrated manner. A fundamental question may be raised, however. Does a monistic view of the origin of natural forces really constitute support for a monistic religious view any more than it supports the biblical view of the one God who creates and sustains? Isn't the choice of religious implication derived from quite nonscientific inputs and not impelled by the scientific model at all?

The answer must be yes unless there is some reason to believe that Christianity leads to the conclusion that all natural forces cannot by their very nature be scientifically describable in a single unified mode; there appears to be no such reason.

Nor is there any reason why the acceptance of the possibility for a common origin for all natural forces should lead one to believe that this violates the practical macroscopic observation of separation between force domains. It is common experience in modern physics that one can treat the radioactive decay of a large number of decaying atoms quite deterministically, even though the scientific description of the process for a particular atom is completely a chance description.

The major question is not whether all forces can be described in a unified field theory, but whether or not there exists some hitherto unknown force of quite different nature from the four forces known today. On the latter question there appears to be considerable difficulty in obtaining relevant specific evidence, and no unambiguous evidence for such a force of "mind" is yet at hand.

Appeal for Christians. Some Christians highly value scientific support for their religious convictions. While, on the one hand they commonly reject scientific descriptions that appear to conflict with their theological descriptions, they are also so much a part of the scientific age that they value demonstrations by "true science" that their religious picture is true. Unfortunately they are often so eager for scientific support that they embrace pseudoscience without critical evaluation and sometimes play havoc with their basic position in the long run.

This appeal of what is presently on the borderline of science and pseudoscience with strong leaning toward pseudotheology, is one of the major dangers of these developments for the Christian. Many Christians delight to embrace the evidence that these phenomena testify against a materialistic interpretation of the universe, in the conviction that through these phenomena we are getting evidence for biblical spirituality. They quickly translate this into meaning that we have scientific evidence for the existence of soul and spirit.

Whatever phenomena may or may not exist, whatever mystic energy field may or may not be associated with human mind, one fact remains: none of these phenomena occurs without the participation of human beings and human beings are material creatures. One might as well argue (and some have!) that electromagnetic or gravitational fields are evidence of a spiritual realm. There is no evidence of any kind for the power of human "mind" without the presence of a living human brain. The claims of the parapsychologist who extrapolates into pseudoreligious interpretations are far more compatible with Christian Science than they are with biblical Christianity.

Christians often find themselves in a curious dilemma. Should they side with the mystics of the new consciousness because they welcome their belief in the supernatural – along with many other beliefs that the Christian denies? Or should they side with the humanists who deny the existence of God and the supernatural, but seem to have a level head on their shoulders when it comes to being skeptical about mystical esoterica? Not surprisingly Christians must do neither in spite of the strong pulls that they may experience.

Philosophical Implications of Quantum Mechanics

Because of the common claim that quantum mechanics gives rise to a revolutionary philosophical perspective on the universe that causes us to change our entire way of thinking, it is appropriate that we consider what may seem to be a somewhat arcane subject at slightly greater length. In particular, it is often claimed that quantum mechanics has shown that there is no objective reality. Therefore, we each create our own reality. Griffiths [102, 103] has given a very useful brief summary of the different ways of drawing philosophical implications from quantum mechanics.

One of the most significant features about the interpretation of quantum mechanics for the Christian to realize is that, although scientists generally agree on how to use quantum mechanics in the pursuit of their research, they do not agree on its philosophical interpretation. A mixture of humility and common sense should warn non-specialists in quantum mechanics to be extremely cautious about making dogmatic interpretations on their own, when the scientists themselves are still having troubles.

There are today four basic philosophical schemes that have been proposed for the interpretation of quantum mechanics, which yield quite different philosophical conclusions from one another.

Hidden Variables. In one interpretation, it is argued that our present description via quantum mechanics is incomplete, and that appearances of chance and probability at a fundamental level are only present limitations. There is a set of variables hidden from us and underlying the phenomena of interest to us, which we do not yet know, but which when known will enable us once more to give a totally deterministic view of nature.

In keeping with his religious aversion to indeterminacy in nature, expressed by his famous statement, "God does not play dice," this was the position taken by Einstein. [104, 105] The kind of approach supported by Einstein, known as "local hidden variables theory" was apparently shown to be indefensible by experiments done in Paris in 1982 [106, 107], in which experimental results agreed with those predicted by standard quantum mechanics, but disagreed with those predicted by local hidden variables theory.

Another kind of hidden variables theory also exists, known as "nonlocal hidden variables," and advocated by Bohm. [108-110] This form has been constructed to give the same results as quantum mechanics, and at the present time there is no way to distinguish between nonlocal hidden variables theories and standard quantum mechanics itself. As long as the nonlocal hidden variables theories remain untestable, they do not really enter into the meaningful realm of scientific theories. Present trends do not seem to favor such a development.

The Orthodox Interpretation. Calculations in quantum mechanics involve the calculation of the spatial and time variation of a mathematical function, called a wavefunction and denoted by the Greek symbol psi, ψ. In the "orthodox interpretation," accepted by the majority of physicists (primarily for historical reasons), the wavefunction ψ can be used to calculate the probability of results to be obtained by measurements. The wavefunction ψ does not represent physical reality when measurements are not being made. Some adherents of the "orthodox interpretation" stretch this to conclude that there is no reality between measurements – that all we can meaningfully talk about is the results of measurements.

It is a small step from this conclusion to the position that has received the most popular press: namely, that the world does not exist except when it is being measured, that in a sense the very nature of reality is determined by what we choose to observe. We create reality when we decide to make a measurement. It is important for us to realize that such a conclusion is possible if the interpreter chooses a philosophical frame of reference compatible with it (just as it is possible to interpret modern physics in terms of analogies to Eastern religion), but it is by no means necessary, and therefore is not binding on everyone.

Splitting Universes. A third proposed interpretation of quantum mechanics [111] is radically different, in that it proposes that there is a precise correspondence between the wavefunction ψ in a non-interacting system and the physical reality it is describing. The system to be considered includes the measurement apparatus and the observer. With the passage of time, the system may develop from one state of affairs into two or more quite different states of affairs which are mutually exclusive.

A standard example is provided by "Schroedinger's cat" as described above. In a quantum mechanical description, one finds one part of the wavefunction ψ_{live} describing the live cat, while another part ψ_{dead} describing the dead cat. What is the physical situation in the box at a later time? The orthodox interpretation would respond that the act of measurement, e.g., looking inside the box, will "collapse" the wavefunction so that only one state is measured with a certain calculable probability: either we see a live cat or a dead cat, but not both. But the "splitting universe" interpretation proposes that the whole wavefunction describes physical reality, and that when the chance process releases the poisonous gas, it "splits" the universe into two equally real universes, one inhabited by a live cat and the other inhabited by a dead cat. This kind of thing is going on continually, producing a very large number of universes, each of which is different from the others and is continually splitting into still others. This interpretation truly deserves the appellation "mind-blowing"!

Consistent Histories. Griffiths [102] has proposed a fourth interpretation of quantum mechanics, designed to overcome some of the objective and subjective problems associated with the other interpretations. This interpretation applies only to closed systems, including the measurement apparatus and the observer, and thus avoids the "measurement step" which characterizes the orthodox interpretation. Unlike the "splitting universes" interpretation, it does not attribute direct physical significance to the wavefunction ψ, but regards it as a useful mathematical tool to calculate probabilities as a function of time of ordered sequences of events that satisfy a mathematical condition of consistency. If a sequence of events satisfies the consistency condition, then it has a probability; if it does not, then it is "meaningless" and can be given no meaning.

While providing an apparent alternative between the orthodox and the splitting universe interpretations, the consistent history interpretation is characterized by two features that might be considered problematic. (1) The description it gives is probabilistic instead of deterministic. Although there are still some who feel that there are profound philosophical or even theological problems with this state of affairs, there does not appear to be any ultimate necessity for this to be the case. (2) Classical logic cannot be applied when "quantum phenomena" are being considered. Although this may also seem troublesome to classicists, it does not appear to pose any crucial issues. We can accept that classical physics does not adequately describe all of the features of the real world; we should be open to the possibility that classical logic is also not adequate for the task.

We can be seriously misled by our efforts to describe quantum mechanical effects using words from common experience that do not apply. The question of where the photon comes from when an electron drops from an excited state to the ground state of the hydrogen atom, for example, has no answer. To get meaningful answers from a scientific model, one must ask questions consistent with the nature of that model. If we insist that quantum mechanics must supply the same kind of answers as classical physics, we have made the decision that classical question-answering must be normative.

The world of electrons, protons, photons etc. exists and behaves (as far as we know today) the way that quantum mechanics describes. Our perception of the total world structure may well include the consequences of our actions in the ways that quantum mechanics describe. But the nature of this total structure is quite independent of us.

There is a qualitative difference between the classical and quantum worlds. This difference must be accepted as indicating the actual properties of the natural world at the quantum level, just as the universal constancy of the speed of light is accepted as indicating the actual properties of the natural world at the relativistic level. There is no known scientific reason today that would cause one to deviate from this position. These issues are described in a helpful way by Polkinghorne. [22]

At the conclusion of his review of interpretations of quantum mechanics, Griffiths offers the following advice,

> In the meantime it is, in my opinion, inadvisable for amateurs to rush in and try to erect important philosophical or theological structures on top of the shifting sands. I wish the situation were otherwise, but I am convinced that genuine progress in working out the philosophical implications of quantum mechanics will have to wait for the physicists to do some more work to put their (our) house in order.

At the very least, Christians should be aware that the visions of the New Age are not based upon the sure foundations of modern science. Still, our thinking in the future may well be challenged by developing interpretations of modern physics.

There are other tantalizing issues raised by the apparent consequences of quantum mechanics applied to the observable world. Polkinghorne [22], for example, discusses briefly the Einstein-Podolsky-Rosen effect.

> Once two quantum entities have interacted with each other, the one retains a power to influence the other, however far apart they may subsequently separate. A measurement on one of the particles produces a collapse of their joint wavefunction which has an immediate consequence for the other particle....
> The quantum world has its own nature of reality. ... it is by no means clear that one would have the kind of situation described by the wilder flights of an alleged "observer-created reality." The more modest phrase of an 'observer-influenced reality' would be a more appropriate account.

In fact, Polkinghorne invokes the unexpected, difficult to believe, inconsistent with "common sense" concepts derived from quantum mechanical descriptions of the world as a kind of insight.

> People sometimes feel that in a scientific age the doctrines of
> traditional Christian theology need remodeling and simplifying to
> bring them into line with "what an educated person might be
> expected to be able to accept."

Perhaps it is the very unexpectedness, mystery and "intellectual
profundity" of the traditional Christian doctrines of a tripersonal God,
the incarnation, the atonement of the cross, the resurrection, and the
new life in Christ, which correspond most clearly to the surprising
kinds of implications in our description of the natural world now being
suggested by quantum mechanics.

Our living in the future will be challenged by efforts to read new
social guidelines out of interpretations of other branches of modern
science as well.

Environmental Concerns

Attempts to develop models to guide Christian response to
environmental issues have frequently taken in recent years some kind of
New Age flavor.   The general argument is that the traditional biblical
view of the human/environment interaction is too human-centered, too
concentrated on human authority over nature, and too missing in the
crucial nature of the interactions that occur between human beings and
the rest of the created world in which they live.   The question naturally
arises, "What is the intrinsic value for the natural world and how does it
relate to human values?"   Three major models exist with fairly direct
consequences if consistently followed.

Three Major Models . In the first model the natural world has value
only because of its usefulness to human beings.   Nature is violent and
dangerous, and it is the job of human beings to tame it.   This can be a
fairly broad view, including not simply various forms of environmental
exploitation, but even efforts to preserve the environment based only on
the conviction that conservation is in the best selfish interest of human
beings.   Of course the natural world does have *a* value because of its
relationship to human beings, but the position that this is the only
source of its value – like the position that the individual has value only
because society gives it – is ultimately insufficient to meet the
requirements of a total worldview. This is the view attributed to
scientific reductionism and an indifference to the natural world as having
value in itself.

In the second model, often advanced in direct reaction to the first, the
natural world is considered to have the same value as human beings.

Usually advanced in the pantheistic framework of Eastern religions, this view attempts to remove the lordship of human beings over the natural world by identifying human beings with the natural world and frequently divinizing or spiritualizing both. Although the divinization of the natural world might be conceived as raising it to identification with human beings, the final effect is to dehumanize human beings to the level of the natural world.

Neither the view that exalts human beings over nature or that reduces human beings to nature is the view presented by the biblical record. It is recognized that nature has intrinsic value as nature because of Creation; a tree has value as a tree because God made it as a tree. The value of nature to human beings is then a second source of value in addition to this intrinsic component. Second, it is recognized that on the level of creation, human beings are part of the natural world and cannot ever forget this interdependence, but as the only creatures made in the image of God, human beings are also distinct from nature and responsible for its care before God. Discussions of these issues can be found by DeWitt et al. [112] and by Schaeffer [113], who dramatically expresses the essence in the words,

> But I must be clear that I am not loving the tree or whatever is standing in front of me, for a pragmatic reason. It will have a pragmatic *result*, the very pragmatic results that the men involved in ecology are looking for. ... When we have learned this – the Christian view of nature – then there can be a real ecology; beauty will flow, psychological freedom will come, and the world will cease to be turned into a desert. Because it is right, on the basis of the whole Christian system – which is strong enough to stand it all, because it is true – as I stand and face the buttercup, I say, "Fellow creature, fellow *creature*, I won't walk on you. We are both creatures together."

Major Biblical Themes. <u>Creation</u>. The earth is a gift given in trust to us by God. The end purpose of the creation account is the appearance of human beings, called to be God's stewards (caretakers, deputies, or custodians) over the earth. The earth belongs to God; he appoints men and women as his stewards over it. The law of Leviticus and Deuteronomy reveals God's concern for the land. The concept of ownership is revised - we do not own in some absolute sense, but we care for it (or abuse it) for God. "The land shall not be sold in perpetuity, for the land is mine..." (Lev. 25:23). The moral faithfulness of God's people is linked with the condition of the earth in Hosea 4:1-3 and Isaiah 24:4-6. The created order will share in the redemption won by Christ (Romans 8:19-22).

Stewardship. The concept of environmental stewardship expresses our responsibility for the care of all things in the created universe that God has given into our trust (Genesis 1:26-30): living creatures, land, water, air, energy, natural resources - everything that characterizes our "Spaceship Earth." [114]   We've lost the sense of global stewardship because we think that everything *belongs* to us. Of course, if it really belongs to us, there is no meaning in stewardship; for a steward is one who serves another to whom all things truly belong.

The Bible teaches that *stewards are required to be faithful.* Stewards are not necessarily called to be *successful* , but rather to be faithful now. Stewards are not called to solve all the problems, but rather to be faithful where they are.   Such faithful stewardship is a personal commitment.   We are called to live in this way not only because it is effective, not only because it works, but primarily because we desire to live in the way that we believe God wants us to.   Stewards are not responsible for all the master's work - but we are responsible for *what we can do.*

Our weakness is not always that we don't know what we should do. The weakness is in our being willing to do what we already know we should do. This is essentially a religious problem. The power to break the patterns of selfishness, waste, unconcern, and exploitation can come ultimately only through a restored relationship with God in Jesus Christ.

It is also a complex problem. Simple answers, simple causes, simple motivations, simple solutions are almost always false and illusory when we are dealing with the problems of the biological, sociological and spiritual aspects of human life on this planet. The need is for informed, dedicated and creative thought and action. Although we are now daily being forced to change our perspective, we have – one might say from the beginning of the human race until the recent past – lived as if the earth were not finite, as if it were so big that it remained constant and unaffected by our presence and our activity. We have thought of ourselves as living *on* the earth, but we have not reckoned with the fact that this kind of separation is to a large extent a fiction: our lives and the environmental welfare of the earth are bound together.

The New Age Perspective on Environmentalism . Convinced that the traditional framework of the biblical view is incapable of dealing with the environmental issues now facing the human race, and searching for new stimuli for dedicated and responsible action, some have been led into the search for a new worldview that will, in their opinion, be capable of sustaining their goals. They have turned to the results of modern science and have attempted to construct from these results a new view of the environment – a view that is often surprisingly like the old views of animism and pantheism.   In the framework of Pattern 6 they have elaborated many views expressed in dramatic and visionary poetic language to describe the new situation when science and religion are joined together in one environmentally supportive   role.   Upon inspection, however, it turns out that the major fault with these claims is that they are simply not true - they do not express valid and necessary conclusions derived from science, but instead often express conclusions that scientific results contradict.   To be more specific, we consider a few examples.

Rowthorn [115] has many valuable comments to make about the role of the Christian with respect to environmental issues.   But her belief that the desacralization of nature has led to our present environmental problems, leads her to call strongly for a "resacralization" of nature.   If by this is meant that we need to see nature as a creation of God and thereby invested with intrinsic value, well and good; but if it means that we really need to resacralize nature so that we perceive natural objects and creatures as being identified with God himself, we have moved down the path toward pantheism in our effort to preserve environmental concern.   The theology becomes clouded with such questions as   "Can we evolve spiritually and emotionally in time to control the overwhelming evil that our advanced and rational intellect has created?"

Dowd [116] also calls for us to see the divine in everything that lives, and focuses on what he considers to be a "new cosmology" arising from the findings of modern science that enables us to save the material world by declaring it to really be spiritual.   The claims for this "new cosmology" are not rooted in scientific or theological reality. Modern science simply does not provide the insights or results that Dowd calls for.

It is not true that "scientists have come to see that all matter has a mysterious, psychic/spiritual dimension."   Modern science has shown us, as indicated above, that the basic descriptions currently available for the very small and the very fast do not correspond to our common sense expectations from macroscopic experience.   But there is absolutely no connection with a "psychic/spiritual dimension."

It is not true that "physicists are beginning to tell us that every atom of the universe has an inner intelligence which is non-material and ultimately unknowable."   There is absolutely no basis for such a claim from modern quantum mechanics.

It is not true that "the earth is alive and we are the Earth's reflexive consciousness." Such a statement is fantasy.

It is not true that "there is nothing in existence that does not have subjective experience."

It is not true that "every being, from individual atoms, to individual persons, to individual solar systems, to individual galaxies, has a non-material center, an inner intelligence." There appears to be here the usual problems associated with preductionism (as we called it earlier) in which the reality of life, consciousness, intelligence at the more complex levels of living creatures including human beings, is attributed to the existence of these qualities in the atomic matter of which we are composed.

Some of this "new perspective" also expresses itself in theological statements that lack basic support. It is not true that "this cosmology can be understood as an integral part of what the church has traditionally anticipated as 'the second coming of Christ.'" It is not true that "ignorance, not evil, seems to be the root of the problem." It is not true that the commandments of God are found "through empirical observation of the universe." It is not true that "Nature is the primary Bible." As far as ecological responsibility is concerned, Dowd is led to claim, "We are neither stewards, nor caretakers, nor anything else that assumes we are separate from nature. We have no existence apart from the living Earth. We *are* the Earth."

Finally we see the attempt to enliven the environmental movement by attributing personal life to the earth itself. Indeed the earth is an entity that has on its surface an intricate and interacting ecosystem with all kinds of plant and animal life. But the effort has been made to treat the earth as if it were a kind of Earth Mother, a living personal organism. Lovelock [117] proposes the Gaia hypothesis, where Gaia is the name for the earth viewed as a living organism. "Gaia is a religious as well as a scientific concept ... I have tried to show that God and Gaia, theology and science, even physics and biology are not separate but a single way of thought." Berry [118] joins in the same kind of expression, "One of the finest moments in our new sensitivity to the natural world is our discovery of the earth as a living organism .. Personal designation of the earth as Gaia is no longer unacceptable in serious discussion."

In many ways such extreme advocates of Pattern 6 proclaim the arrival of a new age, but instead attempt to roll back the years to a day of animism and pantheism, when people worshipped the planets – to an old day indeed.

Chapter 10

Pattern 7: Christian Theology and Science: Complementary Insights

Finally we come to the last in this sequence of seven possible patterns for relating science and faith.   With its appropriate limitations and openness, it seems to have the most consistent relationship to the characteristics of authentic science and authentic Christian theology. [5, 7, 9, 19, 20, 22, 24, 119-122] It is the perspective of complementarity – the holding of both scientific and theological descriptions together, while recognizing their differences and yet appreciating their similarities, with the effort to integrate them into one whole picture that does justice to them both as different insights into the nature of reality.   Effective complementarity demands insights from authentic science and authentic theology, rejects inputs from pseudoscience and pseudotheology, and proceeds to the task of integrating these insights with caution and discernment.

The description of Pattern 7 is given by: *Science and theology tell us different kinds of things about the same things. Each, when true to its own authentic capabilities, provides us with valid insights into the nature of reality from different perspectives. It is the task of individuals and communities of individuals to integrate these two types of insights to obtain an adequate and coherent view of reality.*

With its definition in terms of providing different kinds of insights from science and theology, Pattern 7 differs from Patterns 1, 2, 4, 5, and 6, all of which are based on the assumption that science and theology give us the same kinds of information. While Pattern 7 agrees with Pattern 3 that science and theology give us different kinds of insights, it differs crucially from Pattern 3 in insisting that the insights obtained from science and theology are insights into the *same* reality.

What Complementarity is Not

The complementarity perspective of Pattern 7 is so often misunderstood that it is worthwhile to state clearly what it is *not* before proceeding with our discussion of what it is. Some of these points will be elaborated further in the following discussion.

It is important to recognize that complementarity is not simply a matter of preference, as though there might well be a better choice than complementarity. It is a matter of necessity in many areas of communication. Complementarity is not a cop-out, but an effort to respect the integrity of different, authentic insights into the nature of reality.

Not Compartmentalization . Complementarity is not equivalent to the compartmentalization of Pattern 3 (Chapter 6). Unlike Pattern 3, which simply puts the insights from science and theology into two separate airtight compartments, never to interact, the complementarity of Pattern 7 brings the insights from science and theology together and seeks to understand how both can be a faithful and consistent insight into the same reality. This is a very common misinterpretation of complementarity. Moreland [53], for example, describes complementarity as

Science and theology are non-interacting, complementary approaches to the same reality that adopt very different standpoints, ask and answer very different kinds of questions, employ very different epistemic attitudes (e.g., objectivity and logical neutrality in science, personal involvement and commitment in theology), and /or are constituted by very different language games.

Now the major part of this definition could be accepted as describing complementarity insofar as complementarity has respect for the possibilities and limitations of authentic science and of authentic Christian theology. But the implication that complementary approaches are non-interacting is not a description of complementarity, but of compartmentalization.

It is true that a complementary set of descriptions can each be totally complete on its own level of description without leaving gaps on that level for other disciplines to fill, and without demanding some kind of conflict. For example, it is conceivable that we might be able to describe the physics, chemistry and biology of the origin of life from non-living matter under suitable conditions without leaving any necessary gaps *in our scientific description* for the intervention of God in ways that cannot be described scientifically. We would then understand our whole scientific description (whether in the form of determinism or chance) as our description of God's activity in bringing life into being.

This in no way diminishes the basic biblical revelation of the role of God in the creation of life, nor of insights into the nature, value and meaning of life that we obtain from Christian theology, nor does it demand that there must be gaps in our scientific description in order for the theological description to be valid. Complementarity recognizes that valid insights from science and theology both deal with the same reality and must be integrated. It does not hold the two different insights to be totally unrelated without interaction or effects on one another.

Science and Theology are Not Mutually Exclusive. Complementarity does not claim that no aspects of theology are or should be affected by science, or that no aspects of science are or should be affected by theology. It is indeed maintained that science is incapable of providing the foundation for ethics, for example, or of providing us with knowledge about the relationship between God and human beings, and that theology does not generally provide us with mechanistic information about the "how" questions of the physical universe. But it is also freely recognized, as discussed earlier, that the form of theological models can and has been affected by growth in scientific understanding of the way in which God has actually created the world, rather than simply forming these models using cultural frameworks of the past. And it is also freely recognized that one's choice of problems in the physical sciences, or even one's choice of an integrating, descriptive model in the more culturally related sciences of psychology or sociology, where worldview can play as large a role as actual research results, can be affected by theological insights.

Not an Acceptance of Contradiction. Complementarity is not a thoughtless acceptance of contradiction, paradox, or dualism. It is a recognition of those circumstances where two or more different but valid insights are available to describe and understand something beyond the abilities of known models to encompass. If it is possible by more complete understanding to resolve the paradox, then this is the course of action that must be taken. But if this is not possible in a particular case, then the full benefits of integrating complementary insights are needed.

When Complementarity is Necessary

Some of the problems associated with complementarity have been described by Haas. [123, 124] It is interesting that there are not that many choices for dealing with the broad aspects of relating science and Christian theology. We have broken them down into seven patterns in this book, but one might argue that on a simpler level there are just three essential perspectives: (1) a *conflict* perspective, in which it is believed that science and theology tell us the same kinds of things about the same things (Patterns 1, 2, 4, 5, 6 in this book), (2) a *compartmentalization* perspective, in which it is believed that science and theology tell us different kinds of things about different things (Pattern 3 in this book), and (3) an approach that is based on the claim that science and theology tell us different things about the same reality without inducing conflict or contradiction – the current *complementarity* position of Pattern 7. The appropriate response to complementarity is integration.

It is essential to note that it is complementary *descriptions* that are the focus of attention. Scientific descriptions are valid when scientific categories and methods of description are used, and theological descriptions are valid when theological categories and methods of description are used. What should be the relationship between two descriptions in order for them to be called complementary? And what does this mean?

The application of the term "complementary" to two descriptions stems from the fact that any description of what is unknown must be given in terms of what is known, by telling what the unknown is like. It is in this sense that scientific and theological models can be recognized as similes, metaphors, or allegories, as described by Poythress. [125-127]

If to the request, "Describe an apple for me," from one who has never seen an apple, I reply, "An apple is usually red like a cherry, juicy like a peach, and firm like a pear," I have used three similes. Each gives a partial insight into the reality of an apple but no one separately, or even all three together, gives a totally accurate description of an apple. By knowing all three similes I know more about an apple than by knowing only one or two of them. If to these similes I add, "An apple is like a Japanese persimmon except that its inside is white rather than pink," I would know still more about an apple, while still not knowing exactly what an apple *is*. Such similar descriptions could be multiplied many times over, giving a greater and greater awareness of what an apple is, but never converging on a totally accurate statement of what an apple is. Descriptions that give partial insights (with limited accuracy, exactness, or correspondence with reality) may be said to be *complementary*.

Why do we give such complementary descriptions? There are two fundamental reasons. The everyday example of the apple illustrates both of these reasons. In the first place our descriptions are complementary because we are forced to use similes, metaphors, or allegories to describe the unknown in terms of the known; such metaphorical descriptions are bound to be complementary. In the second place each of our descriptions focuses on a different range of categories of the apple: its color, its reaction with our taste sensors, its feeling to the touch, and its general appearance and texture. Since each description arises out of a different category, it again follows that their contributions to our understanding must be additive, and that the individual descriptions can be properly viewed as complementary one to the other. We consider next a few other illustrative examples.

Limitations on the Known to Describe the Unknown. The first reason that it becomes necessary for us to use complementary descriptions is that we do not have the needed "tools" among the known to adequately describe the unknown with a single model or description. Reality in all its complexity is not apprehensible by the human mind in many cases. Thus we often find it both expedient and necessary to use more than one simile or metaphor to give a number of possible different perspectives on the unknown, providing a more complete representation than a single simile alone. As in the old story of the blind men describing an elephant, we know more completely what an elephant is like if we know that it is like a tree (its leg), a rope (its tail), a sail (its ear), a wall (its side), and a hose (its trunk), than if we had only one or two of these similes at our disposal (yet is clear that we are a long way from knowing by this process what an elephant actually is). Such helpful and necessary multiple similes can properly be considered to be complementary to one another.

Scientific descriptions commonly consist of models of the world being observed and described. These models do not describe the world completely or fully accurately (they certainly do not in any sense fully explain the world). But we believe (as a matter of personal scientific faith) that the better the model is, i.e., the more it corresponds to our perceptions of the world when tested, and allows us to accurately predict new perceptions that can be tested, the more completely it images for us what reality is like (never necessarily what reality is). Such models are always changing as we gain new information and as we formulate new pictures and ways of looking at things more in agreement with our new information. Particular models give particular insights into the nature of reality, but they of necessity convey partial and incomplete truth. It follows that more than one model is needed in the effort to encompass the full dimensions of reality.

This kind of complementary description usually arises in the context of science and Christian theology when descriptions are selected from the same area as the phenomenon to be described. Thus scientific similes or metaphors are used to describe scientific phenomena, and theological similes and metaphors are used to describe theological phenomena.

The typical example from within science is the description of an electron as a particle, and the description of an electron as a wave. The concept "particle" and the concept "wave" are drawn from our macroscopic experiences. When we attempt to apply these macroscopic concepts to the microscopic world of the electron, we are enabled to say what an electron *is like*, but not what an electron *is*.   Which model is applicable depends on the kind of experiment we subject the electrons to.   When we do experiments involving the motion of electrons in an electric field in vacuum, for example, then we can say that electrons behave like particles.   When we do experiments involving the motion of electrons through slits or involving diffraction from crystals, then we can say that electrons behave like waves. If we could invent a sufficiently ingenious model that would transcend the macroscopic concepts of "particle" and "wave," then we *might* be able to resolve the complementarity between "particle" and "wave" descriptions by arriving at a model in categories more faithful to the properties of an actual electron.   This is the kind of achievement reached at least partially through quantum mechanics.

Biblical inspiration takes account of the limitations imposed by the necessity to describe the unknown in terms of the known and secures for us the assurance that the models so presented do indeed provide us with reliable partial insights into reality.   Consider, for example, the persistently difficult issue of describing the relationship between God's sovereignty and human responsibility (or between predestination and free will, or between determinism and free will as applied to human beings). [128]   Theological models provide us with useful and partially valid insights as long as we remember their limited nature (their complementary character).

Just as the question, "What is an electron like?" cannot be answered without knowing the answer to the correlated question, "What kind of experiment are you talking about?", so also the question, "What does the Bible teach on the relationship between God's sovereignty and human responsibility?" can be answered only if we know the context of the question. If the question is, "Does God have to wait for human beings to act before he can accomplish his purpose?" the answer is no. But if the question is, "Must human beings commit themselves to God in order to play a positive role in fulfilling God's purpose through them?" the answer is yes. From God's perspective his sovereignty is unquestionable; from the human perspective our responsibility is equally unquestionable.

What is the cause of this situation? Our human concepts of sovereignty, election, determinism, responsibility, predestination, free will etc., to say nothing of our human concepts of time and interaction, are sufficiently limited that we cannot construct with these human concepts alone a single fully adequate description of the divine dynamics of life. Because of this, the biblical writers have provided us with several complementary models in order that we might not be misled into believing either that God really "runs the show" without our involvement and our sense of responsibility is only an illusion, or that God's sovereignty is really reducible to his foreknowledge of what we in our free will do.

This is equivalent, by analogy, to the use of complementary descriptions to prevent us from believing that an electron is really a particle which just looks like a wave once in a while, or that an electron is really a wave which just looks like a particle once in a while.

Theological descriptions also make use of models (or metaphors) to reveal to us what God is like and what his relationship to the world is like. God himself is pictured for us in the Bible under the models of father, king, husband, bridegroom or even hen. This means, for example, that there are attributes of fatherhood that accurately depict some of the qualities of the character of God. It certainly in no sense implies that God is wholly like a human father or that our human concept of fatherhood is adequate to describe the actual characteristics of God.

Another familiar example within the Christian context is the biblical teaching on the atonement. Here the biblical writers invoke a whole series of different similes in order to convey in some sense as much of the true nature of the mysteries of the atonement as it is possible to do when limited to the categories of everyday human experience. Thus the biblical writers tell us that the atonement is *like* healing and wholeness (salvation), *like* being bought back from slavery (redemption), *like* recovering from estrangement (reconciliation), *like* triumph over the devil (victory), *like* having a legal debt paid by another (sacrifice). Each of these models give us a true and reliable insight into the meaning, purpose, and accomplishments of the atonement. Our understanding of the atonement is enriched by considering them all, yet without encompassing the totality of the atonement. These are complementary biblical descriptions of the atonement.

Are the complementary statements describing biblical doctrine *exactly* the same kind of statements as those describing the properties of an electron? Perhaps not. But their origin is the same: the limitations imposed on us when we try to describe the unknown in terms of the known.

Descriptions Drawn from Different Realms of Discourse .

Descriptions are given within a particular realm of discourse. Thus the color of an apple can be described by a variety of similes, but always within the categories of the color spectrum. Another occasion for the development of complementary descriptions arises quite independently of our limitations on describing the unknown in terms of the known: the limitations that we ourselves impose on a description by choosing its context in a particular set of categories.

This kind of origin for complementary descriptions can also be seen within a particular discipline, for example, science. In fact the various branches of science, extending from physics and chemistry to sociology through biology, botany, zoology, psychology and many others, each define the domain of its own descriptions. The claim that there is only one domain within which a valid description can be given is known as reductionism, and we have previously commented on the shortcomings of this approach. Thus a description of an event in the life of a living creature can be given in terms of the physics of the event, the chemistry of the event, the biology of the event, the psychology of the event, and the sociology of the event, if we choose to remain within the scientific spheres as a whole. We do not expect these different kinds of description to give the same information, but neither do we expect them to contradict one another. Rather we expect them to be complementary. Phenomena involving human beings must be described scientifically with contributions from all these different domains; the goal is to integrate them into a total perspective.

The questions that we ask and the context in which we ask them may limit the appropriate categories of the responding descriptions. If we ask for the appearance of a classic painting, but insist that our answer must come from what we see when observing it with a microscope (thereby limiting ourselves to a particular set of impersonal categories), our response is quite different from what it would be if we stood back twelve feet from the painting and saw it within its full context and human correlations. The two descriptions that we would offer in this way might very well be said to be complementary since they apply to the same object but are drawn from different realms of discourse, as dictated by the examination procedures prescribed.

Descriptions drawn from science and descriptions drawn from Christian theology come from different realms of discourse. That there exists a viable description from science does not a priori mean that no viable description from theology can be given; conversely, that there exists a viable description from theology does not mean that no viable description from science can be offered. Because of the orientation of the two realms, science being a subset of the disciplines of which theology is the most completely integrating, there may well be special cases where no scientific description can be given (e.g., miracles), whereas there are no cases in which some theological description would not be appropriate, even if it were simply to see the event or the object as the result of God's activity.

Healing from disease can be appropriately described both in terms of antibiotic defense against infection and as the healing activity of God. To eliminate one description or the other decreases our understanding of the whole process; both are needed. The coming of rain can be appropriately described both in terms of hot and cold air masses and as the activity of God to provide support for the growth of crops. Although we do not yet have all the information necessary, it is likely that the origin of life can be appropriately described in terms of physical, chemical and biological processes, and at the same time in terms of the creative activity of God bringing something new into being. Ethical issues concerned with the beginning and ending of life must be informed by insights drawn from the biological and psychological scientific areas and from insights provided by biblical perspectives on the value of human personhood.

In this sense, then, it appears that we may meaningfully speak of scientific descriptions and theological descriptions having the capability of being complementary: when they deal with the same phenomenon of reality and when they give descriptions of that phenomenon out of their own realms of discourse using categories and methods appropriate to those realms.

Insights into Complementarity

In recent years the advocacy of Pattern 7 leads quickly to the foundational work of Donald MacKay. [9, 20, 119] No discussion of the subject would be complete without including a quote from MacKay:

To keep scientific and Christian doctrines rigidly apart would be silly as well as potentially dishonest. To try to make them into one by chopping bits from each and pasting them together, or by treating them as rival ways of giving identical information, would be equally to miss the point. We can come to relate them properly only by holding both constantly together in our minds, until little by little there comes to us some glimmering of that greater whole of which they present complementary aspects, the activity and character of God himself: not God seen only in the gaps of the scientific picture, nor God deduced only as the conclusion of a scientific argument, but God revealed as the Author of the whole story . (p. 35)   [20]

This emphasis on the importance of seeing God as the "Author of the whole story" is a fundamental one. It is cast into a somewhat striking, popularized form by asking "What would happen if God turned himself off?"   A variety of answers to this question are commonly suggested, once the people questioned accept the "thought experiment" nature of the question, seeking to probe one's ideas on the actual relationship between God and the world.   One answer is that the laws of nature would gradually start to fail; the implication is that God is needed to keep the laws working.   Another answer is that people would gradually become more immoral; the implication is that God is needed to maintain human morality.   Now it is important to recognize that these kinds of answers do not do justice to the basic biblical revelation that God is the source and sustainer of existence for everything that exists: he is the "Author of the whole story."   If God were to turn himself off, all of the universe would simply cease to exist (in somewhat the same way that the "story" being told on a television screen ceases to exist when the plug is pulled).

Other authors have been critical of the concept of complementarity if widely used without caution.   Barbour [129], for example, prefers to think of science and theology as alternative languages, and would reserve the term "complementary" only to different descriptions within science or different descriptions within theology.   He prefers to use the concepts of "dialogue" and "integration" for the interaction of science and theology.

He concludes a discussion [130] by saying,

There are dangers if either scientific or religious ideas are distorted to fit a preconceived synthesis that claims to encompass all reality . We must always keep in mind the rich diversity of our experience. We distort it if we cut it up into separate realms or watertight compartments, but we also distort it if we force it into a neat intellectual system. A coherent vision of reality can still allow for the distinctiveness of differing types of experience.

The shortcomings of simplistic views of complementarity were early recognized by MacKay, who wrote [131],

> Complementarity is not a universal panacea, and it is a relationship that can be predicated of two descriptions only with careful safeguards against admitting nonsense. Indeed the difficult task is not to establish the possibility that two statements are logically complementary, but to find a rigorous way of detecting when they are not. ... A good deal of consecrated hard work is needed on the part of Christians to develop a more coherent and more biblical picture of the relationship between the two.

Jeeves [7] reports the conditions that MacKay stipulated for two or more descriptions to be called logically complementary.

> These he says are (1) that they purport to have a common reference, (2) that each is in principle exhaustive (in the sense that none of the entities or events comprising the common reference need be left unaccounted for), yet (3) they make different assertions because (4) the logical preconditions of definition and/or of the use (that is the contexts in which they are set) of concepts or relationships in each are mutually exclusive, so that the significant aspects referred to in one are necessarily omitted from the other.

Polkinghorne [22] is sympathetic to the concept of complementarity:

> The appeal of some form of complementary-style understanding is even greater when we consider the most significant area in which science and theology impinge upon each other, namely in their account of what it is to be human.   ...Elsewhere I have suggested that it might be possible to approach the age-old problem of mind and brain ..following a complementary metaphysics.
> (p. 27)

It is interesting that in *Religion and the Natural Sciences: the Range of Engagement* [25], with 48 papers by 47 different authors, the index contains no reference to complementarity.   On the other hand, in *Real Science, Real Faith*, [24] with 16 chapters by 16 different authors, the index lists 7 references to complementarity.   From this book, we may note the statements by Humphreys [132],

> Thus I believe that science and Christianity describe the same territory, the same building of truth, but from different viewpoints.

by Jeeves [133],

> The way to an integrated understanding of man is not to hunt for gaps in any particular scientific picture so that we can fit in other entities, whether it be the soul or whatever, but to explore how the accounts at the different levels are related. It is not that we translate what is happening at one level into what is happening at another. The descriptions we give at the different levels are complementary, not identical or independent.   ... It is possible for an explanation to be complete in its own terms but not to render superfluous another explanation given at a different level.

by Berry [134],

> Science and faith have different methodologies, but they are complementary, not contradictory; a faith without reason is as stultifying as a reason without faith. (p. 195)

and by MacKay [135],

> Explanations in terms of scientific laws and in terms of divine activity are thus not rival answers to the same question; yet they are not talking about different things. They are (or at any rate purport to be) complementary accounts of different aspects of the same happening, which in its full nature cannot be adequately described by either alone. (p.205)

The consensus appears to be that different types of insights into reality derived from different disciplines and backgrounds, and using different languages, can appropriately be considered as being complementary.   They both provide valid insights into the nature of reality, and our response to them should be to attempt to visualize a whole that is faithful to both sets of insights. This does not mean that all philosophical issues in the nuances attributed to this term have been resolved, and we may perhaps expect our understanding to be increased in time.

Illustrations of Complementarity

To complete our discussion of the implications of Pattern 7, we consider further a few examples where the concept of complementary descriptions plays a key role.

The Origin of New Properties and the Structure of the World .
Reflections on the scientific description of the structure of the world
have led many thinkers [78, 136, 137] to conclude from different
orientations that this structure can most adequately be conceived as of a
hierarchically arranged system composed of interrelated parts and
wholes. [80, 138-140]

This structure can be described as an order corresponding
approximately to increasing complexity of interaction as consisting of
the following representative "levels": energy, elementary particles,
atoms, molecules, inorganic matter, organic matter, living cells,
plants, animals, human beings, and human society.   A simple
illustration is given in Table 2. Corresponding to these various levels
are the specific sciences: physics, chemistry, biology, physiology,
botany, zoology, anthropology, psychology and sociology.

There are three main qualitative breakthroughs in this hierarchy; they
occur at (1) the transition from non-matter to matter, (2) the transition
from non-living to living, and (3) the transition from non-human to
human.   Among the material-based levels (i.e., excepting "energy") an
apparent parts/whole relationship exists, e.g., a cell is the whole for an
electron that is a part, or a cell is a part of an animal that is the whole.
This same relationship can be alternatively pictured as a
subsystem/system relationship. Reflection on the structure indicates
that the wholes have properties that are not manifested by the parts
(there are systems properties not exhibited by the subsystems).

As is the case with all scientific "facts," the "fact" of the structure
does not provide its own interpretation. Nor does the structure itself
indicate the origin of the novelty manifested by the new properties of
the wholes. The interpretation of this hierarchical structure depends
critically on which pattern relating science and Christian theology is
chosen to guide the interpretation.

In the complementarity view of Pattern 7, the hierarchical structure of
the world is interpreted to represent the different levels on which
meaningful scientific descriptions can be given . Scientific descriptions
suggesting known or possible mechanisms or processes by which the
hierarchical structure may have originated or may be understood today
are applicable to all the levels of this structure and are not *a priori*
excluded from any level or transition between levels. Similarly
theological descriptions concerning the structure of the world and its
relationship to God are not restricted to some particular gaps in human
knowledge, but are relevant to the whole hierarchical structure,
revealing it to be our present understanding of the nature of God's
activity in that portion of reality susceptible to scientific description.
In the normal course of events there is no need for God to provide

Table 2

A Scientific Description of the Structure of the World

Properties	Science		Major Distinctions
		ENERGY	*Non-matter*
	Physics	_____ (1)	
form	and	"PARTICLES"	
structure	Chemistry	ATOMS	
			Material but non-living
vibration		MOLECULES	
solids		NON-LIVING MATTER	
		_____(2)	
		THE CELL	
motion	Biology	LIVING MATTER	*Living but non-human*
replication	Botany	PLANTS	
reproduction	Zoology	ANIMALS	
		_____(3)	
self-awareness	Anthropology	HUMAN BEINGS	
God-conscious-ness	Psychology		*Human*
politics	Sociology	HUMAN SOCIETY	
language			
crime			
war			

(1) The transition from non-matter to matter.
(2) The transition from non-living to living.
(3) The transition from non-human to human.

non-scientifically describable interventions at various stages of the structure in order to manifest his presence and activity.   Rather the entire structure itself, its very existence with all of its observable properties, is the consequence of God's creative and sustaining activity.

The complementarity approach of Pattern 7 also gives particular insight into the question of the origin of new properties as this is posed by the hierarchical structure.   (See our previous discussion in connection with Pattern 4 in Chapter 7).   In general the whole is more than the sum of its parts.   The whole has properties that are not exhibited by the parts. These properties are not necessarily added to the parts from outside, but may often (if not always) arise from the specific pattern of interaction in which the parts are dynamically arranged (according to the creating and sustaining activity of God).   Thus the complementarity approach of Pattern 7 leads to the concept of the hierarchical emergence of new properties in which the unique properties of more complex organizations of matter are real (as opposed to reductionism), but are not present in the parts making up the whole (as opposed to preductionism).   Rather these new properties emerge as a characteristic of the whole (a systems property) when the pattern of the interactions making up the whole is suitable to sustain them.   The unique properties of the whole are not present even implicitly in the parts, but emerge when the parts participate in a particular, suitable pattern of interaction.

For a simple analogy to the development of new properties, consider the situation where the temperature of a piece of wood is increased, so that the carbon in the wood reacts with the oxygen in the air and much heat is developed. This heat shows itself in the appearance of a flame, a new property of the interacting system that is the result of electronic transitions between excited states of the atoms. If the wood is cooled down or all of the carbon is consumed, the flame disappears.   Is the flame real or is it only an illusion?   It certainly is real and can be carefully analyzed with a suitable spectrograph.   Now the flame wasn't present in the wood or in the air before the fire started.   The flame wasn't added to the wood and the air "from outside." And the flame didn't "go" anywhere (e.g., to "flameland") after the fire went out. But, just because the flame wasn't present in the wood or the air, and didn't go anywhere after the fire went out, doesn't mean that the flame wasn't "real." A real flame existed as long as the interaction between the wood and the air was appropriate to maintain its existence.

It is the pattern of interaction that is responsible for the real properties of the whole, a pattern that is not demanded by the properties of the parts but shapes and focuses their interaction in the same way that boundary conditions shape and focus the solutions of a differential equation. Where do these boundary conditions come from? From the perspective of scientific description, the appearance of novelty often requires the use of a scientific chance description (rather than a scientific deterministic description).

But let us be quick to repeat one more time (at the risk of being redundant) that encountering an event that can be described scientifically as chance (since it is not scientifically determined) can and should be properly described as the consequence of the activity of God. *A scientific chance description does not mean that God is not active.* What we call "chance" can well be God's way of producing design in the universe. We have already given several examples of this. It need not be some special, intervening activity, but simply the consequence of the fact that *all of the reality, all of the existence, and all of the properties described in Table 2 depend for their very existence and identity moment-by-moment upon the continuing creative and sustaining activity of God.* It is precisely at this point that the complementary theological description of new properties arising from God's free activity makes its most significant contribution.

Being Human.. Some of the most illustrative examples of complementary descriptions have to do with different kinds of descriptions of a human being and human relationships. To speak of a human being as the product of "genes" is to use a scientific description; to speak of the same human being as a living "soul" is to use a theological description. Both descriptions are valid; neither can be ignored. If the description of "soul" is abandoned in favor of a description only of "genes," the human being is reduced to an organic machine. If the description of "genes" is abandoned in favor of a description of "soul," the human being becomes a kind of non-biblical "ghost in the machine."

A complementary approach recognizes that "genes" is a description of a human being on the biological level, whereas "soul" is a description of a human being on the theological level. One way of integrating them that does not do violence either to authentic science or to authentic theology is to see the soulful properties of a human being as emergent properties of the whole, resulting from the particular patterned interactions of the biological parts expressing the creative activity of God.

Specific examples can also be drawn in the area of ethical issues concerned with the beginning and ending of life. Each of these must be informed by insights drawn from the biological and psychological scientific areas, and from insights provided by biblical perspectives on the value and significance of human personhood. [141]

Let us consider some of these issues in a little more detail. If the question, "What do you mean by human?" is asked on the spur of the moment to a variety of people, a number of different answers may be given. [142] When these are all sorted through, we find that there are three basic criteria for assigning the *adjective* "human": (1) a minimum necessary and sufficient criterion, a biological criterion, the presence of "human" genetic material in the form of DNA; (2) an ordinary criterion, a social criterion, the appearance and behavior like other "humans"; (3) a transcendent criterion, a spiritual criterion, made in the image of God and capable of fellowship and personal relationship with him. In the normal course of development, an individual is *biologically human* before he is socially human and *socially human* before he is *spiritually human*. The distinction human/not-human occurs only at the biological level; a creature that is biologically human is "human" regardless of the stage of development. Otherwise distinctions are only between exhibiting some of the characteristics of "humanness" and exhibiting more or less of these traits.

Much of this discussion of the meaning of "human" can be repeated from a different perspective involving the concepts of "body, soul, and spirit," as illustrated in Table 3.

Table 3

Body, Soul and Spirit

BODY	Chemistry Biology	DNA, Genes	Looks human	*soma*
SOUL	Psychology Sociology	Self Consciousness Emotions	Acts human	*psuche*
SPIRIT	Theology	Spiritual	Relates to God	*pneuma*

Here the first column refers to the three terms usually used in English to describe the three attributes of human beings, the second column lists the fields of description directly involved, the third column gives the major characteristics, the fourth column gives the typical manifestations, and the fifth column gives the words used in the Greek New Testament to express these ideas.

It appears that "body" (*soma*) is an appropriate term to describe the essentials of the biological criterion for humanness, that "soul" (*psuche*) is an appropriate term to describe the essentials of the psychological and social criterion, and that "spirit" (*pneuma*) is an appropriate term to describe the essentials of the spiritual criterion for humanness.

In the Greek New Testament [143] *psuche* means "(a) *life* - without any psychological content, (b) an *individual* , or (c) psychical *desire* ." It corresponds to the modern conception of *self* .   We may therefore see that the word "soul" refers to a set of properties of a whole living being: to be soulful is to be a living individual self.   Therefore I do not "have" a soul; rather I "am a soulful being."

Similarly in the Greek New Testament *pneuma* means "(a) *wind*, and (b) *breath* - that which distinguishes a living from a dead body. In the New Testament, *pneuma* almost always refers to the higher nature in human beings, the product of the divine Spirit." We may therefore see that the word "spirit" refers to a set of properties of a whole living human being. To be "spiritual" is to be a living, human, individual self, capable of relationship with God's Holy Spirit. Therefore I do not "have" a spirit; I "am a spiritual being."

By *body*   the Bible speaks about the physical, chemical and biological aspects of the human being. By *soul* the Bible speaks about the life, the emotional, mental aspects of the human being, which we might call psychological and social aspects.   By *spirit* the Bible speaks about the ability of the human being made in the image of God to be in relationship with God, to be responsible before Him, to be guilty of sin, and to be in need of a Savior.

But such a reference to body, soul and spirit should not be used to separate a human being into three separate parts. The human being *is* the "I". The "I" *is* a body-soul-spirit: a *pneumopsychosomatic unity* : a whole person.

To complete this particular example of how the complementarity of Pattern 7 integrates scientific and theological insights into the nature of the human being, it is necessary to make one further observation. Sometimes in popular speech the words "soul" or "spirit" are used to indicate a person's "identity" that is maintained in continuity from the mortal self of this life to the immortal self of the next.   When treated as synonymous with individual identity, the terms "soul" and "spirit" are pressed into a different role. When "soul" or "spirit" is used to mean individual identity, there is meaning in speaking of an "immortal soul," for this "identity," resting wholly on God at all times, is by its very nature "immortal," i.e., dependent only on God and not on man. Confusion can result, however, if the words "soul" or "spirit" are used interchangeably and without distinction to mean both the attributes of a living human being and the individual identity of that human being. Attributes are changing continuously through life from conception to resurrection; identity is held secure in the mind of God.   Harris expresses it well when he says, [144]

> In much popular western thought, the soul is simply one part of man, distinguishable from his body not only in thought but also in reality.   As a result, "the immortality of the soul" implies nothing more than the persistence beyond death of that aspect of man which may be called the soul. The New Testament, however, with its basically monistic anthropology, promises the transformation of the whole person, not the survival of a disembodied *ego*. Immortality is not assignable to only a part of man.

Christian Conversion. Consider the great experience of Christian conversion, in which a person is enabled to recognize the relationship between himself and his Creator, and to commit himself to God and to Jesus Christ as Savior and the Lord of his life. How shall we describe this event, and how shall we interpret the description?

Conversion is a personal theological event involving interaction with God and a spiritual restructuring of all of life; it requires a theological interpretation.   Conversion is also an event that may be describable in terms of social interactions, arising from and bringing with it activity and changes on the social level; it requires a sociological interpretation. Conversion is also an event that may be describable in terms of psychological interactions, arising from and bringing with it activity and changes in a person's psychological outlook; it requires a psychological interpretation. Conversion is also an event that may be describable in terms of biological interactions, arising from and bringing with it activity and changes in a person's biological structure and functioning; it requires a biological interpretation.   Since when biological changes occur, they may also be described in terms of chemical and physical changes, it may be likewise maintained that conversion involves such chemical and physical changes, and therefore also requires a physical interpretation.

The theological event of conversion changes a person's life.   A person's life does not change unless his relationship to others and to him/herself changes.   Total personal perspectives, ways of thinking, and bases for relationships do not change unless there are biological, chemical and physical changes.

The perspective of complementarity allows one to integrate all of these inputs, all of these changes into one coherent picture.

Descriptions of one type do not rule out descriptions of other types. Conversion is not *only* a physical event, not *only* a biological event, not *only* a psychological event, not *only* a social event, not even *only* a theological event. Which of these descriptions can be left out without depleting the total understanding of what has happened in conversion? To be sure, the focus of the conversion experience is the relationship on the theological level between a person and God, but it could be no experience at all if it did not have its effects on the subsystems of the person, on his sociology, psychology, biology and physical processes. The possibility of exhaustive description on a single level does not exclude the meaningfulness, validity, or necessity of descriptions on all other levels.

Systems properties – properties of the wholes constructed from the parts – are not illusions, or meaningless, or neglectable because the operation of subsystems can be exhaustively described without reference to the systems property.   Life is a systems property of nonliving matter; but life is no illusion.   Personality is a systems property of impersonal, soul-less matter; but personality or soul is no illusion. The dilemma of how it is possible for the living to arise from the nonliving or of how it is possible for the personal to arise from the impersonal can be answered in a way that preserves the correlation and the reality of the systems property at the same time. It is the *pattern* of the interaction that supplies the organizing and enabling basis for these developments. And the pattern is neither derived from the parts, nor imposed from the whole, but somehow is given to them.

If it is demanded that science provide the answer to the question of where this pattern comes from, it may well be able to answer only that there are no scientifically determinable causes. In such a situation, science has no other choice within its own discipline but to say that the pattern arises "by chance."   There are no other types of scientific description.

But the reality of God's designing activity encompasses and surpasses any possible scientific description that we can come up with, or even our failure to come up with one at all.   Even if our scientific description is stated as "chance," our complementary theological description enables us to affirm without doubt that what has happened is the result of the creative activity of God – possibly working in ways too wonderful for us to understand.   We have seen now several times that God is great and designs as he pleases.   God as Creator rules out Chance (a meaningless, atheistic perspective) as a worldview.   But as we attempt to describe his activity scientifically, we may be led for the time being into scientific deterministic descriptions (cause and effect relationships are well known and scientifically definable) or scientific chance descriptions (cause and effect relations are not known, only probabilistic descriptions can be given).

God is the Author of the whole story!

Chapter 11

Epilogue: A Christian Philosophy of Science

We have taken a look at some of the major ways in which attempts have been made to relate science and Christian theology. For many of these we have had some critical comments to make, as practices caused departures from the guidelines leading to authentic science or authentic Christian theology. In conclusion, we here present a brief positive summary of the characteristics of authentic science as encompassed within a worldview guided by authentic Christian theology. [145] This is intended to supplement and to integrate some of the material previously discussed in this book.

It is convenient to describe the principle characteristics of science within a Christian perspective in terms of five terms all starting with the letter "p": purpose, possibility, presuppositions, posture, and potential.

Purpose

The primary purpose of science is to describe the world in which we live in natural categories, insofar as this is possible. This description is carried out in terms of models (approximations, pictures, projections) of the way the real world is, in a simpler kind of framework. Such models are successful when they describe to a sufficient accuracy what we observe in the natural world.

There are two fundamental reasons why scientific descriptions are sought. We describe (1) in order that we may understand the world, and (2) so that we may know how to control as responsible stewards in caring for the world.

Although many people assume that it is a good and worthwhile activity to understand and control, the Christian position provides a foundation that others must somehow assume or perhaps take for granted without probing into the reasons underlying it. That it is good to understand, to have a theoretical knowledge of the world, and to control, to have an applied technology that enables us to act intelligently and responsibly in the world, must be based ultimately, if on anything at all, on the biblical doctrines of Creation and Providence. According to the biblical doctrine of Creation, the world is a good world according to the creative purpose of God, and the evil that is all too real is an aberration upon this good world. God sustains the world moment by moment by his continuing activity, and without this activity the world itself would cease to exist. As we learn to describe the world more and more accurately, to understand it more completely, and to carry out properly the mandate given in Genesis 1:28, we are carrying on a Christian activity, as well as a human, useful and pleasing one.

Scientific description is not the only possible kind of description, nor does it exclude all other kinds of descriptions. A scientific description is one particular kind of description. It 's a description in which we deliberately say, "We are going to approach the world around us in a specific way. We are going to make those observations and measurements in which we can use our senses, both our natural senses and our extended senses through equipment. When we have the results of these measurements, we will interpret them in accordance with the laws of logic and reasonable evidence to construct models of what reality appears to be like. Sometimes we will be able to propose a scheme of cause and effect that describes the world deterministically; at other times we may be led into a probabilistic (chance) description either because of our ignorance of underlying causes or because the nature of reality appears to be intrinsically probabilistic to us. We will, however, insist that the things we see and describe *in science* will be described in natural categories."

Because we are limited by and concerned with natural categories, science itself never produces supernatural descriptions. No matter what we address ourselves to scientifically, it may be that we can describe it scientifically or that we cannot. But if we have a scientific description, it is going to be by definition in natural categories. In this way scientists attempt to be consistent within their own limiting methodology.

A scientific description is also only one possible kind of meaningful description. There are many kinds of description of the same event, process or being, some of which cannot be tested by the scientific method because they are not susceptible to analysis by sense contacts in the way that scientific descriptions must be. To say that something is not scientific does not imply in any way that it is either false or unimportant. There are many aspects of life, in fact some of the most important aspects of life, which cannot be exhaustively described scientifically. The relationship between loving husband and wife could be partially described in terms of their physics and chemistry, their biology and psychology. But if it were supposed that this is an exhaustive description of their relationship, that there is nothing more to say about this personal interaction than what is contained in this kind of scientific description, the main point would be missed as to what is meant when they say that they love each other.

There are at least two ways in which every event that happens must be considered. One way is to say, "What is the description of this event in terms of natural cause and effect categories; what is the scientific description?" But we must also ask, "What is the meaning of this event? What is the purpose of this event? How does this event relate to God, to his purposes, to the flow of history, to ultimate reality?"

What is a cow? Is it sufficient to reply only in terms of bovine biology? If such a description of a cow is ultimately adequate, then it is assumed that the insight that the cow is a creature made by God is unimportant. But if indeed God has made the cow, this knowledge is extremely significant. To know that a cow is a creature made by God for specific purposes, that it deserves at least the respect appropriate for a creature made by God, is something worthwhile knowing that cannot be derived from the scientific description alone. Human attitudes toward the earth are quite different if we believe that the earth is there only for our own benefit, or if we believe that we are entrusted with responsibility for care of the earth by God himself.

It is essential to realize the possibility of – indeed the necessity of – parallel descriptions, different kinds of descriptions that are not mutually exclusive, but which reinforce each other although they are derived from asking different kinds of questions. If this were done consistently, we would be able to overcome many of the conflicts of our own and of the history of Christianity and science by leaving open the possibility that we need to look at things in more than one way in order to see them in their totality. Such problems as the brain vs. the mind, the body vs. the soul, determinism vs. free will, Calvinism vs.

Arminianism, the non-living vs. the living, evolution vs. creation – all of these historic, profound and life-upsetting supposed conflicts ought not to be thought to involve contradictory and exclusive descriptions so that either one or the other must be chosen. Rather it is that in many cases they represent situations in which one must ultimately choose both options in different situations as one attempts to answer different kinds of questions. Such sets of parallel descriptions were illustrated in Table 1.

Possibility

How do we know that science is possible? Why should science be possible? Why should it be possible for us to approach the world scientifically and obtain at least partially valid, reliable and useful descriptions? Why does the world not constantly change before us? Why are our minds adequate to the task? Why are our finite imaginations sufficient to do as much as they have?

The question, "Is science possible?" is a fundamental question that must be asked in science and cannot be simply glossed over. Those who take a non-Christian position do not hesitate to ask Christians or other theists, "Does God exist?" Then this question is followed with the inevitable, "Prove it." There is a ready response; it is to ask, "Is science possible?" They would reply, "Oh, yes, of course." Then must follow the request, "Prove it." Of course it can't be "proved" logically, and evidence regarding it cannot be obtained except by the doing. It's the doing that gives evidence for its possibility, and the situation with respect to God's existence is quite similar. The evidence that God exists can be personally known only through relationship with him. It is not possible to know that God exists outside that relationship by which God becomes real to a person . (Not that God requires the relationship, but that the person requires it.) Just as one cannot possibly do science while believing it impossible, so one cannot possibly come to know whether or not God exists when believing that he does not.   Both science and Christianity start with faith. A person says, "I believe that science is possible; I'll go out and test it." A person says, "I believe that God exists; I will relate myself to him, using if I must that well-known prayer, 'Oh God, I don't know if you are there or not, but if you're there, please answer my prayer.'" There is no other way that we can gain assurance in either area than through this kind of act of faith.

Actually any act of significance starts with a faith commitment, because an act of faith is always required when we don't have complete knowledge. But we never have complete knowledge. All we have is sufficient evidence to justify our faith; that is all we really ask for in either science or Christian theology. As science becomes possible as its possibility is accepted on faith, so also the knowledge of God's existence becomes a reality as we accept it on faith and test it.

The possibility of science in the Christian perspective once again depends upon the biblical doctrines of Creation and Providence. It is because God has made something that it is possible for us to investigate, and because God does act today in sustaining the world, that it is possible for us carry on from day to day the pursuit of science.

Presuppositions

What are some of the presuppositions of science that are needed in order to lead to that step in faith that makes science possible?   We have already fairly exhaustively summarized these in our discussion of authentic science, and they do not need much further discussion now: the world is understandable through rational process of the human mind, the human mind can conceive models that adequately describe the natural world, natural phenomena are reproducible in some general and universal sense, patterns of order exist that can be identified.   These presuppositions must be accepted on faith and actions made based on them before it can be ascertained that they are in fact reliable.

These presuppositions are ultimately seen to be valid and reasonable because there is a given structure, there is an objective reality, there is subject matter for the pursuit of science. We are made in the image of God and have therefore the possibility of understanding at least partially what this structure is like.

Posture

The posture of science derives from the fact that a structure of reality has been given to us, to which we must be open. In doing science, the universe and its characteristics are normative, and not we. We must subject ourselves to the world, not subject the world to our inclinations. There are, of course, problems with a position like this, for in doing science we do become involved in our scientific investigation, both in the quantum mechanical sense, and the more so as our science is more personally and less physically oriented. Nevertheless, an effective science is one that says simply that we will be open to what is. In our science we wish to find out not what should be, not what might be, not what could be, but only what *is*, and we will do our best to find out what is from the world rather than trying to impose our ideas arbitrarily upon it.

Is there anything basically Christian about this posture? Others who are not Christians may take a similar attitude. But it may be argued that if this posture is viable, the basis for it must once again be found in the biblical doctrines of Creation and Providence. There is a created structure given to us; our pursuit of the knowledge of truth requires us, not to fabricate or invent a structure, but to determine what the given structure is like. Even the theoretician, with his most beautiful theory, must ultimately say, "Now comes the crunch. Does my theory correspond to the way things are insofar as this can be tested by experiment?" The real structure must be contacted and tested in order to see whether any concept, any model of it is adequate to describe it. If the proposed theory cannot be tested - a possibility in some of the extended theories of cosmology and nuclear physics today - then it may, of course, continue to be considered, but it exists at best on the boundary between science and metascience.

The commitment of a Christian view of science is to explore and understand this given structure on its own terms. Although we have argued earlier that no fact interprets itself, that every experiment is affected by the theoretical context in which it is planned, that every interpretation is guided by what we think it should be – nevertheless, authentic science attempts to avoid this kind of problem just as much as is possible. Authentic science tries to survey the results of one's experiments with as open a mind as one can achieve (within a creative flexible conceptual scheme) so that we may come as close as possible to "hearing" what the world has to say to us as we carry on our experiments. The posture of science is one in which the created universe is trusted to be a faithful witness to itself.

One might raise the question, "Why are non-Christians so successful in science?" Non-Christian are successful in science when, and only when, they, without basic justification, adopt a Christian-like view of the world, even though they themselves may not or will not admit it. Non-Christians are successful in science when they are open to the created order, when they adopt the methodology based on saying, "There is something given to us and we will be open to it." As soon as non-Christians (or, of course, Christians too) say, "Reality is subjective and susceptible to our opinions, so that we can enforce our political or religious ideas upon it," they cease to be scientists immediately. It does not matter whether the motivation for this statement is ecclesiastical (as in some of the unfortunate interactions between the church and science) or political (as in the Lysenko case in the former Soviet Union). Science comes to a dead stop when someone says,

"This is the way the world must be philosophically, and therefore you better find it that way scientifically." People may try very hard to do this, and even appear to be successful for a time, but ultimately the given structure of the world wins out and they fail. An Aristotelian view of the universe ultimately falls before the reality of the existing universe; the biological theory capable of producing more and better corn must be faithful to the real world, not only to Marxist dialectical materialism. For Christians the world *is* given; for non-Christians success in science demands that they act *as though the world were given.*

Once this posture of openness is adopted, we have freedom in our scientific activity, freedom from conflict between our preconceptions of what we must find in science and what we do find in science. If we attempt to force a scientific perspective upon our theology, we have pseudotheology; if we attempt to force a theological or philosophical perspective upon our science, we have pseudoscience. There is no need for either. Our scientific description cannot be expected to be identical to our theological description; if this were the case, we would not have the need for both. But we do need both kinds of description since they are complementary and not mutually exclusive.

Potential

The posture of science in which openness to the created structure is emphasized represents the passive aspect of science: here effort is made to allow the structure to impress itself upon us. The potential of science emphasizes the active aspects of science: here effort is made to apply the knowledge gained through scientific inquiry in responsible action.

First of all, science is a human endeavor. It is a process and a practice carried out by human beings. It therefore has no more intrinsic claim to universal helpfulness than any other human endeavor. Whether science or any other way of advancing knowledge produces a good or an evil result depends upon the way we use it. And the way in which we use it is not derivable from science itself, but must be decided on other grounds that transcend science alone. A scientific investigation does not prescribe its own application.

Science is not a competitor of Christian theology. It is rather a helpmate; it enables us to exercise our moral and ethical directives intelligently rather than foolishly. Science is one means by which Christians can seek to serve the world. Science is *per se* no more distinctive than education, or social service, or politics, or other kinds of human endeavor by which we, as well as non-Christians, seek to serve in this world. It has its own unique powers, its own unique methods, its own unique possibilities.

In discussing the potential of science in terms of service, it is helpful to see the emphasis provided to us by the biblical doctrine of Redemption. Here is an opportunity for Christians who have been personally redeemed by Christ to serve him and their fellowmen in a particular mode of life, a particular approach to the needs, desires and necessities of living in this imperfect world. In some small and perhaps insignificant way the scientist as Christian has the possibility of showing in his own limited sphere the first fruits of the ultimate redemption. God has claimed all things for himself in Christ and will claim them ultimately in fact. Christians living today have the opportunity and the privilege to live as "minute men" of the complete redemption. This calls for service and for commitment.

Christians do science recognizing that it does have a potential but that its potential is limited. They look to the future in order to do what needs to be done here and now in the present. They look to God in the face of what seems to be temporal pessimism so that the optimism generated from eternity may enable them to serve here and now in the way in which they are called. The realistic faith required to carry on science in spite of the ambivalence of its consequences requires trust in the ultimate control of God over all things.

References

Bibliography

1. L.Gilkey, *Maker of Heaven and Earth: the Christian Doctrine of Creation in the Light of Modern Knowledge* (Doubleday, 1959)
2. A. van der Ziel, *The Natural Sciences and the Christian Message* (Denison: Minneapolis, Minn., 1960)
3. W. G. Pollard, *Physicist and Christian* (Seabury: Greenwich, Conn., 1961)
4. D. MacKay, *Christianity in a Mechanistic Universe* (InterVarsity Press: London, 1965)
5. I. Barbour, *Issues in Science and Religion*, (Prentice Hall: N.J., 1966)
6. R. H. Bube, ed., *The Encounter Between Christianity and Science* (Eerdmans: Grand Rapids, Michigan, 1968)
7. M. A. Jeeves, *The Scientific Enterprise and Christian Faith* (Tyndale: London, 1969)
8. R. H. Bube, *The Human Quest: A New Look at Science and Christian Faith* (Word: Waco, Texas, 1971)
9. D. MacKay, *The Clockwork Image* (InterVarsity Press: Downers Grove, 1974)
10. C. F. H. Henry, ed., *Horizons of Science: Christian Scholars Speak Out* (Harper & Row, San Francisco, 1978)
11. A. R. Peacocke, *Creation and the World of Science* (Clarendon Press: Oxford, 1979)

12. A. R. Peacocke, *Intimations of Reality: Critical Realism in Science and Religion* (Univ. of Notre Dame Press; Notre Dame, Indiana, 1984)

13. L. Gilkey, *Creationism on Trial* (Winston: Minneapolis, Minn., 1985)

14. R. H.Bube, *Science and the Whole Person* (ASA: Ipswich, MA, 1985)

15. R. H. Bube, "The Relationship between Scientific and Theological Descriptions," *Journal of the American Scientific Affiliation* **38**, 154 (1986)

16. C.E. Hummel, *The Galileo Connection: Resolving Conflicts between Science and the Bible*, (InterVarsity Press; Downers Grove, IL 1986)

17. D.C. Lindberg and R. L. Numbers, *God and Nature: Historical Essays on the Encounter between Christianity and Science* (Univ. of California Press: Berkeley, 1986)

18. A. R. Peacocke, *God and the New Biology* (Harper & Row: San Francisco, 1986)

19. H. J. Van Till, *The Fourth Day: What the Bible and the Heavens are Telling us About Creation* (Eerdmans: Grand Rapids, 1986)

20. D. MacKay, *The Open Mind*, M. Tinker, ed., (InterVarsity Press: London, 1988)

21. I. Barbour, *Religion in an Age of Science* (Harper Collins Pub., 1990)

22. J. Polkinghorne, *Reason & Reality: The Relationship Between Science and Theology* (Trinity Press Internat., Philadelphia, 1991)

23. R. H.Bube, "How Can a Scientist Be a Christian in Today's World?" in *Can Scientists Believe?* N. Mott, ed. (James & James: London, 1991), p. 109-120

24. R. J. Berry, ed., *Real Science, Real Faith* (Monarch: Eastbourne, 1991)

25. J. E. Huchingson, ed., *Religion and the Natural Sciences: the Range of Engagement* (HBJ College Pub.: Orlando, Florida, 1993)

26. A brief synopsis of this book has been published as: R. H. Bube, "Seven Patterns for Relating Science and Christian Faith," *Journal of Integrated Studies* (Taegu, Korea, 1993); also in *Science and Creation*, (Hillsdale College: Hillsdale, Michigan, 1993)

References from the Text

27. See, for example, Ref. 8, Chapter 2.

28. We offer two other non-sophisticated definitions of important terms used in the above discussion: (a) *reality* corresponds to "what is," and (b) *truth* is that which corresponds to reality.

29. R. H. Bube, "Penetrating the Word Maze: Describe/Explain," *Perspectives on Science and Christian Faith* **40**, 170 (1988)

30. R. H. Bube, "Penetrating the Word Maze: Prove," *Perspectives on Science and Christian Faith* **40**, 104 (1988)

31. *Webster's Ninth New Collegiate Dictionary*, Merriam-Webster, Springfield, MA 1987

32. M. Buber, *I and Thou*, 2nd edition, Scribner's 1958, pp. 3, 6

33. C. F. von Weizsaecker, *The Relevance of Science* , Collins, London 1964, p. 20

34. See Ref. 3, p. 21

35. R. H. Bube, "Deduction vs Induction: Understanding Differences Between Biblical Christians," *Journal of the American Scientific Affiliation* **37** ,189 1985)

36. See Ref. 8, pp. 72-76

37. These themes are developed in detail in Ref. 1.

38. See Ref. 8, Chapter 9; Ref. 13; Ref. 14, Chapters 12 and 13; R. B. Fischer, *God Did It, But How?* Cal Media, La Mirada, California 1981

39. R. H. Bube, "Original Sin and Natural Evil," *Journal of the American Scientific Affiliation* **27**, 171 (1975)

40. See Ref. 14, p. 139

41. V. Ya. Frenkel, "Some Remarks on Scientists and Religion, by a Simplicio of Our Time," in *Can Scientists Believe?* N. Mott, ed. (James & James: London, 1991), p. 121-127

42. See, for example, Ref. 8, Chapter 6; R. H. Bube, "Man Come of Age?" in Ref. 14, pp. 41-47; R. H.Bube, "The Failure of the God-of-the-Gaps" in Ref. 10 and its reprinting in Ref. 25; Ref. 23.

43. Dietrich Bonhoeffer, *Letters and Papers from Prison*, rev. ed., ed. Eberhard Bethge, New York: Macmillan Co., 1968, p. 142

44. See, for example, M. Ruse and E. O.Wilson, "The Evolution of Ethics," in Ref. 25, p. 308.

45. See Ref. 7, p. 103

46. See Ref. 43, p. 188

47. R. H. Bube, "Penetrating the Word Maze: Supernatural/Natural," *Perspectives on Science and Christian Faith* **41** , 109 (1989)

48. N. Mott, "Christianity Without Miracles?" in *Can Scientists Believe?* N. Mott, ed. (James & James: London, 1991), p. 3

49. R. W. Maatman and R. H.Bube, "Dialogue: Inerrancy, Revelation and Evolution," *Journal of the American Scientific Affiliation* **24** , 80 (1972);

50. See also Ref. 8, pp. 117-125;   Ref. 49; R. H. Bube, " A Perspective on Scriptural Inerrancy," *Journal of the American Scientific Affiliation* **15**, 86 (1963)

51. B. Ramm, "The Relationship of Science, Factual Statements and the Doctrine of   Biblical Inerrancy,"*Journal of the American Scientific Affiliation* **21** , 98 (1969)

52. J. P. Moreland, *Scaling the Secular City : A Defense of Christianity,* (Baker Book House: Grand Rapids, Michigan, 1987)

53. J. P. Moreland, "Is Natural Science Committed to Methodological Naturalism?" in *Science and Creation,*   (Hillsdale College: Hillsdale, Michigan, 1993)

54. B. Fraser, "A Christian Perspective on Time," *Perspectives on Science and Christian Faith,* **42,** 177 (1990)

55. A. Plantinga, "When Faith and Reason Clash: Evolution and the Bible," *Christian Scholar's Review* **21**, 8 (1991).

56. In *Christian Scholar's Review* **21** (1991) see also:
           H. Van Till, "When Faith and Reason Cooperate," p. 33;
           P. Pun, "Response to Professor Plantinga," p. 46;
           E. McMullin, "Plantinga's Defense of Special Creation," p. 55;
           A. Plantinga, "Evolution, Neutrality, and Antecedent
           Probability: A Reply to McMullin and Van Till," p. 80

57. W. Hasker, "Evolution and Alvin Plantinga," *Perspectives on Science and Christian Faith* **44**, 150 (1992)

58. H. J.Van Till, D.A. Young and C. Menninga, *Science Held Hostage: What's Wrong with Creation Science AND Evolutionism* (InterVarsity Press, Downers Grove, IL 1988)

59. H. M. Morris and J.C. Whitcomb, Jr., *The Genesis Flood ,* (Presbyterian and Reformed Publishers, Philadelphia, 1961)

60. D. A. Young, *Creation and the Flood: An Alternative to Flood Geology and Theistic Evolution* (Baker, Grand Rapids, MI 1977)

61. D. A. Young, *Christianity and the Age of the Earth*   (Zondervan, Grand Rapids, MI, 1982)

62. R. L. Numbers, *The Creationists. The Evolution of Scientific Creationism* (Knopf, New York, 1992)

63. P. Johnson, *Darwin on Trial*   (InterVarsity Press, Downers Grove, IL, 1991)

64. P. Johnson, "What is Darwinism," in *Science and Creation*, (Hillsdale College: Hillsdale, Michigan, 1993)

65. K. Barth, *Dogmatics in Outline* (Harper & Row, New York, 1949)

66. W. A. Whitehouse, *Christian Faith and the Scientific Attitude* (Philosophical Library, New York, 1952)

67. I. Barbour, "Ways of Relating Science and Religion," in Ref. 25, p. 13

68. See Rev. 22, p. 56

69. S. Berry, "Genes, Genesis, and Greens," in Ref. 24, p. 182

70. R. H. Bube, "A Reasonable Faith," a script for a television "spot" for "100 Huntley St.", Burlington, Ontario (1992)

71. A. Plantinga, *God and Other Minds* (Cornell University Press: Ithaca, N.Y., 1967)

72. See Ref. 71, pp. 4,5

73. See Ref. 71, pp. 27, 28

74. J. W. Montgomery, *Evidence for Faith: Deciding the God Question* (Probe Books, Dallas, Texas 1991)

75. S. Hawking, *A Brief History of Time: From the Big Bang to Black Holes* (Bantam Books, N.Y., 1988)

76. W. Pollard, *Man on a Spaceship* (The Claremont Colleges, Claremont, CA, 1967), pp. 44, 49

77. R. H. Bube, *Electronic Properties of Crystalline Solids* (Academic Press, New York, 1974), p. 70

78. P. Teilhard de Chardin, *The Phenomenon of Man* (Harper Torchbooks, N.Y., 1959)

79. J. D. Barrow and F. J. Tipler, *The Anthropic Cosmological Principle* (Clarendon Press, Oxford, 1986)

80. R. H. Bube, "Reductionism, Preductionism and Hierarchical Emergence," *Journal of the American Scientific Affiliation* **37,** 177 (1985)

81. See Ref. 14, p. 56

82. J. W. Sire, *The Universe Next Door: A Basic Worldview Catalog* (InterVarsity Press, Downers Grove, IL, 2nd ed., 1988)

83. R. H. Nash, *Worldviews in Conflict* (Zondervan, Grand Rapids, MI, 1992)

84. J. M. Templeton and R. L. Herrmann, *The God Who Would be Known: Revelations of the Divine in Contemporary Science* (Harper & Row, San Francisco, 1989)

85. R. J. Russell, "Christian Discipleship and the Challenge of Physics: Formation, Flux, and Focus," *Perspectives on Science and Christian Faith,*" **42,** 139 (1990); and R. H. Bube, "Reflections on

'Christian Discipleship and the Challenge of Physics,'" *Perspectives on Science and Christian Faith* **43,** 193 (1991)

86. R. J. Russell, "Theological Implicationsof Physics and Cosmology," in *The Church and Contemporary Cosmology,* J. B. Miller and K. E. McCall, eds. (Carnegie Mellon Univ. Press, Pittsburgh, 1990)

87. F. Capra and D. Steindl-Rast with T. Matus, *Belonging to the Universe : Explorations on the Frontiers of Science and Spirituality* (Harper San Francisco, San Francisco, 1991)

88. R. H. Bube, "Pseudo-Science and Pseudo-Theology: Scientific Theology," see Ref. 14, p. 25

89. R. W. Burhoe, "The Human Prospect and the 'Lord of History,'" *Zygon* **10,** 299 (1975)

90. R. W. Burhoe, "Attributes of God in an Evolutionary Universe," see Ref.25, p. 298

91. R. H. Bube, "Tension in Theology: Creation vs Redemption," *Journal of the American Scientific Affiliation* **32 ,** 1 (1980)

92. M. Fox, "Elements of a Biblical Creation-Centered Spirituality," *Spirituality Today* , Dec. 1978, p. 368

93. J.White, *The Meeting of Science and Spirit: Guidelines for a New Age: The Next Dynamic Stage of Human Evolution, and How We Will Attain It* (Paragon House, New York, 1990)

94. W. A. Tiller, quoted in R. Williams, *Qantas Airways,* May/June (1976), p. 8

95. F. A. Wolf, *Star Wave: Mind, Consciousness, and Quantum Physics* (MacMillan, New York, 1984)

96. V. Mangalwadi, *When the New Age Gets Old: Looking for a Greater Spirituality"* (InterVarsity Press, Downers Grove, IL, 1992)

97. E. P. Wigner, "Remarks on the Mind-Body Question," in *The Scientist Speculates* (W. Heinemann, London , 1961)

98. E. P. Wigner, *Symmetries and Reflections* (Indiana Univ. Press, Bloomington, Indiana, 1967)

99. A. Petersen, *Quantum Physics and the Philosophical Tradition* (MIT Press, Cambridge, 1968)

100. F. Capra, *The Tao of Physics* (Wildwood House, London, 1975)

101. G. Zukav, *The Dancing Wu-Li Masters: An Overview of the New Physics* (Morrow, New York, 1979)

102. R. B. Griffiths, *Journal of Statistical Physics* **36,** 219 (1984)

103. R. B. Griffiths, "Philosophical Implications of Quantum Theory," Conf. of the American Scientific Affiliation and the Research Scientists' Christian Fellowship of Great Britain, Oxford University, July 1985

104. A. Einstein, A. Podolsky and N. Rosen, *Physical Review* **47**, 777 (1935)

105. A. Einstein, in *Albert Einstein Philosopher-Scientist* , P.A. Schilpp, ed. (Tudor, New York, 1951)

106. A. Aspect, P. Grangier, and G. Roger, *Physical Review Letters* **49**, 91 (1982)

107. A. Aspect, J. Delibard, and G. Roger, *Physical Review Letters* **49** , 1805 (1982)

108. D. Bohm, *Causality and Chance in Modern Physics* (Van Nostrand, Princeton, N.J., 1957)

109. D. Bohm, *Wholeness and the Implicate Order* (Routledge and Kegan Paul, London, 1980)

110. D. Bohm, *Physical Review* **85**, 166, 180 (1982)

111. H. Everett III, *Reviews of Modern Physics* **29**, 454 (1957); reprinted in J. A. Wheeler and W. H .Zurek, eds., *Quantum Theory and Measurement* (Princeton University Press, Princeton, N.J., 1983)

112. C. B. DeWitt, ed., *The Environment and the Christian : What Can We Learn from the New Testament?* (Baker Book House, Grand Rapids, MI, 1991)

113. F. A. Schaeffer, *Pollution and the Death of Man: The Christian View of Ecology* (Tyndale, Illinois, 1970)

114. W. G. Pollard, *Man on a Spaceship* (Claremont Colleges, CA, 1967)

115. A. Rowthorn, *Caring for Creation* (Morehouse Publishing, Wilton, CT, 1989)

116. M. Dowd, *The Meaning of Life in the 1990's: An Ecological, Christian Perspective* (Living Earth Christian Fellowship, Woodsfield Ohio 1990)

117. J. Lovelock, "God and Gaia," in Ref. 25, p. 383

118. T. Berry, "Human Presence," in Ref. 25, p. 388

119. D. MacKay, *Human Science and Human Dignity* (Hoddern and Stoughton: London, 1977)

120. R. H. Bube, "The Appeal (The Necessity?) of Complementarity," *Journal of the American Scientific Affiliation* **35**, 240 (1983)

121. R. H. Bube, "Reductionism, Preductionism and Hierarchical Emergence," *Journal of the American Scientific Affiliation* **37**, 177 (1985)

122. R. H. Bube, "The Relationship between Scientific and Theological Descriptions," *Journal of the American Scientific Affiliation* **38** , 154 (1986)

123. J. W. Haas, Jr., "Complementarity and Christian Thought. 1. Classical Complementarity," *Journal of the American Scientific Affiliation* **35**, 145, 203 (1983)

124. J. W. Haas, Jr., "Complementarity and Christian Thought. 2. Logical Complementarity," *Journal of the American Scientific Affiliation* **35**, 203 (1983)

125. V. S. Poythress, "Science as Allegory," *Journal of the American Scientific Affiliation* **35** , 65 (1983)

126. V. S. Poythress, "Newton's Laws as Allegory," *Journal of the American Scientific Affiliation* **35**, 156 (1983)

127. V. S. Poythress, "Mathematics as Rhyme," *Journal of the American Scientific Affiliation* **35** , 196 (1983)

128. R. H.Bube, "The Relevance of the Quantum Principle of Complementarity to Apparent Basic Paradoxes in Christian Theology," *Journal of the American Scientific Affiliation* **8**, 4 (1956)

129. I. Barbour, *Myths, Models and Paradigms* (SCM Press, 1974)

130. I. Barbour, "Surveying the Possibilities: Ways of Relating Science and Religion," in Ref. 25, p. 6

131. D. M. MacKay, *The Christian Graduate* **6**, 163 (1953)

132. C. J. Humphreys, "Can Science and Christianity Both Be True?" in Ref. 24, p. 107

133. M. A. Jeeves, "Brains, Mind and Faith" in Ref. 24, p. 149

134. R. J. Berry, "Genes, Genesis and Greens" in Ref. 24, p. 182

135. D. M. MacKay, "Science and Christian Faith Today" in Ref. 24, p. 196

136. H. Dooyeweerd, *New Critique of Theoretical Thought* (Presbyt. and Reformed Pub. Co., Philadlephia, 1953); *In the Twilight of Western Thought* (Presbyt. and Reformed Pub. Co., Philadelphia, 1960)

137. M. Polanyi, "Life Transcending Physics and Chemistry," *Chemical and Engineering News*, Aug. 21, 1967; "Life's Irreducible Structure," *Science* 160 (1968)

138. R. H. Bube, "The Whole and the Sum of It Parts: A Unifying Perspective on Man and the World," *Journal of the American Scientific Affiliation* **18**, 8 (1966)

139. H. H. Pattee, ed., *Hierarchy Theory* (George Braziller, N.Y., 1973)

140. R. H. Bube, "The Structure of the World" in Ref. 8, p. 134

141. R. H. Bube, "Of Dominoes, Slippery Slopes, Thin Edges of Wedges, and Camels' Noses in Tents: Pitfalls in Christian Ethical Consistency," *Perspectives on Science and Christian Faith* **42**, 162 (1990)

142. R. H.Bube, "The Significance of Being Human" in Ref. 14, p. 56

143. A. Souter, *A Pocket Lexicon to the Greek New Testament* (Oxford Press, 1915)

144. M. Harris, "Resurrection and Immortality: Eight Theses," *Themelios* 1 , 50 (1976)

145. R. H. Bube, "The Philosophy and Practice of Science," in Ref. 14, p. 12

Index

About the Author

Richard H. Bube received his Sc.B. degree in Physics from Brown University in 1946 and his Ph.D. degree in Physics from Princeton University in 1950. Between 1948 and 1962 he was a senior member of the research staff at the RCA David Sarnoff Research Laboratories, Princeton, New Jersey, and finally Section Head for photoelectronic materials, where he was concerned with the photoelectronic properties of luminescent and photoconducting materials. Dr. Bube received the RCA Achievement Award for research in 1952 and 1957. He joined the faculty of the Department of Materials Science and Engineering in 1962 with a joint appointment in Electrical Engineering. From 1975 to 1986 he served as Chairman of the Department of Materials Science and Engineering; in 1990 and 1991 he served as Associate Chairman. In September 1992 he became Emeritus Professor of Materials Science and Electrical Engineering after 44 years of continuous involvement in scientific research, continuing in an active role.

In 1948 he married Betty Jane Meeker; they have four children: Mark T. Bube, General Secretary for Foreign Missions of the Orthodox Presbyterian Church; Kenneth P. Bube, Professor of Mathematics at the University of Washington; Sharon E. Bube Tilley, Clinical Psychologist; and Meryl Lee Bube Issichopoulos, accounting processing. They have five grandchildren: David R. Tilley, Jonathan H. Tilley, Douglas O. Issichopoulos, Amy L. Issichopoulos, and Jane E. Bube.

His major fields of scientific research include photoelectronic properties of materials, luminescence, photoconductivity, photovoltaic effects, semiconductors, insulators, amorphous semiconductors, trapping, properties of imperfections, photoelectronic analysis techniques, surface properties, transport in thin films and polycrystalline layers, heterojunctions, and solar energy conversion.

Dr. Bube is the author of *Photoconductivity of Solids* (1960, 1978), *Electronic Properties of Crystalline Solids* (1974), *Electrons in Solids* (1981), 2nd Edition (1988), 3rd Edition (1992), *Fundamentals of Solar Cells* (1983) (with Alan L. Fahrenbruch), *Photoelectronic Properties of Semiconductors* (1992), *Photo-Induced Defect Interactions in Semiconductors* (1995) (with David Redfield), and is the author or co-author of over 280 research publications.

He is a Fellow of the American Physical Society, the American Association for the Advancement of Science, and the American Scientific Affiliation, past Editor of the *Journal of the American Scientific Affiliation* (1968-1983), past Associate Editor of *Annual Review of Materials Science* (1968-1983), Member of the Editorial Advisory Board of *Solid State Electronics* (1975-   ), past Associate Editor of *Materials Letters* (1982-1989), and Member of the Editorial Board of *Christians in Science* (Leicester, England) (1992-   ). He is a Life Member of the American Society for Engineering Education, and a member of Sigma Xi, and the American Division of the International Solar Energy Society.

Dr. Bube has lectured at the NATO Summer School in Ghent, Belgium (1962), and the Ecole Polytechnique Federale Lausanne in Lausanne, Switzerland (1984). He was a Visiting Professor at the Institut fuer Physikalische Elektronik at the University of Stuttgart (1986), and at the Institut de Microtechnique at the University of Neuchatel (1986). He is a member of the Science and Technology Review Committee of the Solar Electric Research Division/SERI (1985-   ).

A Faculty Sponsor for the InterVarsity Christian Fellowship at Stanford University, a member of the Advisory Council of the InterVarsity Graduate Student Ministry, and a member of the Board of the International Students Christian Outreach at Stanford, he is the editor and co-author of *The Encounter Between Christianity and Science* (1968), the author of *The Human Quest: A New Look at Science and Christian Faith* (1971), and *Science and the Whole Person* (1984), and over 125 papers on the interaction between science and Christianity. He is a member of the National Advisory Board for *The Crucible: A Journal for Christian Graduate Students* . He became a Christian at St. Paul's Evangelical Lutheran Church, Missouri Synod, in Providence, Rhode Island in 1938, and served on the founding board for the Lutheran Church of the Messiah, Missouri Synod, in Princeton, New Jersey in 1947. He has also been a member of the Orthodox Presbyterian

Church; the United Presbyterian Church; and the Evangelical Covenant Church. He has served as Adult Education leader and lay preacher in several congregations.

At Stanford he has taught an Undergraduate Seminar on "Interactions Between Modern Science and Christianity" for 25 years.   In this capacity he has served as Adjunct Professor of Theology and Science at Fuller Theological Seminary, Pasadena (1974) and at Regent College, Vancouver (1976), as a Staley Distinguished Christian Scholar Lecturer (1975, 1979, 1982, 1983, 1986, 1988, 1990), as a Pew Lecturer (1978), as an invited speaker at conferences on Science and Christian Faith at Oxford University (1965, 1985), and Hillsdale College (1992), as a Templeton Lecturer at Stanford University (1992), and as a Visiting Professor at New College Berkeley (1993). He has lectured on science and Christianity on the campuses of over 60 colleges and universities.